THE SUCCESSION (SCOTLAND) ACT 1964

AUSTRALIA
Law Book Co.
Sydney

CANADA and USA
Carswell
Toronto

HONG KONG
Sweet & Maxwell Asia

NEW ZEALAND
Brookers
Wellington

SINGAPORE and MALAYSIA
Sweet & Maxwell Asia
Singapore and Kuala Lumpur

THE
SUCCESSION (SCOTLAND) ACT 1964

Fifth Edition

By

Michael C. Meston
M.A., LL.B. (Aberd.) , J.D. (Chicago)

EDINBURGH
W. GREEN/Sweet & Maxwell
2002

First published 1964
Reprinted 1967
Second edition 1969
Reprinted 1976
Third edition 1982
Reprinted 1988
Fourth edition 1993

W. Green & Son Ltd
-21 Alva Street
Edinburgh EH2 4PS

www.wgreen.co.uk

*Printed in Great Britain by Athenaeum Press Ltd,
Gateshead, Tyne & Wear*

No natural forests were destroyed to make this product;
Only farmed timber was used and replanted

A CIP catalogue record for this book is available from the British Library

ISBN 0414 01453 7

To Doris

PREFACE

When faced with the multitude of problems which arise in practice, anyone who thinks that the law of succession is an unchanging backwater rapidly discovers the truth even in areas which seem to have been settled for years. The importance of the subject is being recognised more widely, especially as a result of the increase in personal assets brought about by the inflation of house prices, but there is at last a wider study of the implications of the law of property.

The major changes in the law of succession recommended by the Scottish Law Commission in 1990 in its Report on Succession (Scot. Law Com. No. 124) have still not been implemented but there is as yet no indication of whether or when time will be found for the necessary legislation. This is yet another symptom of the neglect of valuable reforms which do not seem to have political mileage. It seems probable that it will now take several years before the changes come into force, and the desultory amendments of specific figures in the Act will continue to lag far behind the reality of current values. In consequence the original purposes of the Act are being steadily eroded. There is an attempt in Chapter 10 to analyse the broad consequences if the Commission's proposed reforms were to be enacted in the form of the draft Bill attached to the Report, but there has been no attempt at a detailed commentary, given that the Act which may eventually result will undoubtedly be subject to alteration.

This new edition is now necessary to take account of the multiple changes since the appearance of the last edition in 1993. Testators continue to be ingenious in framing clauses which are difficult to interpret and one suspects that birling can be heard in several graveyards over the results which have actually happened. The law is stated as at August 2002.

The main statutory change has been the Requirements of Writing (Scotland) Act 1995 with its dramatic changes to the whole process of execution of deeds. That great icon of Scots law, the holograph will, is no more in that form, since the only requirement for basic validity is that a testator subscribes the will, irrespective of whether the text of the will is in the testator's writing. The magical incantation "adopted as holograph" no longer has any function, which spoils my favourite speculation of how any signature could ever have been holograph of a firm of solicitors rather than of an individual. The Act also makes a substantial step forward by recognising a mark as a signature and subscription in many circumstances, including the important provision that it is a signature if the testator *intended* it as his signature.

Chapter 7 has been considerably expanded to give a general account of wills rather than the previous comment on the changes effected by the Act. Some illustrations derived from the author's published volume of opinions have been included and it is hoped that this work will continue to provide a useful service to the student and to the profession.

My thanks are due to reviewers of previous editions for their helpful comments.

M. C. MESTON

University of Aberdeen.

PREFACE TO FIRST EDITION

The purpose of this work is to state and to explain the substantial changes in Scots law made by the Succession (Scotland) Act 1964. The main effects of the Act are in the law of intestate succession, but there are very important provisions making completely new arrangements for the property consequences of divorce and a number of provisions affecting testate succession and inter vivos deeds. Taken together, these changes amount to the most important reform of Scottish private law in recent years.

It is hoped that this book will provide a guide through the provisions of the Act which will be of assistance to practitioners and to students and others concerned with the law of succession. An attempt has been made to present a complete picture of the law of intestate succession in Scotland, with a new Table of Heirs and some illustrations of particular situations in the Appendices. Those parts of the previous law left in existence, e.g., in the field of legal rights, are considered, albeit briefly, along with the changes made by the Act. In relation to the other topics dealt with by the Act, comment has been limited to the specific changes made. Any suggestions for improvement will be gratefully received.

Although the Act will not come into force until September 10, 1964, the text has been written as if this had already happened.

My thanks are due to my colleagues for the willingness to act as guineapigs on whom ideas could be tried out, and in particular to Professor D. M. Walker and Professor J. Bennett Miller who suggested valuable improvements.

M. C. MESTON

Faculty of Law,
University of Glasgow,
July, 1964.

CONTENTS

PART I

PART II

APPENDICES

TABLE OF CASES

TABLE OF STATUTES

CHAPTER 1

INTESTATE SUCCESSION IN SCOTLAND
BEFORE SEPTEMBER 10, 1964

The Succession (Scotland) Act 1964[1] came into force on September 10, 1964. It does not purport to be a code in itself, for it adopts the device of requiring succession to be regulated by the provisions of the Act and by "any enactment or rule of law in force immediately before the commencement of this Act which is not inconsistent with those provisions and which, apart from this section, would apply to that person's moveable intestate estate, if any."[2] Nonetheless, when read with the subsequent amending legislation, it does in fact state most of the law relating to intestate succession in Scotland (together with various other topics) and it was certainly the first attempt to set out intestate succession as a coherent body of rules.

Despite the passing of nearly 40 years since the Act came into force on September 10, 1964, it remains necessary to understand the previous law. This is particularly true for succession to heritage, for an apparently never-ending series of cases still produces situations in which the title to land was not completed when a death occurred prior to 1964. In one case, which was referred to the author recently, the last recorded title was dated 1899 and a chain of wills and intestacies had to be unravelled before the owner of a particular piece of ground could be determined. Very often the trigger for the need to establish a recorded title is a purchase by a public authority, perhaps only of a few square yards for a telephone box. It seems to have been very common for a member of the family of a deceased owner to continue to live in the "family" house whether or not a will had been made and without any attempt to make up title. Sharply increased house values mean that disputes, and inheritance tax, have become significant in many estates which would previously have been too small, so that title to the house now becomes vital on the death of the occupier. The older law is necessary to guide one through possibly several generations of inheritances in order to provide a good title to a purchaser.[3]

The system of intestate succession in Scotland prior to the passing of the Succession (Scotland) Act 1964 was one based on common law (which itself derived partly from feudal law and partly from canon law) with a succession of piecemeal amendments contained in a variety of statutes. The general

---

[1] (c.41).
[2] s.1(1).
[3] See for example *Meston's Succession Opinions*, No.8, pp.17–18.

principles were tolerably well known, but the exceptions and special statutory provisions were such that difficulties could be experienced in applying them to practical situations.

For example, the Intestate Moveable Succession (Scotland) Act 1855[4] gave the deceased's father in certain circumstances a right to one-half of the intestate's "moveable estate." That phrase was defined by section 9 as "the whole free moveable estate on which the deceased ... might have tested, undisposed of by will." The Intestate Husband's Estate (Scotland) Act 1911 gave to the widow of a man who died intestate and without lawful issue a prior right to the first £500 out of his estate. The deceased might clearly have tested on this £500, even though he did not in fact do so. Thus it was difficult to establish that the £500 was meant to be deducted before the father took one-half of the balance under the 1855 Act, although that was the only sensible course. The difficulty was not resolved until the passing of the Intestate Moveable Succession (Scotland) Act 1919,[5] which deemed any sums due from an intestate's estate to the surviving spouse not to be estate on which the intestate might have tested.

Representation

Similarly, when the 1855 Act first introduced the concept of representation in intestate moveable succession[6] it did so in the broad general form that "the lawful child or children of such person so predeceasing shall come in the place of such person, and the issue of any such child or children, who may in like manner have predeceased the intestate, shall come in the place of his or their parent predeceasing, and shall respectively have right to the share of the moveable estate of the intestate to which the parent of such child or children, or of such issue, if he had survived the intestate, would have been entitled." This broad assertion of the principle of infinite representation among descendants did however use the term "next of kin" to describe the person predeceasing the intestate and this use of a technical term led to the remarkable decision by the Court of Session in *Turner v. Couper*[7] that representation was not in fact complete among descendants, and commenced only at the nearest class of descendants in which there were any surviving members. This peculiarity still bedevils our law and should be reformed to avoid the enormous variations in benefits which occur under the present law through the accident of whether or not a single member of a previous generation happens to have survived the deceased.[8]

---

[4] (18 & 19 Vict., c.23), s.3.
[5] (9 & 10 Geo. 5, c.61), s.4(1).
[6] s.1.
[7] (1869) 8 M. 222.
[8] Meston, "Representation in Succession" (1995) 1 Scottish Law & Practice Quarterly pp.83–92.

Proof of death and of survivorship

The law of succession prior to the Succession (Scotland) Act 1964 began with the usual problems of establishing that the deceased had in fact died and that potential beneficiaries had survived. Then, as now, the rules of succession depended on proof of the death of the person whose estate was being divided. In most cases this prerequisite is so obviously satisfied that it is seldom considered beyond the steps necessary to obtain a death certificate, but in cases of disappearance proof of the fact of death and of the date of death can become matters of considerable difficulty.

Actions were available, both at common law and under the Presumption of Life Limitation (Scotland) Act 1891,[9] for settling the question of death and the date on which it occurred.

The common law action was based on a general presumption that human life, once shown to have been in existence, continued until the extreme limits of human age. It was never completely clear what those limits were, but they seem to have meant that life was presumed to continue until the missing person would have been between 80 and 100 years old.[10] The effect of this was that the onus of proving an earlier date of death fell upon the persons propounding it, and if no clear evidence of earlier death could be produced, the result was that the missing person had to be regarded as still alive and 40 or 50 years might have to elapse before the missing person's property could safely be distributed on the basis of his or her death.

The statutory action under the 1891 Act solved some of the problems by introducing the seven-year rule. The statutory procedure came to be widely used and the result usually was that, in the absence of fairly cogent evidence pointing to an earlier date of death, a missing person was presumed to have died exactly seven years after he was last known to be alive.[11] However, the Act dealt only with property, and did not affect other issues such as the continued existence of the missing person's marriage. Conversely, dissolution of marriage on the ground of presumed death under the Divorce (Scotland) Act 1938[12] had no effect on the succession to the missing person's property, and in theory it was necessary for the representatives of the missing person to raise a number of separate actions to establish death for different purposes.[13]

Closely linked with the question of establishing the death of the owner of the property in question is the problem of establishing that the beneficiary survived the date of the previous owner's death. Again this requirement is so obviously met in most cases that it is not considered, but problem situations can arise in which the issue is by no means clear. The approach taken is that, unless a potential beneficiary can be affirmatively proved to have survived the

---

[9] (54 & 55 Vict., c.29).

[10] Stair, IV, xlv, 17, nineteenthly; Bankton, Inst., II, vi, 31; *Secretary of State for Scotland v. Sutherland*, 1944 S.C. 79.

[11] 1891 Act, s.3. If he reappeared, the missing person had a right to recover his property for a period of 13 years from the registration of title to it or the transfer of possession, as appropriate: ss.6 & 7.

[12] (1 & 2 Geo. 6, c.50).

[13] *Report on Presumption of Death*, Scot. Law Com. No. 34 (1974).

deceased, he has no claim on the succession.[14] The problem which caused the greatest difficulty was that arising out of the common calamity. There was, until the passing of the 1964 Act, no presumption of survivorship in such cases. Thus if, for example, a husband and wife died intestate in a common calamity without proof that one survived the other, the result was that neither set of representatives could claim their predecessor's share of the estate of the other. The practical result was much the same as if the husband had predeceased his wife and the wife had also predeceased the husband, but in fact predecease was not established either. All that was established was that neither had been proved to have survived the other. Thus if two persons, whether or not they were spouses, died in an incident in which there was no proof of survivorship by either of them, and left wills in each other's favour, neither could be proved to qualify as a beneficiary in the other's estate. Equally, however, neither could be proved to have predeceased the other, so that even if the wills provided for an alternative disposal in the event of the "predecease" of the other, the alternative could not be used either and the result would be intestacy.[15] Under section 31 of the 1964 Act this is still the case when the common calamity involves husband and wife, but there is now a presumption of survivorship for other cases.

Once these preliminary questions of death and survivance had been considered, the rules of division came into play.

Fragmentation of approach

The pattern of the 1964 Act in having several different sets of rules, with different characteristics, any or all of which might be applicable in a given case, was also evident before it. Three different sets of rules had to be considered before the precise division of a particular estate could be established. These were first, the preferable right to the first £5,000 of a deceased's estate given in certain circumstances to the surviving spouse, secondly, the legal rights of spouses and children, and thirdly, the ordinary law of intestate succession. These three sets of rules had to be considered in that order, and if all were applicable, the preferable right would first be deducted from the estate to which legal rights applied. Then the entitlement to legal rights would be applied and deducted, leaving the balance subject to the ordinary law of succession.

Statutory preference of the surviving spouse

This right was created by the Intestate Husband's Estate (Scotland) Acts 1911 to 1959.[16] Despite the title of the Acts, the right applied in favour of a

---

[14] "Survivance is in every case a matter of proof, and ... when a claimant whose claim depends upon proof of survivorship is unable to establish the fact of survivance, his claim necessarily fails." *Drummond's J.F. v. Lord Advocate*, 1944 S.C. 298, *per* Lord President Cooper at 302.

[15] *Ross's J.F. v. Martin*, 1955 S.C. (H.L.) 56.

[16] (1 & 2 Geo. 5, c.10); (9 & 10 Geo. 5, c.9); (3 & 4 Geo. 6, c.42), s.5; (7 & 8 Eliz. 2, c.21). The figure was raised from £500 by the 1959 Act.

husband in his wife's estate as well as vice versa. Where one spouse died
intestate and without lawful issue, the surviving spouse had an absolute right to
the first £5,000 of the free estate, with interest at four per cent, from the date of
death until payment, taken rateably from heritage and moveables belonging to
the intestate. If the intestate's total estate was less than £5,000, and the
conditions were satisfied, the surviving spouse took the whole estate. If the
deceased's intestacy was only partial, the surviving spouse had this right in the
estate undisposed of but had to deduct from the £5,000 any legacy left to him
or her. The new "prior rights" created by the 1964 Act have obvious
similarities of approach.

Legal rights of spouses and children

As a result of the feudal relic expressed in the differentiation between
heritage and moveables, these rights were divided into rights in heritage and
those in moveables.

(1) The rights exigible from heritage existed only in favour of a surviving
spouse of the deceased, and were of an income nature. A widow's right was
known as terce and gave her a liferent of one-third of the heritage owned by
her husband at the date of his death. (Note the important difference from the
Anglo-American concept of dower which could apply to land owned by the
husband at any time during the marriage.) Even after the removal of some
peculiarities deriving from a rule that terce existed only in heritage in which
the husband was infeft,[17] certain items of heritage were still not subject to terce,
e.g. the principal mansion house of an estate, feuduties[18] and minerals.[19] The
practical value of the right was usually negligible, being to one-third of the net
income after payment of local rates, interest on heritable debt, etc. The
corresponding right of a widower was known as courtesy, but it was a liferent
of the whole of the heritage belonging to the wife at her death. It has been said
that it was awarded to the husband more as father of an heir than as husband of
an heiress, for it applied only if a live child had been born of the marriage, and
that child was at some time the wife's heir.

(2) The rights exigible from moveable estate were full rights of fee, and
were available to both surviving spouse and to children. There were three
possible units of division, namely *jus relictae* (widow) or *jus relicti* (widower),
being the surviving spouse's share; legitim, being the surviving children's
share; and dead's part, which fell to be regulated by the ordinary law of
intestate succession (or of which the deceased was completely free to dispose
if he left a will). If there was a surviving spouse and also surviving children,
the moveables were split into three for the purposes of legal rights, one share
going to each of the units above. If there was a surviving spouse, but no
surviving children, the moveables were split into two shares, the spouse taking
one share as *jus relictae* or *relicti* as the case might be, and the other share
going to dead's part. Similarly, if there were surviving children, but no

---

[17] Conveyancing (Scotland) Act 1924 (14 & 15 Geo. 5, c.27), s.21(4).
[18] *Nisbett v. Nisbett* (1835) 13 S.517.
[19] *Grosset v. Grosset*, 1959 S.L.T. 334.

surviving spouse, the children shared one-half of the moveables as legitim and the other half as dead's part. In the division of the legitim fund so arrived at, the doctrine of collation *inter liberos* was applied to preserve equality. Any child claiming legitim who had received an advance, *e.g.* for setting him up in life, could be required by other children claiming legitim to collate that advance by adding it to the legitim fund and taking his rateable share of the total fund.[20]

Prior to the commencement of the Succession (Scotland) Act 1964, "surviving children" had to be literally interpreted for the purposes of legal rights. There was no representation in legitim, and thus only those of the immediate children of the deceased who survived him were entitled to it. The issue of predeceasing children could not in any circumstances represent their parents in claims for legitim, nor could they have independent claims in their own right.

The best known feature of legal rights was, as it still is, that they were indefeasible, apart from certain exceptions, and operated as a bar to capricious disinheritance by a testator. The origin of legal rights in moveables in Scotland seems to have been in a germanic system of common family ownership of property,[21] and in theory a testator had no power to deal with any part of his moveable estate other than the one-third or one-half included in the dead's part. Legal rights could, of course, be evaded by transactions during the deceased's own lifetime, *e.g.* by making a gift of the fee of his whole estate *inter vivos* and reserving only a liferent, which left nothing at his death on which legal rights could operate.[22]

Of more importance from the point of view of intestate succession was the fact that legal rights might be excluded, either by an express discharge granted by the party prospectively entitled,[23] or by exclusion in the deceased's ante-nuptial marriage contract.[24]

The ordinary rules of intestate succession

These rules applied to the estate left after any statutory preference and legal rights had been deducted. For historical reasons, there were entirely separate bodies of rules applying to the succession to heritage and to the succession to moveables respectively. They were similar to the extent that both employed the same general notions of propinquity in seeking heirs. Instead of using either the civil law or the canon law system of computation of degrees of relationship through a common ancestor, Scots law used (and to some extent still uses) a modified version of the parentelic system. This system employs the principle of lines of succession, so that the whole of the first line must be exhausted without finding a surviving heir before any member of the second

---

[20] *Coats's Trs v. Coats*, 1914 S.C. 744.

[21] J.C. Gardner, *Origin and Nature of Legal Rights in Scotland*.

[22] *Campbell v. Campbell's Trs*, 1967 S.L.T (Notes) 30.

[23] *Melville's Trs v. Melville's Trs*, 1964 S.C. 105.

[24] *Panmure v. Crokat* (1856) 18 D. 703; *Dunbar's Trs v. Dunbar* (1902) 5 F. 191; *Galloway's Trs v. Galloway*, 1943 S.C. 339.

line can take. Thus the claim of any member of the second line, however close by a system of degrees, is postponed to that of any member of the first line, however remote. Within a particular line, the order of priority is determined by the number of steps from the head of the line.

In the version employed in Scotland the first line consisted of the children and other more remote lineal descendants of the deceased. In the absence of such descendants, the succession opened to the second line, consisting of the collaterals of the deceased and their descendants. Note that the second line did not (and does not) commence with the parents of the deceased as in a true parentelic system such as that in Germany. Failing successors in the categories of descendants or collaterals, the succession opened to ascendants. But, although both used these basic principles, intestate heritable and moveable succession were very different in detail.

A. *Intestate heritable succession* operated on the principle of picking out the one individual who would succeed as heir at law to all the heritage of the deceased. This was based on the necessity under the feudal system of preserving the unity of landed estates so that the appropriate military services might be rendered, but in certain circumstances in which the succession opened to females, a group of females might be regarded as a collective heir and were known as "heirs portioners". The principles on which the heir at law was selected were as follows:

(1) The succession opened first to lineal descendants of the deceased.

(2) In the absence of descendants, the succession opened to collaterals of the deceased and their descendants.

(3) In the absence of descendants or collaterals, the succession opened to ascendants of the deceased. Emphasising the importance of direct blood relationship in this system, and also the feudal preference for males to perform military services, this meant that the mother and maternal relations were excluded and ascendants meant the father, whom failing the father's collaterals or their descendants, whom failing the paternal grandfather or his collaterals or their descendants, and remoter ascendants *ad infinitum* on the same principles.

(4) Preference of males applied in any given category. If there were one son and several daughters, the one son took the whole of the heritage. Only if there were no males in that category did females succeed. Thus, if the deceased left only daughters, they could inherit the heritage, but they took it as heirs portioners, which meant that they were a kind of collective heir at law. Heirs portioners shared the heritage equally, except that any indivisible items of heritage went to the eldest daughter as her *praecipuum*. The main examples were titles of honour and the principal mansion house of a landed estate with its garden and ornamental policies.

(5) Primogeniture was used as the principle to select the one male descendant of a given category to succeed as heir at law, *i.e.* the eldest son had this position. Primogeniture did not however apply among collaterals, so that the selection of the one brother of the deceased (or the brother of his lineal paternal ascendant) in cases in which the succession opened to such collaterals was not carried out by primogeniture. It also did not apply to succession by females, except to the extent that items regarded as indivisible fell to the eldest heir portioner.

(6) Representation was unlimited in every degree of intestate succession to heritage. This rule of genuine representation was entirely different from the position in moveables (and indeed is entirely different from the present day position — except for titles of honour). Any descendant, however remote, and whether male or female, of someone who would have been entitled to inherit if he or she had survived could stand in that ancestor's shoes. It did not matter if the whole of an intervening generation had died. Thus if the eldest son predeceased the intestate, his issue, however remote, could represent him and take in preference to the second son of the intestate. Primogeniture and preference of males operated to select the person to act as representative, but even if the representatives were a class of females they were still preferred to the second son of the intestate. If sisters would have inherited as heirs portioners, their children took their respective shares. It did not matter if all the sisters had predeceased the intestate. The issue of each still took the share which their mother would have taken, and did not divide the estate per capita among all the grandchildren. Note that this genuine representation was entirely different from the rules of succession to moveables, and the fact that there was genuine representation in heritage seems to have been totally ignored in the modern law.

(7) Exclusion of the mother and all maternal relatives was complete in heritable succession. While the child was heir to its mother, the mother and anyone tracing relationship through her could never be the heir at law of the child.

(8) The full blood excluded the half blood in all degrees of succession. This meant that any collateral who shared both parents with the deceased took in preference to any collateral sharing only one parent with the deceased. However, if there were no collaterals of the full blood, or their issue representing them, the half blood consanguinean could inherit. This meant that collaterals sharing the same father with the deceased could inherit in these circumstances. The complete exclusion of the mother and maternal relations in heritable succession had the consequence that collaterals of the half blood uterine (sharing the same mother with the deceased) were completely excluded from the succession.

(9) The rule that heritage descends was applied in cases where the succession opened to brothers of the intestate or of his lineal paternal ascendants, but was not applied where sisters succeeded collectively. Although the intestate might have had elder brothers, the rule of descent pointed out the next younger brother to the deceased as his heir at law. Failing that brother (or his issue by representation), the next brother down the line was entitled. Failing younger brothers, or their representatives, or if the intestate was himself the youngest of three or more brothers, the succession opened to the immediate elder brother in preference to the eldest.

(10) The Crown, as *ultimus haeres*, was entitled to the heritage of anyone dying intestate without other lawful heirs entitled to the succession. The Crown's interests were, and still are, represented by the Queen's and Lord Treasurer's Remembrancer, a position which is now part of the functions of the Crown Office.

The process by which the heir at law proved that he was the heir at law and obtained a judicial declaration to that effect was service of heirs. Until 1964 all sheriff courts had jurisdiction in services. For the continuing flow of cases in which it is necessary to obtain a service in respect of deaths prior to 1964, the process has been centralised with the Sheriff of Chancery in Edinburgh.[25]

B. *Intestate moveable succession* operated on the different principle that all surviving members of the class nearest in degree to the intestate should share equally in his moveables, as "next of kin". This at least was the common law principle, although it was subject to various statutory modifications. The general rules of propinquity to the intestate were the same as in intestate heritable succession, but the special rules of primogeniture and preference of males applied to heritable succession in order to select the one member of the class to take the whole did not apply to moveables. Further, since the principle at common law was that only the next of kin, *i.e.* the *surviving* members of the class nearest in degree to the intestate, could succeed, there was at common law no representation in intestate moveable succession. Thus at common law the next of kin, even if the class consisted of only one person, took the entire moveable succession in preference to any number of people in the next or remoter degrees of propinquity.[26]

Statutory amendments to the common law

The various statutory amendments to the common law of moveable succession had the effect of creating a dichotomy between the next of kin identified on the common law principles and the heirs *in mobilibus*, *i.e.* the persons who actually took the moveable estate. As a result of the changes, the heirs *in mobilibus* became a class including the next of kin, but not limited to the next of kin. The three major statutory changes were the introduction of representation in moveables to a limited extent, improvements in the position of the parents of the intestate, and the grant of limited rights in favour of collaterals of the half blood uterine.

Representation in succession to the free moveable estate was introduced by section 1 of the Intestate Moveable Succession (Scotland) Act 1855.[27] Apparently copying a provision of the English Statute of Distribution of 1670, the 1855 Act limited the principle of representation to descendants and collaterals of the deceased. The moveable estate in which representation became possible was defined as "the whole free moveable estate on which the deceased ... might have tested".[28] As it was well established that a testator had power to test only on the dead's part, and not on the part of his estate subject to legal rights, the result of this definition was that there was no representation in legitim. When the succession opened to ascendants and their collaterals, representation was no longer applicable. Thus, after the introduction of

---

[25] For forms and procedure, see Act of Sederunt (Chancery Procedure Rules) 1996 (S.I. 1996 No. 2184)
[26] *Ormiston v. Broad* (1862) 1 M. 10.
[27] (18 & 19 Vict., c.23).
[28] *ibid.*, s.9.

representation in 1855, grandchildren could not share in legitim along with surviving children, but could share with them in the dead's part by representation. Nephews and nieces could share by representation along with surviving brothers and sisters, but one survivor of the class of uncles and aunts would take the whole free moveable estate in preference to cousins by virtue of his position as next of kin at common law.

The improvements in the position of the parents of an intestate were effected by the 1855 Act and by the Intestate Moveable Succession (Scotland) Act 1919.[29] At common law the father of an intestate ranked next after the intestate's collaterals and before his own collaterals, forming in effect a special class of next of kin. The mother of the intestate had no rights as such.

Presumably in recognition of the oddity of treating the second line of succession as excluding parents, section 3 of the 1855 Act gave the father an extra right to share in moveables in a situation where the succession would not otherwise have opened to him. It provided that he was to have one-half of the moveable estate in preference to brothers and sisters of the deceased or their descendants. The mother's position, finally contained in section 1 of the 1919 Act, was effectively a right to represent the predeceasing father, so that if the father had predeceased the intestate, the mother took over his right to one-half of the free moveable estate in preference to collaterals or to the whole free moveable estate if the intestate left no collaterals.

At common law collaterals of the half blood uterine had no rights of succession to moveables, although the half blood consanguinean had full rights postponed only to collaterals of the full blood. Section 5 of the 1855 Act gave uterine collaterals a right limited in all circumstances to one-half of the moveable estate (the balance went to the Crown if there were no other heirs). This right applied only if the intestate died without issue, without collaterals of the full blood or of the half blood consanguinean, and predeceased by both parents.

C. Collation inter haeredes was a doctrine which arose as a result of the existence of different rules of succession applying to heritable and to moveable property respectively. In mixed estates with both heritage and moveables it qualified the separation of the two lines of succession by permitting, in appropriate circumstances, the massing together of the heritage and the moveables and the distribution of the combined fund by the rules normally applicable to moveable property only. Accepting the inequality which arose from giving all the heritage of an intestate to his heir at law, the object of collation *inter haeredes* was to make some show of equality in the distribution of the intestate's moveable property.

A person succeeding as heir at law to the heritage was normally barred from sharing in the moveable estate.[30] However, provided that he was a member of the class entitled to succeed to the moveables of the intestate (which was not always the case)[31] he could choose to throw his heritage into a common pool with the moveables and to take his proportionate share with the other heirs *in*

---

[29] (9 & 10 Geo.5, c.61).
[30] *Law v. Law* (1553) Mor. 2365.
[31] *McCaw v. McCaws* (1787) Mor. 2383; *Colville's J.F. v. Nicoll*, 1914 S.C. 62.

mobilibus in the composite fund. He had a completely unfettered option and, naturally, a decision to collate would normally be made only when the heir's share of the combined fund was more valuable than the heritage to which he succeeded as heir at law.

However, if there was no heritage, no question of collation could arise. Collation was a doctrine applicable only to mixed estates, and if the estate was wholly moveable the heir at law simply took his appropriate share of moveables along with the other heirs *in mobilibus*. He was excluded from sharing in the moveables only so long as he actually took heritage from the intestate's estate. Equally there could be no collation if there were no other heirs *in mobilibus* to share the moveables. In that situation he simply took the whole estate, heritable and moveable, since there was no one with whom to collate.

History of the attempts to achieve reform

For the earlier background one can do no better than to quote the Report of the Mackintosh Committee on the Law of Succession in Scotland published in 1950.

"Amendment of our law of intestate succession is a matter which has been under the consideration of the legal profession in Scotland at least since 1924. Following on the passing of the Law of Property Act 1922 (now embodied in the Administration of Estates Act 1925), which made radical reforms upon the law of succession in England, the whole question of the alteration of the law of intestate succession in Scotland was fully explored by Committees of the Society of Writers to H.M. Signet and of the Faculty of Procurators in Glasgow, and Reports recommending change were made by the Committee of the former body in 1924 and again in 1927 and by the Committee of the latter body in 1925. The most detailed of these Reports was that of 1927 which was approved by the W.S. Society on May 30, 1927. From these Reports and the investigations which preceded them the following common factors of agreement were separately arrived at by the two Committees and represent, we were informed, what is still the considered view of their parent bodies:

(1) That for the purpose of intestate succession, heritable and moveable property should be blended and form one estate.

(2) That the law of primogeniture should be abolished.

(3) That the differentiation between the sexes in intestate succession should be abolished.

(4) That there should be succession through the mother as well as through the father, and

(5) That in any alteration of the law the principle of legal rights should be retained, though these would require readjustment consequent on the abolition of primogeniture and the blending of heritable and moveable estate.

In 1927 a Bill was promoted by a private member of Parliament entitled 'The Succession (Scotland) Bill' which proposed inter alia certain alterations in the law relating to intestate succession including the abolition of primogeniture. This Bill did not proceed, the view taken of it by the legal societies being that a much more sweeping and general amendment of the law of succession was required, and that the legislative action which was necessary in the matter was not such as should be left to the initiative of individual Members of Parliament. In their Report of 1927 the W.S. Society recommended that the Law Officers of the Crown be memorialised with a view to the appointment of a Departmental Committee for consideration of the subject. For one reason or another no such appointment was made until our Committee was set up...

During the Bill stage of the recent Adoption of Children Act 1949 the question arose as to whether sections 9 and 10 of the Act--which in effect for all purposes of succession gave adopted children the status and rights of children born in wedlock--should be applied to Scotland. The conclusion then reached was that the sections in question should not be applied to Scotland because of the legal complications which might ensue under our existing law of intestate succession, more particularly because of its rules of primogeniture and preference of males over females. This in turn brought to the fore once more the issue as to whether a comprehensive review of our law of intestate succession ought not now to be undertaken. It will be seen, however, from what has been said above, that while the question which arose under the Adoption of Children Act 1949 may have furnished the immediate occasion which led to the present Inquiry, the causes for this Inquiry lie deeper and are of long-standing duration."

The Committee was appointed on July 30, 1949, and reported on December 9, 1950,[32] but the history of delay noted in the section of the Report quoted above was by no means over.

The Morton Committee on the law of intestacy in England was appointed on October 13, 1950. A Bill giving effect to most of its recommendations received the Royal Assent as the Intestates' Estates Act 1952 on October 30, 1952. Although time was thus speedily found for the English measure, the proposals for Scotland in the Mackintosh Committee Report were allowed to languish despite periodical prodding by Scottish Members of Parliament. In February 1952, in answer to a question in the House it was "hoped to make a statement at an early date", but in November 1953 it was "not proposed to introduce legislation on this subject during the present session." Not until May 1957 was another question asked in the House, when the reply was again evasive. It is perhaps symptomatic of the consistent delay that a letter to the editor of the Scots Law Times on the anomalies of the law of succession, printed early in 1957, could reappear in that journal, identically worded, late in 1958.

---

[32] Cmd. 8144 (1950).

Pressure for the introduction of legislation was stepped up from then on. Two questions were asked in the House in 1958, and some concrete results were achieved when a private member's Bill to raise the amount of the surviving spouse's prior right from £500 to £5,000 received governmental blessing and was enacted as the Intestate Husband's Estate (Scotland) Act 1959. This appeared to provoke action, and in the Queen's speech at the opening of the new session of Parliament in October 1959, legislation to effect the long-awaited reform of the law of succession was promised for that session. A draft Bill was in fact circulated for comment but ran into a variety of technical objections, and the Bill lost its place in the legislative queue. A series of questions in 1960 and 1961 could elicit no more than the stock reply that it could not yet be said when it might be possible to introduce a Bill.

In April 1961 the Intestacy (Scotland) Bill was introduced by a group of Scottish private members, including those who had been most active in putting pressure on the Government, but it made no progress. Admittedly, however, the drafting would not have been satisfactory as an Act. 1962 appears to have been quiescent, and finally in May 1963, completely out of the blue, came the publication of the Law Reform (Succession, etc.) (Scotland) Bill. While too late to be enacted in that session of Parliament, it was at least an earnest of good intentions, and provided an opportunity for detailed consideration of the proposals. Some of the fruits of that consideration were apparent when the Bill, under its new title of the Succession (Scotland) Bill, was reintroduced in the following session of Parliament on November 14, 1963. The Act came into force on September 10, 1964, since when various amendments have been effected, particularly by the Law Reform (Miscellaneous Provisions) (Scotland) Acts of 1966 and 1968, the Law Reform (Parent & Child) (Scotland) Act 1986, the Age of Legal Capacity (Scotland) Act 1991 and the Requirements of Writing (Scotland) Act 1995.[33]

Further major reform is likely when the Scottish Law Commission's Report on Succession[34] is accepted and the proposed Bill is introduced into Parliament. However the history of delay continues. The present author was doubtful whether the previous edition of this book would have a long currency before the reforms. That was more than 10 years ago and there is still not the remotest sign of any action being taken to implement the Law Commission's recommendations even although the fixed sums have become increasingly outdated, despite periodic amendments. The possible effect of the Commission's reforms is discussed in Chapter 10.

---

[33] See the annotated text of the Act, amended to the date of publication of this edition, in the Part II.
[34] Scot. Law Com. No. 124,(1990)

CHAPTER 2

INTESTATE SUCCESSION AFTER THE 1964 ACT

Commencement

The 1964 Act came into force on September 10, 1964 to regulate the succession to the estates of persons dying after midnight on the night of September 9, 1964.[1] The provision in section 5 of the Law Reform (Miscellaneous Provisions) (Scotland) Act 1966[2] designed to cure a hiatus in the succession rights of some adopted persons[3] came into force on August 3, 1966. It applies to cases where the adopting parents died before September 10, 1964, and the natural parents died on or after August 3, 1966.

The increased but limited succession rights of illegitimate children created by Part I of the Law Reform (Miscellaneous Provisions) Scotland) Act 1968[4] came into force in respect of the estates of persons dying on or after November 25, 1968, as did the provisions in Part II of the same Act bringing crofting tenancies within the scope of the Succession Act. Virtual abolition of the status of illegitimacy and the creation of equality in succession for children formerly classed as illegitimate has applied in respect of deaths on or after December 8, 1986.[5]

Substantial increases in the financial limits of the prior rights of a surviving spouse were effected by the Succession (Scotland) Act 1973[6] for deaths on or after May 23, 1973. That Act also gave the Secretary of State power to effect further increases by statutory instrument and such increases have so far been made by the Prior Rights of Surviving Spouse (Scotland) Orders of 1977 (deaths on or after December 31, 1977), 1981 (deaths on or after August 1, 1981), 1988 (deaths on or after May 1, 1988), 1993 (deaths on or after November 26,1993) and 1999 (deaths on or after April 2, 1999).

Policy of the changes

The main policy of the alterations made by the 1964 Act was one of taking account of changing social conditions. The previous law was framed in such a way as to be relevant mainly to the large landed estate and, although modifications had been made from time to time, it still bore the marks of the feudal system in which these landowners might be called on as such to provide

---

[1] s.38(3).
[2] (c.19).
[3] See p 72, *infra*.
[4] (c.70).
[5] Law Reform (Parent and Child) (Scotland) Act 1986 (c.9).
[6] (c.25).

military services. Changed conditions, however, demanded a different approach. This change had taken place over many centuries. For example the valuation roll for Aberdeenshire in 1674 displayed a much larger number of small landholdings than the equivalent valuation roll for 1548 when Mary Queen of Scots (or her advisers) anticipated an invasion by England.[7] By 1964 not only had the typical estate left by a deceased person changed from a large landed estate to one of a substantial number of much more modest estates, but there had been steady progress in the equalisation of the sexes and a growing feeling that a surviving spouse, especially a widow, was not properly catered for by the law of intestate succession.

All this meant that the law of intestate succession in Scotland was completely out of touch with the expectations of a large section of the population. Many a solicitor was abused, or suspected of improper dealings, by disappointed relatives who found that they were to get no share of the estate. It was not easy to justify the privileged position of the heir at law to his younger brothers. It was not easy to tell a mother that she had no right to her deceased child's heritable estate and that it might go to the Crown rather than to her. Even if, as an act of grace, the Crown did make a gift of the heritage to her, she rightly would consider that the fact that this was necessary, let alone the expense, was ridiculous. It was not easy to tell the cousin who had nursed the deceased for years prior to his death that, because the deceased had made no will, the whole of his moveable estate went to his Aunt Jemima in Timbuktu, and that, devoted or not, the cousin got nothing. And in particular, it was not easy to tell a widow that the amount of capital which she had to live on after her husband's death might be substantially less than she had expected. Many a widow imagined that the whole estate of her husband automatically passed to her on his death and was disappointed when the truth emerged.

The reforms therefore attempted to bring the law of intestate succession into line with modern conditions. In the well-known phrase of the Mackintosh Committee Report, "we have throughout kept in view the principle that when a man dies without a will the law should try to provide so far as possible for the distribution of his estate in the manner he would most likely have given effect to himself if he had made a will".

It is probably true that no general provision for intestacy can provide a result which will be that most likely to have been selected by every deceased person, whatever the size of his estate. Fears were expressed in Parliament as to the effect the Act would have on larger estates, but it was pointed out that intestacy was far commoner in small estates than in large ones. Thus, although ideas as to what constituted a "small" estate varied widely, the Act was framed with the medium to small estate in mind.

Figures obtained from a survey of confirmations granted in 1961 were quoted in the House of Lords to illustrate the proposition that the Succession Act had to be mainly concerned with the smaller estates. Of 26,943 confirmations granted in 1961, 17,273 (or approximately two-thirds) were cases where wills had been made. Only 9,670 (approximately one-third) were

---

[7] *The Aberdeen Stylebook 1722,*(Stair Society,Vol. 47).

intestacies. Of the 9,670 intestacies only 32 were estates with a gross value over £25,000, and in only five cases was the heritable portion of an intestate estate valued at over £10,000. Intestacy was thus rare when the estate was large, and extremely rare when there was substantial heritable estate. As this would suggest, experience since 1964 has allayed fears that the Act would cause wholesale subdivision of country estates and farms.

Even these figures do not give the full picture. Although there were 26,943 confirmations in 1961 there were 63,928 deaths in Scotland in that year. For many years the annual number of deaths in Scotland had been stable at around 63,000 (which is almost the same as the number of deaths in 1855). Thus although deaths in a given year need not necessarily lead to confirmation in that year, the proportion of confirmations to deaths in any year gives useful evidence, being set against a relatively stable number of deaths. Some of the deaths will have been of persons whose estates were wound up elsewhere, but that should be counterbalanced by deaths elsewhere of domiciled Scots. Allowing for these factors, there were therefore in 1961 approximately 37,000 cases, over and above the 27,000 in which confirmation was granted, in which it must be assumed that the estate was so small that confirmation was not obtained.

A survey carried out at Aberdeen in the mid-1980s produced similar results. In the five years from 1980 to 1984, the Scottish average of confirmations as a proportion of total deaths was about 43 per cent. This conceals variations between different parts of the country. In Aberdeen and Stonehaven sheriff court districts confirmations averaged around 50 per cent of relevant deaths, with the obvious conclusion that in other areas the proportion was less than the national average of 43 per cent. It is rather startling to the solicitor accustomed to winding up estates and obtaining confirmation to realise that only about two-fifths of the persons who die in Scotland leave estate of sufficient value to be worth the expense of obtaining confirmation of an executor.

It seems probable that there is a correlation between the proportion of estates in which confirmation is obtained and the proportion in which there is a will. Although not yet fully established, it seems that there is a higher proportion of testate to intestate confirmations in areas where the proportion of confirmations to deaths is also higher than average. Put crudely, more confirmations seem to equal more wills. If this correlation exists, then there seems to be a strong possibility that the deaths in respect of which no confirmation was obtained will include a high proportion of intestacies. Although the estates may have been small, the rules of intestate succession would still be of importance. The figures clearly indicate the need for the law of intestate succession to be relevant to the small and very small estate rather than to the large estate.

These figures also cast doubt on the frequently quoted ratio of one-third intestacy to two-thirds testacy. Although the figure is not readily verifiable, it may be true that about 66 per cent of confirmations are in respect of testate estates. However, if one makes the heroic assumption that not more than one-fifth of the 57 per cent of people whose deaths do not lead to confirmation will have left any testamentary provisions, the result would be a true figure of about 39 per cent testacy to 61 per cent intestacy.

In order to bring the law into harmony with changed conditions, the 1964 Act effected a variety of changes. First, there was a greatly reduced emphasis on the importance of heritage in succession. While the distinction between heritage and moveables in succession was not totally removed, the privileged position of the heir at law was. Apart from the special case of titles and coats of arms, he no longer has any rights which are not shared by the other heirs. Scotland cannot reasonably be accused of undue haste in making this change, for it was one of the very last countries in the world to abolish the special rules of succession to land.

Similarly, there was a substantial reduction of the feudal emphasis on direct blood relationship through the male line. This shows itself in various ways. The position of the surviving spouse of an intestate was substantially improved, partly by changes in prior rights, and partly by being for the first time included in the list of heirs to the free estate after providing for prior and legal rights. Previously, whatever rights a surviving spouse might have had in the other's estate, he or she was never an heir of the other, and this change represented a substantial breach in the doctrine that succession depends on direct blood relationship. So also did the grant of full rights of succession to adopted children in the estates of their adopting parents. Despite pressure in Parliament, however, stepchildren were not given rights of succession. In this situation the principle of blood relationship was apparently too strong to be overcome.

In addition to the widow's increased rights, there were other changes in the position of women. The preference for males disappeared with the abolition of the need to look for the one member of a given class to take the heritable estate as heir at law and the substitution of the principle that all members of a class share equally in the whole, but equating the sexes was carried further. The mother, and relations through her, were given the same rights as the father and the relations through him, and this had effects such as giving collaterals of the half blood uterine exactly the same rights as collaterals of the half blood consanguinean. Bringing in the maternal relatives substantially widened the potential field of research into the family tree but was clearly necessary in the interests of justice and logic. The argument which was presented against the Mackintosh Committee's Report that "it is contrary to all Scottish feeling for heritage to go out of the family to which it belongs" merely begged the question and was completely out of touch with the practical aspects of the situation. No one is now prepared to justify the preservation of the purity of the male line in succession to land.

As a result of all these changes, not only have the common law principles for the selection of the heir at law become virtually obsolete, but so also have the common law principles for identification of the next of kin. Previously relevant for the purpose of ascertaining the heirs in mobilibus, who were a class including the next of kin, but not limited to them, these common law rules now drop out of the picture altogether — apart from competitions for the office of executor. In place of the principles previously applicable in intestate moveable succession there is now a statutory list contained in section 2 of the 1964 Act.

Assimilation of heritage and moveables

As already noted, part of the policy of the Act was to assimilate heritage
and moveables for the purposes of succession, and in so far as this was
achieved, it was done by section 1 of the Act. However the distinction between
heritage and moveables has by no means been abolished. Although terce and
courtesy are no longer exigible from the deceased's heritable estate, section 10
preserves the rule that *jus relicti, jus relictae* and legitim are exigible out of the
deceased's moveable estate only. In addition the items excepted from the
operation of the Act by section 37 (principally titles and coats of arms) pass
under the pre-existing rules.

Until the further reform proposed by the Scottish Law Commission takes
effect, the preservation of the distinction between heritage and moveables in
legal rights has the effect that the distinction must also be preserved for the
purposes of the surviving spouse's prior rights under sections 8 and 9 so that
precise values may be maintained for the calculation of legal rights. Equally
the law relating to the incidence of liabilities between heritage and moveables
remains unimpaired.[8]

The result is that the assimilation of heritage and moveables affects only the
free estate after satisfaction of the prior rights of a surviving spouse and of the
legal rights of a surviving spouse and descendants. If the free estate consists of
heritage to the value of £30,000 and moveables to the value of £50,000 there is
simply a fund of £80,000 to be divided up according to the provisions of Part I
of the Act. These are broadly similar to the old law of intestate moveable
succession.

Another consequence of the assimilation of heritage and moveables is the
virtual abolition of the status of heir at law. Apart from the items excepted by
section 37, where the status is still relevant, the heir at law and his anomalous
privileges vanish from the law. Sections 27 to 50 of the Titles to Land
Consolidation (Scotland) Act 1868, dealing with service of heirs, were
repealed by the 1964 Act, but had to be revived in 1980 by section 6 of the
Law Reform (Miscellaneous Provisions) (Scotland) Act 1980[9] for the limited
purpose of enabling the heir of a last surviving trustee to establish the
propinquity on which his right to office depended. It was expected that there
would be very few cases of this sort, and that services of heirs of persons dying
before the commencement of the Succession Act would form a minuscule and
vanishing jurisdiction of the Sheriff of Chancery to whom the whole
jurisdiction over services was transferred.[10] However the flow of cases where
title to land depends upon succession to someone dying before 1964 has
continued virtually unabated, with an average of over 40 new cases every year.
New procedural rules for services of heirs have been required to cope with the
cases.

Among other changes consequential on the partial assimilation of heritage
and moveables, the 1964 Act empowered minors to dispose of their heritage by

---

[8] s.14(3).
[9] 1980 (c.55).
[10] (S.I. 1971 No. 743).

will as they already could in respect of their moveables. This has now been extended by the Age of Legal Capacity (Scotland) Act 1991[11] (which abolishes the concepts of pupillarity and minority) to the effect that all children (male or female) have testamentary capacity from the age of 12. This startlingly young age is probably viable only because few people are aware of it and is a candidate for reform. The doctrine of collation *inter haeredes* was also abolished by the 1964 Act. For some time after the Act collation remained relevant in cases where the heir at law succeeded to the tenancy of a croft and had to collate the value of that tenancy in order to share in the moveable estate.[12] However, crofting tenancies, formerly excluded from the operation of the Succession Act, were brought within its scope by Part II of the Law Reform (Miscellaneous Provisions) (Scotland) Act 1968. Thus the heir at law no longer has, as such, any right of succession to crofts, and collation disappeared in that situation also.

The estate subject to the operation of the Act

Peerages excluded

Under section 37(1)(a), nothing in the Succession Act applies to any title, coat of arms, honour or dignity transmissible on the death of the holder thereof or affects the succession thereto or the devolution thereof. This has the result, for example, that succession to peerages is still governed by the principles of primogeniture and preference for males. It also means that adopted and illegitimate children, whose rights of succession are conferred by the Act, cannot succeed to them.[13] Legitimated children can however succeed to titles. This was always true of those legitimated at common law, while those whose legitimation depends upon the Legitimation (Scotland) Act 1968[14] have rights independent of the Succession Act.

Definition of "estate"

Apart from this exception, "estate" is defined in section 36(2) as follows:

> "Any reference in this Act to the estate of a deceased person shall, unless the context otherwise requires, be construed as a reference to the whole estate, whether heritable or moveable, or partly heritable and partly moveable, belonging to the deceased at the time of his death or over which the deceased had a power of appointment and, where the deceased immediately before his death held the interest of a tenant under a tenancy or lease which was not expressed to expire on his death, includes that interest."[15]

---

[11] (c.50), s.2(2).

[12] 1965 S.L.T. (News) 209.

[13] The extension of the rights of illegitimate children by the Law Reform (Miscellaneous Provisions) (Scotland) Act 1968 took the form of inserting the provisions into the Succession Act, while the further liberalization in the separate Law Reform (Parent and Child) (Scotland) Act 1986 contains in s.9(1)(c) an express exemption of succession to titles, etc.

[14] (c.22).

[15] See *Cormack v. McIldowie's Exrs*, 1975 S.L.T. 214 on the nature of qualifying tenancies.

In addition to the general definition there are two provisos. One is that heritage subject to a special destination in favour of a third party is not part of the deceased's estate unless he could and did evacuate that destination. The other provides that if heritage over which the deceased held a power of appointment has not been disposed of under that power, and it is in those circumstances subject to a power of appointment by some other person, it is not to be treated as part of the deceased's estate. Considerable care must be taken over the terms of this definition which is central to the whole scheme of the Act.

Special destinations

The definition expressly states that property subject to an unrevoked special destination is not part of the deceased's estate for the purposes of the Act. It is probably therefore incompetent for the deceased's executor to confirm to it, although it will still be part of the estate liable to taxation.[16]

The commonest example of a special destination is probably the survivorship destination in a title to heritage taken to husband and wife and survivor.[17] Although not necessarily true of other types of property,[18] in this case registration of the disposition immediately confers on each a one-half *pro indiviso* share of the heritage. The survivorship destination concerns only the survivor's right to receive in addition the predeceaser's half. Whether this half forms part of the predeceaser's estate for the purposes of the Act depends upon two factors. One is whether there was power to revoke the destination. The other is whether, even assuming the power to exist, revocation has in fact occurred.

There is no limitation on the power of either of the parties to a survivorship destination to alienate his or her share *inter vivos*, thereby evacuating the destination to that half. The possible limitation applies only to testamentary deeds.[19]

In the absence of express contractual provisions, the existence of a power to revoke by testamentary deed is normally dependent on the source of the finance used in the purchase of the property. If the price was provided at least to a significant extent by both parties the destination is a contractual arrangement which neither has power to revoke.[20] Equally, if the property was a gift from a third party, the destination will be a condition attached to the gift which neither spouse has power to revoke.[21] If the purchase price was provided wholly by one of the spouses, and the terms of the conveyance do not contradict that fact,[22] that spouse may be entitled by will to revoke the

---

[16] See p.33-34, *infra*.

[17] If the Scottish Law Commission's proposals in its report on succession (Scot. Law Com. No. 124) are accepted, this will be the only form of special destination to remain in future but it is not clear that even that form should remain. Too many cases occur in which account has not been taken of the existence of a destination.

[18] See Meston, "Survivorship Destinations and Bank Accounts" [1996] 1 Scottish Law and Practice Quarterly 315.

[19] *Steele v. Caldwell*, 1979 S.L.T. 228; *Smith v. Mackintosh*, 1989 S.L.T. 148.

[20] *Perrett's Tr v. Perrett*, 1909 S.C. 522.

[21] *Brown's Trs v. Brown*, 1943 S.C. 488.

[22] See *Gordon-Rogers v. Thomson's Exrs*, 1988 S.L.T. 618; *Smith v. Mackintosh*, 1989 S.L.T. 148.

destination so far as it provides that his or her one-half of the property is to pass to the other spouse.[23] In the absence of power to revoke, any purported revocation of a destination is totally ineffective.

However, if the power exists, the question of whether revocation has occurred so as to bring the property into the "estate" of the deceased has been simplified by section 30 of the 1964 Act. Briefly, revocation of a destination occurs only if there is an express reference to the destination and a declared intention to evacuate it.[24] The old practice of including a general reference to destinations without specifying them is no longer effective.

Powers of appointment

The provisions concerning powers of appointment are also worth closer attention. For the purposes of the Act, the general proposition in section 36(2) is that the "estate" of a deceased person includes property over which he had a power of appointment, subject only to the proviso excluding heritable property from his estate if his failure to exercise a power of appointment gives rise to a power of appointment in someone else. This might have been thought to mean that (apart from the situation in the proviso) where the deceased had a power of appointment, whether general or special, whether or not he exercised it and indeed whether or not he had a right of fee in the property concerned, the deceased's family could claim rights of beneficial succession in it. The prospect of the widow acquiring prior rights out of property which her husband did not own would have been a startling one. However, this provision appears in fact to be a purely administrative one giving the executor power to obtain a title to the property for the purpose of conveying to those beneficially interested by virtue of the appointment or of the deed creating the power. By a classic example of tortuous draftsmanship, rights of succession to the donee of the power are excluded unless he had the fee of the property over which his power of appointment extended.

The case where the deceased was owner of the property would arise where the power was completely general or where he was given a full liferent with an unqualified power of disposal.[25] No greater problem arises in applying the Succession Act to this type of property than to any other property which he owned.

However, if the deceased had no right of fee in the property over which he had the power of appointment — *e.g.* if either the liferent or the power was qualified in some way — then it will be found that the various rights of succession are set out in such a way as not to apply.

The surviving spouse's prior rights under sections 8 and 9 come out of the intestate estate of the deceased. Similarly, the provisions of Part I for succession to the free estate apply solely to the intestate estate. If the deceased exercised the power of appointment, he was not intestate *quoad* the property subject to the power. However, even if he did not exercise the power, the

[23] *Hay's Tr. v. Hay's Trs*, 1951 S.C. 329.
[24] See p. 92, *infra*.
[25] *MacKenzie's Trs v. Kilmarnock* (1908) 16 S.L.T. 676; 1909 S.C. 472; *Ewing's Trs v. Ewing*, 1909 1 S.L.T. 104; 1909 S.C. 409.

property is still not part of his "intestate estate" as that phrase is defined in section 36(1), because it has been disposed of by "testamentary disposition" within the meaning of the same section. The definition there given is not limited to deeds by the deceased and includes "any deed taking effect on his death whereby any part of his estate is disposed of". If he failed to exercise his power of appointment, the deed by which the power was created takes effect on his death and disposes of part of his "estate". Hence property subject to a power is not part of the intestate estate for the purposes of prior rights or the free estate.

So far as legal rights are concerned, section 10(2) provides that they are to be calculated by reference to so much of the net moveable estate as remains after satisfaction of prior rights. "Net estate" is defined as so much of an estate as remains after "estate duty[26] and other liabilities of the estate having priority over legal rights, the prior rights of a surviving spouse and rights of succession". It would seem that one of the liabilities of the estate having this priority would arise from the duty to transfer property which the deceased did not own to those who have a vested right to it.

Hence one is left with the proposition that property subject to a power is part of the deceased's estate solely for the purpose of completion of title.

Another point is raised by this. It must be carefully noted that the word "estate" is used in different senses in different parts of the Act. Not only must the interpretation section (section 36) be studied closely, but one must also consider special interpretations in particular sections. Thus in Part I of the Act, which deals with the succession to the free estate, the words "intestate estate" are used as meaning only the free estate after prior and legal rights (section 1(2)). In section 9, "intestate estate" is defined as meaning so much of the net intestate estate as remains after satisfaction of the surviving spouse's housing right under section 8 (section 9(6)(a)).

Agricultural property

The special administrative provisions for agricultural units which appeared at one stage of the Succession Bill's history were eventually dropped. The purpose was to ensure as far as possible that farms would be kept in the ownership of a single member of the family. The provisions were highly complex and seemed likely to cause many practical difficulties in operating them. It was also pointed out in the House of Lords that, from a survey of the estates of persons dying in 1961, intestacy was extremely rare among those with heritable estates of over £10,000 (of 9,670 intestacies recorded, only five involved heritage of over £10,000 in value). As £10,000 even then represented a very modest farm, there seemed to be no real substance in the fears that, without special provisions, farms would be split up, or pass out of the family's hands altogether. From the figures, the vast majority of farmers regulate the succession to their farms by will. In any event it would be extremely unlikely

---

[26] Includes CTT and IHT. Inheritance Tax Act 1984 (c.51), Sched. 6, para. 1 and Finance Act 1986 (c.41), s.100(1)(b).

that a farm would be subdivided on intestacy, for the economic facts of life would dictate its continuance as a unit.

Similar reasoning has now led to crofting tenancies being brought within the scope of the Succession Act by the Law Reform (Miscellaneous Provisions) (Scotland) Act 1968. Originally they were excluded from the reforms effected in 1964 and had special rules of succession giving the primary right to the tenancy (and its value) to the heir at law. Now, however, a crofting tenancy is just another item of heritable estate to be dealt with like any other. It has a value, whatever difficulties there may be in ascertaining it, and that value may now have to be divided among those beneficially interested in the estate, although only one person can be the new tenant. This may lead to competition for the office of executor, as the executor controls the transmission of the tenancy.[27]

Death and survivorship

The fundamental nature of the law on this point remains as before. The deceased whose estate is in question must be proved to have died and any person claiming to be a beneficiary must be affirmatively proved to have survived him or her. The onus of proof lies on the person relying on the death or survivorship, and the consequence of failure of proof is the failure of that person's claim on the estate.

Death certificates are sufficient, though not conclusive, evidence of the death, and an action is available under the Presumption of Death (Scotland) Act 1977 for fixing the date of death in cases of disappearance.

Common calamities

The 1964 Act, however, effected a very valuable change in establishing survivorship. In a common calamity, section 31 creates what it calls presumptions of survivorship based on age. In truth they are not really presumptions but rules of law as they cannot be rebutted. If there is proof on the balance of probabilities[28] that one person in a common calamity survived the other, effect is given to that order of deaths. It is only if there is no proof of survivorship that the Act's "presumptions" come into play, so that, by definition, there cannot be evidence to rebut the presumptions.

The general rule in section 31 is that, where two persons have died in circumstances indicating that they died simultaneously or rendering it uncertain which, if either, of them survived the other, the younger is presumed to have survived the elder for all purposes of succession.[29]

However, in two particular cases, different presumptions apply. Where the persons concerned are husband and wife, section 31(1)(a) states a positive presumption that neither survived the other. The different treatment for spouses is intended to avoid a situation in which the estate of the elder spouse

---

[27] MacCuish & Flyn, *Crofting Law*, para. 7.05.
[28] *Lamb v. Lord Advocate*, 1976 S.L.T. 151.
[29] s.31(1)(b). Note that it is not necessary to attempt to prove exactly simultaneous death. It is sufficient to establish that it is uncertain which survived the other.

would pass to the younger by virtue of the presumption and then to the younger spouse's relatives to the exclusion of the elder spouse's relatives. For example, if a childless couple perished in a car crash (or died in independent incidents) without proof of survivorship, the husband's estate might pass out of his family and into his wife's family. It was felt in Parliament that this would be likely to be contrary to the husband's wishes, and thus the presumption in this case is that neither survived the other.

One wonders, however, whether in the case of the husband and wife common calamity is properly catered for. The positive presumption that neither survived is admittedly better than the old lack of any presumption. On intestacy, the husband's estate can be wound up on the basis that the wife did not survive to become a beneficiary and vice versa. But if one spouse makes a will in favour of the other and makes alternative provision in the event of the other "predeceasing," he will none the less die intestate if both spouses perish in a common calamity. The statutory presumption that the other "did not survive" is not proof of predecease, as the deaths might have been exactly simultaneous. Hence the essential precondition of the alternative provision cannot be shown to exist and it cannot take effect. It might have been better to direct the logically impossible presumption that each predeceased the other. The common practice of making testamentary provisions for a spouse conditional upon that spouse surviving for a specified period avoids the problem.[30]

The other special case where a different presumption of survivorship applies is a somewhat complicated one specified in section 31(2). Where two persons other than husband and wife have perished in circumstances making survivorship uncertain, the presumption would normally be that the younger survived the elder. But, if the elder has left a testamentary disposition containing a provision in favour of the younger, and failing the younger, in favour of a third party, and if the younger has died intestate, then it is presumed for the purposes of that survivorship destination that the elder person survived the younger. The effect is that the elder's property will go to the nominated third person. Without such a provision, in spite of the known wishes of the elder person as specified in the survivorship destination, the property so bequeathed would have passed via the younger to those who would be entitled to succeed on the intestacy of the younger person.

The drafting of section 31(2) does not appear to be beyond criticism, even if one accepts the need for this exception to the usual presumption of survivorship. The younger person must die "intestate" before the reversed presumption applies. This is defined in section 36(1) as "leaving undisposed of by testamentary disposition the whole or any part of" one's estate. Thus one dies "intestate" if any part of one's estate is undisposed of.[31] Thus, in the situation envisaged in section 31(2), even if the younger person has made explicit provision in his will for the property which he expects to pass to him

---

[30] The Scottish Law Commission's proposed reforms would introduce a fixed period for all cases. This concept, already in force in England, creates considerable surprise among European lawyers, although they recognise its practical merits.

[31] *Munro's Trs, Petrs*, 1971 S.L.T. 313.

on the elder person's death, he has died "intestate" within the meaning of section 31(2) if he has failed to dispose of any other item of his estate. The younger person being "intestate," the presumption for the purpose of the destination would be that the elder survived him, and the property would pass to the third party nominated in the destination. Only if he had also made a testamentary disposition of every item of his estate would the younger person avoid being "intestate". One might have thought that, if this exception to the usual presumption of survivorship is necessary (which seems doubtful) it would have applied whether or not the younger person made a will, or alternatively only in cases where he was intestate as to the property subject to the survivorship destination. To make it apply where he is intestate as to any part of his estate seems to be a defect in drafting. The Scottish Law Commission proposes reform.

It is to be noted that the reversed presumption in section 31(2) applies only for the purposes of the third party destination, to ensure that the third party in fact receives the property in question. For all other purposes of succession, the younger person will still be presumed to have survived the elder.

The comment has been made that the presumptions contained in section 31 do not cover cases where more than two persons perish in a common calamity, but in fact all cases are dealt with. In any situation one is concerned only with two people at a time. One is winding up X's estate and the question is whether Y survived, or is to be presumed to have survived, so as to qualify as a beneficiary. If Z also died in the same calamity, an entirely separate question of survivorship arises between X and Z.

For purposes of Inheritance Tax, persons dying in a common calamity without proof of survivorship are deemed to die at the same instant.[32]

Posthumous children

A different question of survivorship arises in connection with posthumous children. Wills frequently refer to a beneficiary being "survived by issue", and under the Succession Act there are references to survivorship in sections 9(1), 11(1) and 2(1)(a) in connection with prior rights, legitim and rights in the free estate respectively. The question is whether a posthumous child counts as such a survivor.

In *Elliott v. Joicey*[33] it was held that the deceased did not "leave issue him surviving" when his only child was born posthumously. This was apparently on the basis that a child which was *in utero* at the deceased's death had no separate existence at that time and could not be said to "survive" him in the ordinary meaning of that word.

One may think that the ordinary meaning does include a posthumous child and it might still be possible to present that argument in an appropriate case. Complications do, however, arise from the use of modern technology. Recently a widow has given birth to two children by artificial insemination

---

[32] Inheritance Tax Act 1984 (c.51), s.4(2). This presumption avoids the risk of duplicated taxation, and is also the general rule adopted by some countries, *e.g.* Germany (Verschollenheitsgesetz § 11) for all cases of common calamities.

[33] 1935 S.C. (H.L.) 57.

using her husband's sperm after his death. The second child was born in 2002 fully two years after his death. Does his estate have to be reopened and redistributed to take account of the new child? However, whatever the ordinary meaning may be, it is clear that the courts are ready to deduce that a meaning including posthumous children was intended if the result of that construction would be to the benefit of the child. The main reason for the decision in *Elliott v. Joicey* seems to have been that there was no benefit to the child in holding that it survived its parent. In the vast majority of cases, and in particular cases arising under the Succession Act, there is clear benefit to the child in holding that it survives, and thus this interpretation would be adopted. The maxim *qui in utero est pro jam nato habetur* is of very long standing and gives the posthumous child the same benefits as one born before the parent's death, providing it is born alive.[34] Until recently this meant only that it might be necessary to wait for up to nine months after the death to determine the division of an estate, but the courts have not yet had to face the problem of how to administer an estate when a child is born by the use of frozen sperm some years after the father's death. Executors may be concerned at the possibility of having to pay out to children not even conceived at the time of their father's death although the whole estate had already been distributed to those in existence or *in utero* at the time of his death. Some form of prescriptive period may be necessary to protect executors in this situation. The consequence of prenatal death is that the child is treated as never having existed.[35]

The unworthy heir

In order to qualify as a beneficiary in the division of an estate, it may not always be enough for the person apparently entitled under the rules of testate or intestate succession to establish that he survived the deceased. In certain situations, the person otherwise entitled to succeed may be passed over because of some factor making it inappropriate that he should succeed to that particular deceased. The theoretical basis of this disqualification, and therefore the precise area of its application, are not entirely certain, but considerations of public policy are clearly involved in a determination that an heir is so unworthy that he ought not to be permitted to inherit.

The main situation for invoking the disqualification arises when the potential beneficiary has killed the person whose estate is being distributed. There is statutory provision in the Parricide Act 1594[36] disinheriting anyone convicted by an assize of "slaying" a parent or grandparent, but the Act is limited to these relationships and may apply only to the succession to heritage.[37] It seems, however, that there is also a more general rule of common law that a person who has culpably and deliberately killed another is debarred from succeeding to that other's estate. A rule of this nature is well established

---

[34] *Cox's Trs v. Cox*, 1950 S.L.T. 127; 1950 S.C. 117.
[35] Bankton, Inst., I, xlvii; Walker, *Intestate Succession*, p. 10.
[36] 1594 (c.30); 12 mo. c.224.
[37] Bankton, Inst., II, ccci, 30.

in England, where a common formulation is that it is contrary to public policy for a person guilty of feloniously killing another to take any benefit in the deceased's estate.[38]

Although it was generally accepted in Scotland that there was also a general disqualification at common law, and estates were indeed wound up on this basis when one spouse killed another,[39] there was little direct authority. Such as there was could be found in the principle of insurance law that an insured cannot deliberately produce the circumstances under which he may recover under his policy, which is not very different from the case of the heir accelerating his succession by deliberately creating the death under which his right emerges. Public policy demanded that the same approach be taken to killing the deceased, and the sheriff court case of *Smith, Petr*[40] for the first time expressly held that a wife convicted of culpably killing her husband was barred from taking any benefit in his estate. The degree of culpability was not high, but was sufficient to bring in the exclusion. Since then several cases have confirmed the existence of the common law rule.[41]

The common law disqualification is based upon so important a fundamental principle that it is the only known case in which British courts are prepared to ignore the express and precise terms of statute in favour of a common law rule based upon morality. The statutes regulating intestate succession have no qualifications permitting the exclusion of the deceased's killer, but the courts have been prepared to ignore the statutes in such cases. Despite the strength of the principle of unworthiness, it is interesting that a power to exempt from the forfeiture was introduced soon after the existence of the forfeiture was formally recognised in Scotland. The Forfeiture Act 1982[42] was introduced as a private member's Bill and became law in a form which leaves many questions unanswered. Except in cases where the killer has been convicted of murder, a court is given power to "modify" what the Act calls "the forfeiture rule". It has not been clear whether power to modify includes power to exclude the rule totally, and in Scotland the courts have proceeded on the assumption that it does not. However they have been prepared to go so far as to remove all practical difference between modification and exclusion by awarding the killer the whole of the deceased's heritage and 99 per cent of his moveables.[43]

In its application to Scotland the Forfeiture Act runs into another problem over its definition of the forfeiture rule from which exemption may be granted. It is defined in section 1 as the "rule of public policy" which excludes the person who has unlawfully killed another. It is not clear that this includes the

---

[38] *Re Dellow's Will Trusts* [1964] 1 All E.R. 771.
[39] *e.g.* the estate involved in *Garvie's Trs v. Still*, 1972 S.L.T. 29.
[40] 1979 S.L.T. (Sh. Ct.) 35.
[41] *Burns v. Secretary of State for Social Services*, 1985 S.L.T. 351 (1st Div.); *Paterson, Petr*, 1986 S.L.T. 121; *Cross, Petr*, 1987 S.L.T. 384; *Gilchrist, Petr*, 1990 S.L.T. 494; *Hunter's Exrs, Petrs*, 1992 S.L.T. 1141.
[42] (c.34).
[43] *Cross, Petr (supra)*; *Paterson, Petr (supra)*; *Gilchrist, Petr (supra)*. In *Cross* no account was taken of the Parricide Act, although a son had killed his father, but it may be that the culpable homicide of which he was convicted did not amount to "slaying" for the purposes of the Parricide Act. The proposals of the Scottish Law Commission would replace the Parricide Act with new statutory provisions.

statutory disqualification created in Scotland by the Parricide Act 1594, but the Act was not considered in *Cross, Petr*, where a son killed his father and extensive exemption was granted. The result of a disqualification is clearly spelt out in the Parricide Act for the situations to which it applies, although the disqualification of the killer's posterity may have been repealed in the general repeal of sentences involving corruption of blood.[44] At common law the result is not clearly established. Although there is English authority that the share of the unworthy heir falls to be distributed as if that person died before the deceased,[45] and this will often have to be the practical result, the principle will not be carried so far as to bring into play testamentary provisions depending on the "predecease" of the killer. The Inner House has held in *Hunter*[46] that the disqualification should be applied only to the extent necessary to achieve its object.

As between husband and wife another disqualification may arise under the Conjugal Rights (Scotland) Amendment Act 1861.[47] Property acquired by a wife after she has obtained a decree of judicial separation passes on her intestacy as if her husband had then been dead.[48] In effect this creates a statutory unworthiness of husbands (though not of wives). The disqualification ceases if the spouses again cohabit.

The order of applicability of rules of succession

Under the 1964 Act, as under the old law of intestate succession, there is a fragmentation of approach in deciding how a particular estate is to be divided up. After payment of the deceased's debts and any other liabilities and charges to which his estate is subject, there are under the Act three sets of rules to be considered in their proper order, before the final division can be established. The order is as follows:

1. Prior rights

(a) *The housing right under section 8*

Under section 8, the surviving spouse of an intestate is entitled to the deceased's interest in any one house owned or tenanted by the deceased at the time of his or her death. The surviving spouse must have been ordinarily resident in the house in question at the intestate's death, and the maximum value of the benefit conferred under this section (as at 2002) is £130,000. If the value of the deceased's interest is more than £130,000, the surviving spouse receives that sum. Even if the value is below that limit, in some cases it is only the value of the deceased's interest (and not the interest itself) which passes to the survivor. In addition, the surviving spouse is entitled to the furniture and

---

[44] Criminal Justice (Scotland) Act 1949 (12, 13 & 14 Geo. 6, c.94), s.15(1).
[45] *Re Callaway, deceased* [1956] 2 All E.R. 451. See also for Ireland the Succession Act 1965, s.120(5) and for Germany B.G.B. 2344.
[46] 1992 S.L.T. 1141.
[47] (24 & 25 Vict. c.86).
[48] s.6.

plenishings of the house, up to a maximum value of £22,000, and subject to special provisions in respect of heirlooms.

The fact that the housing right under section 8 is the first in order of priority emerges when it is found that all the other rights are postponed to it.

(b) *The monetary right under section 9*

From what is left after any right under section 8 has been met,[49] the surviving spouse of an intestate is entitled to £35,000 if the intestate is survived by issue or to £58,000 if no issue survive the intestate.

2. *Legal rights*

These are the traditional legal rights, still resting largely on the previous common law. Under section 10(2), legal rights, as amended by the Act, are exigible from any moveable estate remaining after the satisfaction of the prior rights under sections 8 and 9. The main amendments are the abolition of terce and courtesy, the introduction of representation in legitim, and the grant of rights to illegitimate children, so that legal rights are now available to the surviving spouse and to the descendants of the intestate, but in his moveable estate only.

3. *Succession to the free estate*

These rules, specified in Part I of the Act, deal with the succession to the free intestate estate after both of the above sets of rules have been applied,[50] precise values being maintained at each stage.

As before, the rules of succession to the free estate are a modified version of the parentelic system. Apart from specialties such as bringing the surviving spouse into the list of heirs to the free estate and dividing the estate equally between parents and brothers and sisters when both categories survive, it is necessary to exhaust one class (as represented if need be) before moving on to the next class. As before, the order of the classes is issue, then collaterals, then parents, then parents' collaterals and so on *ad infinitum.*

---

[49] s.9(6)(a).
[50] s.1(2).

CHAPTER 3

DEBTS AND TAXATION

Before any estate is available for distribution to beneficiaries, whether under a will or on intestacy, there must be deducted from the gross estate any debts incurred by the deceased and any liabilities to which his estate is subject. It is in the balance after these items have been deducted that the beneficiaries share. Even though a surviving spouse and children are sometimes classed as creditors in respect of their legal rights in a competition with others having ordinary rights of succession, this does not entitle them to participate in the gross estate along with genuine creditors. They are limited to sharing in the net estate after deduction of debts and liabilities and thus in a competition with true creditors, those entitled to legal rights are ordinary beneficiaries.[1] The special privilege of an illegitimate child of being regarded as a true creditor for aliment was removed by the Law Reform (Miscellaneous Provisions) (Scotland) Act 1968.[2] Thus all the rights of succession, under the three different sets of rules mentioned in the previous chapter, are in the net estate after satisfaction of debts and liabilities.

There is no obvious limit to the way in which a deceased person may have incurred liabilities falling to be paid out of his estate. Contractual obligations, for example debts on the deceased's own account or guarantees of the debts of others, may be liabilities of the estate. So also may delictual claims arising from wrongful acts by the deceased. However, typical examples of debts which commonly have to be paid or allowed for before division of the estate are outstanding loans secured over the deceased's house, local council tax, suppliers' accounts, funeral expenses and the expenses of administration of the estate.

Apart from the ordinary run of debts met with in most estates there are some of rarer occurrence. McLaren[3] gives the example of the expenses connected with the birth of a posthumous child, citing the authority of Erskine and two early cases in *Morison's Dictionary*. One can perhaps regard this as a liability incurred by the deceased husband by fathering the child, and it is certainly consonant with reason that the expenses should be treated as a debt due from his estate. In view of the existence of the National Health Service, the point will rarely be of much importance nowadays, but if, in the case of complications, the mother were to be in a private nursing home for a lengthy period, the sum involved could be substantial, and could make a considerable difference to the shares to be taken by the beneficiaries from the estate. At least if the deceased husband expressly or impliedly authorised private

---

[1] *Naismith v. Boyes* (1899) 1 F. (H.L.) 79, *per* Lord Watson at 82.

[2] (c.70).

[3] *Wills & Succession*, i, 127.

treatment for the birth, such an expense should clearly be treated as a debt due from the estate rather than a private liability of the mother.

The right of the deceased's widow (but not, apparently, widower) and family to a reasonable allowance for mournings on a scale suitable to the family's social position is a debt of the estate. Erskine,[4] Bell[5] and McLaren[6] all refer to the cost of mournings as a debt, while Bell goes so far as to treat it as a privileged debt payable even although the estate should be insufficient to meet the claims of the deceased's creditors. The right to mournings is, however, likely to be abolished as anachronistic if the proposals of the Scottish Law Commission are enacted.[7]

Another debt which appears nowadays to be rarely invoked is the right of a surviving spouse to aliment till the next term after the deceased's death. As stated by Erskine[8] and in *McIntyre v. McIntyre's Trs*[9] this is a right available to a widow only, the purpose being to provide funds for her maintenance until her provisions, either on intestacy or under a will, become payable. It would seem, however, that section 4 of the Married Women's Property (Scotland) Act 1920[10] gave a surviving husband a reciprocal right — if he was indigent. Any such rights are specifically saved by the 1964 Act. Section 37(1)(c) provides that nothing in the Act is to "affect any right on the part of a surviving spouse to claim from the representatives of his or her deceased spouse payment of aliment out of the estate of that spouse". In view of the extensive provisions now made for a surviving spouse, it may be that it will rarely be necessary to invoke this right, but it could still be of importance in cases where the deceased has left a will making very little provision for his or her spouse. This right is also liable to be abolished if the Scottish Law Commission's proposals are accepted.[11]

Classification of debts as heritable or moveable

Although there has been an assimilation of heritage and moveables for some purposes, it is still necessary to classify debts as either heritable or moveable. Not only must there be a precise value for the moveable estate from which the legal rights of spouses and issue are due, but the prior rights of a surviving spouse may also be affected. The prior right to the deceased's interest in the matrimonial home is "subject ... to any heritable debt secured over the interest".[12] Thus the benefit taken by the surviving spouse is directly reduced by the whole amount of any debt which can be classed as both heritable and secured over the deceased's interest.

---

[4] Inst., III, ix, 22, 43.
[5] Comm., i, 679.
[6] *Wills & Succession*, i, 127; see also *Sheddan & Ors v. Gibson* (1802) Mor. 11855.
[7] Report on Succession (Scot. Law Com No. 124 (1990)), recommendation 54.
[8] Inst., I, vi, 41.
[9] (1865) 3 M. 1074. See also *Barlass v. Barlass's Trs*, 1916 S.C. 741.
[10] (10 & 11 Geo. 5, c.64) — repealed Family Law (Scotland) Act 1985 (c.37), Sched. 2.
[11] Report (*supra*), recommendation 56.
[12] 1964 Act, s.8(6)(d).

The result is that the liabilities of the estate must still be allocated to heritage and moveables under the old principles regulating the liability *inter se* of heir and executor, even although the heir at law now exists only for succession to titles. Section 14(3) expressly preserves all the old rules, with the general result that debts secured over heritage are payable out of, or form a deduction from, the value of the heritage while all other debts are payable out of the moveable estate.[13]

Debts for which the creditor holds both heritable and moveable securities

One aspect of the general rules which has achieved a new significance in a number of cases is, however, the method of dealing with debts for which the creditor holds both heritable and moveable securities. It is not uncommon for a bank or insurance company which has provided a loan for the purchase of a house to take both a heritable security over the house and an assignation of policies of assurance on the life of the purchaser. If the purchaser dies, the lender will be very generously secured, as the life policies will frequently be sufficient by themselves to pay off the debt. Nonetheless the situation remains that there is a heritable debt secured over the house at the time of death. Assuming that the house is one in which the deceased's spouse is ordinarily resident, the result would be that the value of the surviving spouse's prior right to the house would be reduced by the whole amount of the heritable security if no account could be taken of the creditor's concurrent moveable security.

Thus, as was also the case between heir and executor before the Succession Act, it is necessary to apportion the debt between heritage and moveables so that only the appropriate proportion of the debt is classed as a heritable debt. The heritable element is therefore the same proportion of the total debt as the proportion between the value of the heritable security held by the creditor and the whole value of all the securities held by the creditor. If the heritage held in security is worth £100,000 and the moveable security is worth £50,000, only two-thirds of the debt is a heritable debt.[14] Very difficult questions arise if a life policy assigned in security is a joint one on the lives of two spouses. Depending on the precise terms of the policy, there can arise a debt due by the estate to the survivor of half of the proceeds of the policy.[15] This is on the basis that the survivor's interest in the policy has been used to meet a debt due by the deceased.

Capital Gains Tax

This tax is now mainly governed by the Taxation of Chargeable Gains Act 1992[16]

In principle the tax is levied when an asset is sold on the increase in value of the asset from the time of its acquisition to the time of its disposal. After

---

[13] What little authority exists is very general. See McLaren, *Wills & Succession*, ii, 1305; and Wilson, *Law of Debt* (2nd ed.), para. 29.10.

[14] *Graham v. Graham & Ors* (1898) 5 S.L.T. 319. See also *Meston's Succession Opinions*, No.40, p.117.

[15] Gretton, 1988 J.L.S. 141.

[16] (c.12).

considerable variations, the current position is that only gains from March 1982 are chargeable, and a relief for the effects of inflation is available by means of indexation of the acquisition price. There is also an allowance for losses on other disposals. In addition there is an "exempt amount" for gains made in a particular year, so that taxpayers are liable for CGT only on the net gains greater than the exempt amount which have been realised in the course of that year. The exempt amount for 2001 to 2002 was £7,500[17] and the figure will be increased annually by the amount of the percentage increase in the retail price index.

Executors are obviously liable as a debt of the estate for any CGT already due by the deceased at the time of his death. Until 1971[18] the death of the deceased was treated as a disposal by the deceased, with the consequence that CGT became due in addition to the then Estate Duty levied on the value of the estate at death, but this double charge no longer applies.

The position is now governed by section 62 of the Taxation of Chargeable Gains Act 1992. The assets of which a deceased person was competent to dispose are not deemed to have been disposed of by him at his death,[19] although they are deemed to have been acquired by the executors at their market value as at the date of death.[20] Thus the death does not give rise to a new charge to tax, but does give an uplift to the base value of the assets, from which any future capital gains are calculated. If the assets are transferred to a legatee or intestate beneficiary, that legatee or beneficiary takes the asset with the base value as at the date of the deceased's death, but there is no charge to capital gains tax. However if the disposal is to anyone other than a legatee or intestate beneficiary, it counts as a disposal for the purposes of CGT and tax would be charged on any increase in value from the date of death. This may arise for example if shares are sold by executors to meet inheritance tax.

For fuller and more detailed exposition see Davies, *Principles of Tax Law*,[21] *The Laws of Scotland*, *Stair Memorial Encyclopaedia*[22] and Cumulative Supplement.

Inheritance Tax

Whatever its name, inheritance tax is not in fact a tax upon inheritances received, like the former legacy duty and succession duty, but a tax on capital transferred out of a deceased person's estate. There could be much to be said for the fairness of a tax based on the total sums received by individuals from all inheritances. In particular, the rate of tax could be varied according to the total benefits from inheritances and according to the degree of relationship between the deceased and the beneficiary. However the administrative complications and the record-keeping involved mean that a true inheritance tax

---

[17] (S.I. 2001 No. 636).
[18] Finance Act 1971.
[19] s.62(1)(b).
[20] s.62(1)(a).
[21] (4th ed., 2000), pt III.
[22] Vol. 25, paras 990–998.

is not a practical possibility. Capital transfer tax, which was originally intended as the forerunner for a general wealth tax, ran into the same problem of practicability when it purported to record and tax all chargeable transfers made by an individual at any point in his lifetime, including transfer on his death. It was based on a cumulative total of lifetime transfers, with a charge levied every 10 years. *Inter alia*, the burden of record keeping became impossible and the scheme was dropped before the first 10-year charge would have applied. Hence when the Capital Transfer Tax Act 1984[23] was retrospectively renamed the Inheritance Tax Act ("IHTA") by the Finance Act 1986,[24] the opportunity was taken to convert the tax back to a basic principle not dissimilar to the old estate duty levied on the estates of deceased persons. It is, however, not necessarily limited to inheritance on death.

The value of the estate for the calculation of tax takes account of the liabilities of the deceased[25] and it seems that the liabilities which were accepted as deductions for estate duty and for capital transfer tax are also accepted for inheritance tax. Thus the allowance for mournings remains an allowable deduction for tax purposes.[26] The cost of a tombstone was formerly thought not to be allowable, but since the decision in *Prentice v. Chalmers*[27] it is established that the reasonable cost of a tombstone is now allowable. However, it should be remembered that a particular debt may well be a liability of the estate to be deducted before distribution to beneficiaries even although it is not an allowable deduction for tax.

The amount of the tax due is also a liability of the estate and is deducted from the estate available for the beneficiaries of the estate. It is no longer true that a specific legacy of heritage bears its own tax,[28] with the result that the deceased's executors are primarily liable for payment of the tax in the ordinary case.

Various categories of transfer must be identified if the scheme of inheritance tax is to be understood. "Chargeable transfers" are the fundamental category, as tax is due only if there is something which qualifies as a chargeable transfer. This is helpfully defined as a transfer of value which is made by an individual, but is not an exempt transfer.[29] On death, tax is levied as if the deceased, immediately before his death, had transferred the value of his estate as it then stood.[30]

"Exempt transfers" arise from specific exemptions created in a variety of situations. The most important exemption is however that all transfers between spouses are exempt from inheritance tax.[31] There is no requirement that the

---

[23] (c.51).
[24] (c.41), s.100.
[25] IHTA 1984, s.5(3).
[26] Extra Statutory Concession F1 (1992).
[27] 1985 S.L.T. 168; Practice Statement 7/87.
[28] *Cowie's Trs Petrs*, 1982 S.L.T 326, *sub nom. Re Dougal* [1981] S.T.C. 514. Inheritance Tax Act 1984 (c.51), s.211.
[29] IHTA 1984, s.2(1)
[30] *ibid.*, s.4(1).
[31] *ibid.*, s.18. It has to be borne in mind however that the combined estates will be subject to inheritance tax on the death of the survivor so that it may be wise to make transfers to children on the first death.

spouses should have been living together, the exemption being based on the status only (as in the case of rights of intestate succession). The former problems in the estate duty legislation whereby the value of a surviving spouse's prior rights varied according to whether he or she took the house itself, or a cash sum in lieu, no longer cause trouble. Transfers of up to £3,000 in any one year are exempt from inheritance tax[32] and unused relief may be carried forward for one further year. Small gifts to the same person are exempt.[33] Normal lifetime expenditure out of income is also exempt, even if there may be scope for argument about what is "normal".[34] Marriage gifts are exempt up to limits varying from £1,000 to £5,000 depending upon the relationship of the parties.[35] Gifts to charities and to public bodies are also exempt.[36]

"Potentially exempt transfers" arise when transfers were made by the deceased during his or her lifetime.[37] They are not subject to an immediate charge to tax but if they were made within the seven years prior to the deceased's death they are also subject to inheritance tax.[38] A taper relief reduces the amount of the tax if the transfer was made more than three years before the death. If the transferor lives for more than seven years, there is no tax and the potentially exempt transfer has become actually exempt, but it might still be relevant in calculating the rate of tax on other transfers within the seven years.

"Gifts with reservation of benefit", even if made outwith the seven-year period, may however still be liable to inheritance tax. A fairly obvious method of avoiding tax would otherwise have arisen if parents could transfer the ownership of their house to a child while continuing to live in the house under some tacit or open agreement that they would have a liferent. Thus tax is due on "gifts with reservations" if the deceased had retained an interest in the subject of the gift.[39]

Variations — deeds of family arrangement

It is also possible to alter the disposition of an estate (whether by will or on intestacy) by a deed of variation (family arrangement) or similar instrument. The author has used the method of an assignation by a beneficiary of part of his entitlement in favour of a charity. This affirmation of the very important rule that beneficiaries may rearrange benefits among themselves is significant for several purposes. So far as inheritance tax is concerned, such a variation effected within two years of the deceased's death has the result that the tax charge is on the basis that the agreed variation was the distribution prescribed by the will or the intestacy rules.[40]

---

[32] IHTA 1984, s.19.
[33] *ibid.*, s.20 The current figure is £250 to any one person.
[34] *ibid.*, s.21. See *Bennett v. IRC* [1995] S.T.C. 54.
[35] *ibid.*, s.22.
[36] *ibid.*, ss.23–27.
[37] Defined in IHTA 1984, s.3A.
[38] IHTA 1984, s.3A(1), added by Finance Act 1986, Sched. 9.
[39] Finance Act 1986, s.102. The common case is that where a parent transfers a house to a child, but retains the use of the house without paying a full market rent.
[40] IHTA 1984, s.142.

Rate of Tax

As at 2002, the rate of tax on the first £250,000 of cumulative transfers, including the deemed transfer on death, is nil. For all transfers above that amount the rate is 40 percent.

CHAPTER 4

SURVIVING SPOUSE'S PRIOR RIGHTS

The prior rights created by the Succession Act were probably the most important single change effected by the Act. They are in two parts, the first of which is set out in section 8. This was entirely new, and consists of a right to the house (with its furniture and plenishings and up to specified values) in which the surviving spouse was ordinarily resident at the date of death of the intestate. The second part, stated in section 9, gives a surviving spouse a right to a fixed sum of money, the amount depending on whether the deceased was or was not survived by issue. This was patterned upon the right formerly conferred by the Intestate Husband's Estate (Scotland) Acts 1911 to 1959, but there are important differences. Provision is now made for the spouse even when the deceased is survived by issue (who may be legitimate or illegitimate) and the prior right is now part of the general law of succession of Scotland, instead of being confined to the estates of persons dying domiciled in Scotland.[1]

The rights to the house, to the furniture and plenishings and to a sum of money are quite independent of each other. The fact that the deceased may have had no interest in a house does not increase the value of the monetary right, and therefore the total value to the surviving spouse of prior rights varies according to the form of the estate as well as its total size. This anomaly would be corrected if the recommendations of the Scottish Law Commission were to be put into effect but at present can create totally unjustifiable variations in the benefit to a surviving spouse.[2]

The great social significance of these rights lies in the fact that in the large majority of intestacies, prior rights will exhaust the estate and ensure that the surviving spouse is the sole beneficiary, even although others may have nominal rights of succession.

Intestacy

It is, however, important to emphasise that prior rights can arise only when the deceased died intestate. They do not function as family protection devices, so that if the deceased has disposed of the whole of his estate by testamentary disposition, his surviving spouse has no claim to prior rights, however unjust the will. In that situation the spouse must claim the legal right of *jus relictae* or *jus relicti* if she or he is not satisfied with the provisions of the will, possibly supplemented by claims for mournings and aliment for so long as these claims are possible.

---

[1] See Intestate Husband's Estate (Scotland) Act 1911 (1 & 2 Geo. 5, c.10), s.1
[2] See for example Opinion no.64, pp.199–200 in *Meston's Succession Opinions*.

For prior rights to operate, however, the intestacy need not be complete. Thus if the deceased dies partially intestate the surviving spouse has prior rights in so much of the estate as is undisposed of by will. This appears from the definitions in section 36(1) of the Act, which include the statement that "'an intestate' means a person who has died leaving undisposed of by testamentary disposition the whole or any part of his estate, and 'intestate' shall be construed accordingly". The rights are required by sections 8(1) and 9(1) to be met out of the "intestate estate" which by section 36(1) is defined as "so much of his estate as is undisposed of by testamentary disposition". The only qualification in cases of partial intestacy is contained in the proviso to section 9(1). This provides that legacies left to the surviving spouse in the deceased's will may have to be deducted from the claim for prior rights in the estate which was not disposed of by the will.[3] Thus prior rights are available only to a surviving spouse and operate only in that part of the deceased's estate which has not been disposed of by testamentary disposition.[4]

The housing right under section 8

No recommendation that a surviving spouse should receive the deceased's house was made by the Mackintosh Committee, and this provision did not appear in the pilot version of the Bill introduced into Parliament in May 1963. Concern was, however, expressed in the Scottish Grand Committee on that occasion about the position of a surviving spouse, particularly a widow. It was pointed out that under the previous system it was not unknown for a widow of an intestate to find herself without a roof over her head if the heir at law decided to sell the house. Family squabbles, of the type that every solicitor has encountered, sometimes led to her being put out of the house or feeling bound to go. Sometimes a widow who had worked in order to help her husband to buy a house found on his death that the title was in his name and that it passed to, say, his brother or uncle. While solicitors always endeavoured to ensure that the purchaser of a house considered the question and made a will, there was, and still is, often a reluctance to settle down to consider the terms of a will. The result was that there were from time to time very hard cases which tended to discredit the law and the legal profession. The government took account of the concern expressed and what is now section 8 appeared in the Bill when it was reintroduced in November 1963.

The effect of section 8 is that on intestacy of the deceased spouse, the surviving spouse is entitled to receive, subject to any burdens affecting it, the ownership or tenancy of any one house owned, or tenanted otherwise than under the Rent Acts, by the deceased spouse, plus its furniture and plenishings. Maximum limits of £130,000 and £22,000 are stipulated for the values of the house and furniture respectively. The surviving spouse, but not necessarily the deceased spouse, must have been ordinarily resident in the house in question at the date of death of the intestate.

---

[3] See *infra*, pp.47-48.
[4] *Munro's Trs, Petrs*, 1971 S.L.T. 313.

The right to the house

The substantive right is set out in section 8(1). This provides that where the intestate estate includes a "relevant interest" in a dwelling-house to which the section applies, the surviving spouse is entitled to receive that interest, if its value does not exceed £130,000. If it does exceed that figure, the surviving spouse is entitled to the sum of £130,000. The concept of a maximum limit on the value of the housing right was intended to meet the difficulties which might arise if very valuable houses or mansions passed to the deceased's widow. At one stage in the Succession Bill's progress through Parliament, it was proposed to give the surviving spouse only the value of the house, and not the ownership (or tenancy) of it, if there were "special circumstances of a historical nature" connected with it. This being so vague as to be probably unworkable, the provision was dropped in favour of a maximum value for the interest which is transferred to the surviving spouse.

The limit of £130,000 has not, however, kept up with inflation, despite increases in 1973, 1981,1988,1993 and 1999.[5] The original figure of £15,000 in 1964 represented approximately three times the value of a substantial city house purchased in that year by the author. The current figure of £130,000 is approximately half of the current value of the same house and the protection afforded by the housing right may now be illusory. The intention was that a surviving spouse would be enabled to continue to live undisturbed in the house in which he or she was ordinarily resident before the deceased's death, but values have so changed (and are continuing to change) that the surviving spouse may not be able to afford to remain in it. If the value of the house is over the limit, or if one of the exceptions stated in section 8(2) applies, the survivor receives a cash payment rather than the house itself. If the value of the deceased's interest in the house is below the limit, but one of the exceptions applies, the payment is "a sum equal to the value of the relevant interest". However if the value of the interest exceeds the limit, the surviving spouse is entitled to receive "the sum of £130,000". It is not said that this is in lieu of the interest or that it is a *surrogatum* for the interest. Some doubt may therefore exist whether this right falls to be treated as an interest in heritage or as an interest in moveables.[6] The better view, and the only one which makes sense, is that the right falls to be treated as heritable, as being a *surrogatum* for the house itself.

Relevant interest

It is very important to an understanding of this prior right to observe that it transfers to the surviving spouse not the house itself, but the deceased's "relevant interest" in the house. This is to cope with the various forms of interest which an occupier of a house may have. The purpose was to ensure that the surviving spouse could obtain whatever interest the deceased had and could continue to live as before but the explosion in house values means that

---

[5] Succession (Scotland) Act 1973 (c.25), s.1; (S.I. 1981 No. 806); (S.I. 1988 No. 633); (S.I. 1993 No. 2690) and (S.I. 1999 No. 445).
[6] For possible effects of this doubt on the calculation of the legal rights fund and on private international law, see *infra*, p.135.

this is much less likely to be the result. In contrast to the position with the furniture and plenishings, which must have belonged to the deceased before they can pass as a prior right, it is whatever interest the deceased may have had in the house that is transferred. The deceased may have been the owner or a tenant or may have had some lesser right, but it is that interest which is transferred. The exception — and it is a large one — is that tenancies subject to the Rent Acts 1971 to 1974 do not pass to the surviving spouse as a prior right, but this is because Rent Act tenancies already have their own code of transmission on the tenant's death.

The "relevant interest" as defined in section 8(6)(d) is subject to any heritable debt secured over the deceased's interest. In addition to the problem of how much of a debt is heritable when there is also moveable security[7] this means that it is the net value after allowing for the heritable debt which determines whether the limit on value has been reached. The surviving spouse takes the deceased's interest when the value of the interest (and not of the house) does not exceed £130,000.

If there is a "mortgage protection" policy on the life of the deceased owner of a house, the surviving spouse commonly assumes that this clears the house of debt and that the whole value is transferred as a prior right, subject to the limit. However this is incorrect, for such a policy is just an ordinary policy of life assurance which pays into the estate a moveable sum which happens to be the amount needed to pay off the heritable debt. It does not alter the fact that, at the moment of death, a heritable debt is secured over the house, and the prior right is to the value subject to the burden of that debt. There is no compensation in the monetary right for the reduced value of the housing right and attempts to devise a scheme for tying mortgage protection policies directly to the debt so as to cancel the debt at the moment of death have so far failed.

"Ordinarily resident"

Section 8 applies, by virtue of section 8(4), to any dwelling-house in which the surviving spouse of the intestate was ordinarily resident at the date of death of the intestate. The deceased spouse need not have been resident there, and if the deceased was not resident there, the separation may have been friendly or otherwise. The only qualification for this right is that the surviving spouse was ordinarily resident there (and of course that the interest in the house belonged to the deceased spouse).

Difficult questions do arise with some regularity over the concept of ordinary residence. In one case spouses had been living in rented accommodation but the husband had concluded missives in January 1977 to purchase a house with entry in March of that year. All formalities were complete when the husband died on the very day of entry. The keys were not collected until a few days later and the widow and children did not move in until some time later. It was therefore clear that the widow was not "ordinarily resident" in the new house at the date of her intestate husband's death, and was

---

[7] *Supra*, p.32.

thus entitled only to such minimal value as the tenancy had instead of the value of the new house.[8]

It is, of course, possible to be ordinarily resident in more than one dwelling-house at a time. It may be a rare situation, but could arise, for example, if the spouses had town and country houses and used both regularly, keeping two establishments in being. It seems highly unlikely that a holiday cottage would be sufficient to produce an "ordinary" residence of the surviving spouse unless there were evidence of very frequent use as an alternative principal home. To meet the possibility of there being multiple ordinary residences, the proviso to section 8(1) ensures that the surviving spouse's right applies to the predeceaser's interest in only one of the houses in which the survivor was ordinarily resident. When this situation arises, the surviving spouse has an unfettered discretion to choose the house which is to fall under the right with a period of up to six months within which to reach a decision. In the cases when this right of election arises, the surviving spouse will probably be influenced by the capital values, at least if it is a right of ownership that is involved. Unless there is some particular reason for preferring to occupy the less valuable house, the surviving spouse can always opt to take the more valuable, selling it if need be to provide capital for the purchase of a more conveniently located house. This would apply even more strongly if one of the houses was owned and the other merely leased by the deceased spouse. It will be noted, however, that the value of the furniture and plenishings in the two houses need not be a factor, since an entirely separate election is involved in that case.[9]

Dwelling house

The right is not limited to the actual structure — the stone and mortar. "Dwelling-house" is defined in section 8(6)(a) as including any garden or portion of ground attached to, and usually occupied with, the dwelling house or otherwise required for the amenity or convenience of the house. This would seem to cover not only garden ground physically contiguous to the house but also such things as *pro indiviso* shares in the garden ground in the centre of a square.

It is not clear whether such mobile or temporary residences as caravans and houseboats come within the definition of "dwelling-house". The Matrimonial Homes (Family Protection) (Scotland) Act 1981[10] expressly includes them, along with any "other structure" which has become a family residence, within the definition of a matrimonial home for the purposes of that Act. However, the Matrimonial Homes Act definition sets out to be a comprehensive one, while the Succession Act's definition of a dwelling house does not. The latter merely specifies that some things are included, without stating that others are excluded, and the view is ventured that the definition can extend to caravans, etc.

---

[8] *Meston's Succession Opinions*, no. 64. See also no. 65.
[9] s.8(3) proviso.
[10] (1981 c.59), s.22.

Exceptions where the surviving spouse receives only the value of the house

Recognising that, in some circumstances, considerable difficulties might be created by the transfer of the ownership or tenancy of a house to the surviving spouse, two exceptions are stated in section 8(2). In these cases the surviving spouse is entitled to receive the value of the deceased's interest up to the maximum limit, but is not entitled to insist upon a transfer of the interest itself.

The first of the exceptions arises under section 8(2)(a) when, although the other conditions are satisfied, the dwelling-house forms part only of the subjects comprised in one tenancy or lease under which the intestate was the tenant. A dwelling-house for the purposes of section 8 need not be a complete structure in itself. By virtue of section 8(6)(a) the term includes a part of a building occupied (at the date of the death of the intestate) as a separate dwelling. Thus a flat in a large block clearly falls within the definition. No problem arises if the flat was owned by the deceased spouse, whether or not his title also included the other flats in the block. The flat in which the surviving spouse was ordinarily resident can readily be hived off and conveyed separately to the survivor. But if the deceased had only a lease of the block of flats, in one of which the survivor was ordinarily resident, the landlord could not reasonably be required to grant a separate lease of that flat to the surviving spouse. Hence the exception applies to a dwelling-house forming part of larger subjects tenanted by the deceased and does not arise in cases of ownership.

This exception may prove to be of relatively rare occurrence in practice, but the second exception is a specialized application of the first which is likely to be of greater importance. It arises in cases of both ownership and tenancy by the deceased spouse, and is stated in section 8(2)(b). Again the surviving spouse is limited to the value of the house in question if it "forms the whole or part of subjects an interest in which is comprised in the intestate estate and which were used by the intestate for carrying on a trade, profession or occupation, and the value of the estate as a whole would be likely to be substantially diminished if the dwelling-house were disposed of otherwise than with the assets of the trade, profession or occupation".

The typical example of this exception is a farmhouse. Farming qualifies as a "trade, profession or occupation"; the house is part of the subjects used for that trade, etc., and the value of the estate as a whole would undoubtedly be substantially diminished if the farmhouse were not available along with the farming land. If the purchaser cannot have a house from which to run the farm, the amount by which the value of the farm is reduced is likely to be much greater than the value of the house as such, due to the inconvenience to the purchaser. Similar considerations might apply to cases such as that of the doctor's house with surgery attached. In either case, if the whole unit was merely tenanted by the deceased, the house would also come under the first exception in section 8(2)(a), but even if the deceased was the owner, it would seem that the surviving spouse would be entitled only to the value, and not to the ownership, of the deceased's interest in the house. The fall in the value of the whole unit by reason of the absence of the house would be greater than the value of the house itself, qua house, and hence the "value of the estate as a whole would be likely to be substantially diminished" if the house were not disposed of along with the farm or surgery.

The surviving spouse may not regard the cash value of the house or of the tenancy thereof as adequate compensation for loss of the living accommodation, but the general policy that the survivor should not be left without a roof over his or her head gives way in this instance to the general benefit of the estate as a whole.

It is worth remembering that many farms (and surgeries) are owned by partnerships rather than by individuals. If a farm is owned by a partnership of which the deceased was a partner, his interest is a moveable interest in the partnership. He does not have a direct interest in the individual assets of the partnership, and in particular he would not seem to have any "relevant interest" in the farmhouse unless he has a tenancy agreement with the firm. In the normal case he would be neither owner nor tenant and his occupancy would not be a "relevant interest" so that nothing would pass to his spouse as a prior right under this heading.

Valuation of dwelling-houses

Where any question arises as to the value of a house, or interest therein, for the purpose either of the maximum limit or of the substituted value in cases failing within section 8(2), it is provided by section 8(5) that the question is to be settled by arbitration by a single arbiter. In default of agreement on an arbiter, he is to be appointed by the sheriff of the county in which the intestate was domiciled at the date of his death, or if that county is uncertain, or the intestate was domiciled furth of Scotland, by the Sheriff of the Lothians and Peebles at Edinburgh.

The value to be ascertained will presumably be the market value of the deceased's interest, taking into account any heritable debt secured over it, which should mean that in most cases the net value agreed for estate duty purposes will be accepted by those concerned.

Furniture and plenishings

The right to the house would be of little practical use if the surviving spouse had to restock it. The general aim of section 8 is to further the presumed intention of the intestate spouse that the survivor should be enabled to continue to live in the house which he or she previously occupied with as little disturbance as possible. Accordingly, section 8(3) provides that in addition to taking over any interest which the deceased may have had in the dwelling-house in which the survivor was ordinarily resident and indeed whether or not the deceased had any interest in that house, the surviving spouse is entitled to receive that house's furniture and plenishings so far as belonging to the intestate, subject to a maximum value of £22,000.

It will be noted that this excludes furniture being acquired by the deceased on hire purchase. Section 8(3) gives rights to the survivor when "the intestate estate includes the furniture and plenishings". The whole point of a hire purchase agreement being that the articles concerned do not belong to the hirer until fully paid for, furniture on hire purchase is not included in the deceased's estate and does not pass to the surviving spouse under this provision. Subject to any specialties in the terms of the contract, this would presumably also be true even if insurance had been effected to pay off the outstanding debt in the event of the hirer's death. Credit sale agreements do not give rise to this problem as the property in the goods does then pass to the purchaser leaving the seller with only a claim of debt.

Definition of furniture and plenishings

The "furniture and plenishings" which fall under this right are more restrictively defined than on the first appearance of the Bill. The definition appears in section 8(6)(b), and is not exhaustive of all possibilities, for the term is said to *include* "garden effects, domestic animals, plate, plated articles, linen, china, glass, books, pictures, prints, articles of household use, and consumable stores". It does not include "any article or animal used at the date of death of the intestate for business purposes, or money or securities for money or any heirloom". No mention is made of motorcars although they, with carriages and horses, were included in the version of the Bill which had its first reading in May 1963. One imagines that it might still be possible in some cases to argue that a car was part of the plenishings of a particular house if it were treated as an appurtenance of the house, *e.g.* an estate car kept at a country mansion and used solely for ferrying people and their luggage to and from the nearest station. In most cases, however, a car will prove either to have been used for business purposes, or not to be part of the plenishings of the house at all. Professional practice in drawing up inventories of estates would tend to indicate that a car is rarely regarded as part of the plenishings of a house, for cars are usually entered as separate items of estate.

The heirlooms which are not to be treated as part of the furniture and plenishings of any particular house are (by section 8(6)(c)), any articles which have associations with the intestate's family of such nature and extent that they ought to pass to some member of that family other than the surviving spouse of the intestate. This is a magnificently vague provision which has so far produced surprisingly little litigation. The type of item envisaged by those who pressed for this provision in Parliament was a regimental trophy, but one wonders whether it will not lead to disputes over grandmother's silver teapot or great-grandmother's best tea dishes.

The definition of furniture and plenishings is, of necessity, in fairly general terms, and there is obvious scope for considerable argument over what does and what does not fall within it. It is unfortunate, therefore, that the uncertainty and the scope for litigation is further increased by employing this form of definition as "including" certain items. This merely throws one back on the common law concept of what is furniture and plenishing, with a number of specific examples and exceptions pointed out by the Act. Since every item which is held to pass to the surviving spouse under this head automatically reduces the share falling to other persons interested in the succession, a considerable amount of litigation may arise. Any family animosities are at their bitterest when an estate is being divided up, and these provisions give full scope for this bitterness to erupt into litigation. An executor would be wise to treat the classification of particular items as furniture and plenishings with considerable caution.

Limit on value

Where the value of the furniture and plenishings included in the intestate estate does not exceed £22,000 the surviving spouse is entitled to the whole thereof. If the value is over £22,000, the survivor may select the items which he or she wishes to have up to that value. This limit will be adequate in most estates, and is certainly nearer to a realistic figure than the upper limit placed on the house itself. Its function is to provide for the possibility that the deceased spouse had extremely valuable paintings hanging on the walls of the house.

Disputes as to valuations are to be settled by a single arbiter under section 8(5), as in the case of valuations of the house. However, despite the terms of the arbitration provisions, valuation of the furniture and plenishings can be undertaken only when the deceased was domiciled in Scotland, for only in that situation will Scots law govern the succession to his moveable estate.[11]

The house from which the furniture and plenishings may be taken

In the normal case where the surviving spouse was ordinarily resident in only one house in which the deceased had a "relevant interest" there is no problem. It is the furniture and plenishings of that house which the survivor is entitled to receive.[12] The survivor is still entitled to the furniture and plenishings when the deceased spouse's interest in the house falls within one of the exceptions specified in section 8(2) (or has a value over the limit), so that the survivor receives only the substituted value. Despite the exception, the house in that case is still one to which section 8 applies,[13] and therefore the surviving spouse is entitled to such furniture and plenishings in it as belonged to the intestate by virtue of section 8(3).

In cases where the surviving spouse was ordinarily resident in more than one house at the date of death of the intestate, the survivor is entitled to the furniture and plenishings belonging to the deceased in such one of them as he or she may elect within six months of the death of the intestate.[14] This election is entirely separate from the election of a house from two or more belonging to the deceased in which the survivor was ordinarily resident under section 8(1). It will therefore be possible to elect to take one of the houses with the furniture and plenishings of another, although one imagines that any difference in value of furnishings would rarely justify the removal expenses involved.

The right to furniture and plenishings may arise completely independently of the right to a house, as where the deceased spouse did not have a "relevant interest" in the house in which the survivor was ordinarily resident, but did own some or all of the furniture. Section 8(3) expressly provides that the right to furniture and plenishings exists whether or not the house is comprised in the intestate estate. The commonest case is that of the wife dying intestate when the house is owned or tenanted by the husband. Here no interest in the house is included in the wife's estate, but the husband is entitled to receive as a prior

---

[11] See Chap. 9, *infra.*
[12] s.8(3).
[13] s.8(4).
[14] s.8(3) proviso.

right such of the furniture and plenishings of the house as belonged to the wife, subject always to the £22,000 limit.

Order of priority of the rights under section 8

The surviving spouse's rights to the house and furniture and plenishings under this section are the first items to come out of the deceased spouse's estate. Section 9(6)(a) postpones the second set of prior rights — the monetary provision — to the housing right under section 8. Section 10(2) postpones the traditional legal rights, as amended, to both of these prior rights, and section 1(2) postpones the operation of the rules of succession to the free estate to both prior and legal rights. Hence the housing right is the first to be considered.

Monetary right under section 9

Section 9(1) entitles the surviving spouse to £35,000 if the deceased was survived by issue, or to £58,000 if the deceased left no issue. This right comes out of the intestate estate left after the housing rights under section 8 have been met[15] and is therefore in addition to the right to house, furniture and plenishings.

Interest is payable on the £35,000 or £58,000 as the case may be from the date of the intestate's death until payment. Although the Succession Act originally specified a fixed rate of interest (4 per cent) the rate is variable by the Secretary of State, and currently is 7 per cent.[16]

When the Succession Act 1964 came into force, the surviving spouse's right was restricted to the lower figure only when the deceased was survived by lawful issue. This included adopted children but not illegitimate children. Thus, if a deceased wife was survived only by an illegitimate child, her husband was entitled to a prior right at the higher level even if that entirely defeated the child's claim in the mother's estate. This had also been the case under the corresponding provisions prior to the 1964 Act[17] and still applies in the division of the estates of persons who died on or after September 10, 1964, up to and including November 24, 1968.

However, on November 25, 1968 — the commencement of the Law Reform (Miscellaneous Provisions) (Scotland) Act 1968 — the first major improvement of the position of illegitimate children came into force. Illegitimate children were put on the same footing as legitimate children in the succession to both parents (although only in succession directly to the parents). The result is that, since that date the surviving spouse's prior monetary right has been restricted to the lower figure whenever the deceased was survived by children, legitimate or illegitimate.[18] From November 25, 1968, until the Law Reform (Parent and Child) (Scotland) Act 1986[19] came into force on December

---

[15] s.9(6)(a).

[16] (S.I. 1981 No. 805). From 1964 to 1981, 4%.

[17] *Osman v. Campbell*, 1946 S.C. 204.

[18] 1968 Act (c.70), s.3 and Sched. 1, amending s.9(1) of the Succession Act.

[19] (c.9).

8, 1986, the existence of lawful issue, however remote, of a predeceasing child of the intestate also restricted the surviving spouse's right, but illegitimate offspring of a predeceasing child were not taken into account.

This was because the policy was to grant illegitimate children rights of succession in the estates of their parents, but not to permit them to represent their parents in, for example, the division of the estates of their grandparents. When this policy was applied to prior rights, the result was that the existence of an illegitimate child affected the division of the estate of its father or mother, but not any other estate. Thus, if the intestate's sole child (legitimate or illegitimate) had predeceased him, only the existence of legitimate offspring of that child reduced the surviving spouse's right.[20]

However, the status of illegitimacy has for practical purposes been abolished by the Law Reform (Parent and Child) (Scotland) Act 1986. Section 1 of that Act sets out the fundamental principle that the fact that a person's parents are not or have not been married to one another shall be left out of account in establishing the legal relationship between the person and any other person. The consequence is that the existence of any issue of the deceased spouse reduces the right of the surviving spouse under section 9 to the lower figure of £35,000. The terms legitimate or illegitimate have ceased to have any meaning for this purpose.

The children or issue concerned must, of course, be the offspring of the deceased spouse but need not be the offspring of the surviving spouse. Children of the deceased by a previous marriage or children who would formerly have been classed as illegitimate automatically reduce the surviving spouse's entitlement.

Effect of legacies in cases of partial intestacy

A surviving spouse has prior rights in cases of partial as well as total intestacy. The rights exist in the intestate estate as defined in the Act, and the definition refers to such part of the deceased's estate as is undisposed of by testamentary disposition.[21] If the intestacy is partial, the surviving spouse still receives the house and its furniture and plenishings except to the extent that they have been disposed of by the deceased in his will.[22] Equally, the surviving spouse is still entitled to either £35,000 or £58,000 from the rest of the undisposed of estate, but must deduct from that sum the amount or value of any legacy which he or she is entitled to receive out of the estate of the deceased. However, the survivor does not require to deduct the value of a legacy of any house in which he or she was ordinarily resident at the deceased's death, nor need a legacy of any furniture and plenishings of any such house be deducted.[23] If the survivor was ordinarily resident in more than one house, he or she may take a legacy of all the houses, and of all the furniture and plenishings in all of them, with no limits on value, without having to deduct the legacy from the prior right. This is probably an error but

---

[20] Succession (Scotland) Act 1964, s.9(1)(a), as amended, read with the definition of "issue" in s.36(1).
[21] *ibid.*, s.36(1). See *supra*, p.38
[22] *ibid.*, s.8(1) and (3).
[23] *ibid.*, s.9(1) proviso.

arises because section 8(4) applies the section to any dwelling-house in which the survivor was ordinarily resident, while the proviso to section 9(1) discounts a legacy of any house to which section 8 applies. If the surviving spouse chooses to renounce any legacy affecting the monetary prior right, as might be done if the legacy were of dubious value, the full sum may be claimed.

Section 9(6)(b) defines a legacy for these purposes as including "any payment or benefit to which a surviving spouse becomes entitled by virtue of any testamentary disposition". This gives a very wide interpretation to the term legacy and many benefits may be conferred in deeds which rank as testamentary dispositions which are not normally thought of as legacies. For example, the definition would seem to cover special destinations in favour of the surviving spouse. In a situation where the deceased spouse had purchased heritage with his own funds and recorded a destination, which he did not thereafter revoke, to himself and his wife and the survivor, that part of the destination having testamentary effect, namely the destination to his wife of the one-half share belonging to him at his death, would be a "legacy", the value of which might have to be deducted by the widow from her claim for the monetary element of her prior rights. Provisions in marriage contracts might also be such as to rank as "legacies". Although the definition of legacy in section 9(6)(b) is not limited to testamentary dispositions made by the deceased spouse, what falls to be deducted is a legacy "out of the estate of the intestate".[24]

The valuation of any such legacy is to be made as at the date of the deceased's death.[25]

Estate affected by the surviving spouse's monetary right

Where the amount of the estate available to meet the monetary payments, after deducting the rights under section 8, is less than the specified figures that spouse's right is held to be satisfied by the transfer to him or her of the whole of the available balance, thereby exhausting the estate.[26]

This can have surprising effects, as illustrated by example 1 in Appendix 2. A man dies intestate leaving a widow and two children. The net value of his estate is £170,000 consisting of a house valued at £120,000, furniture and plenishings thereof valued at £20,000, and net moveable estate of £30,000. The widow's prior right under section 8 gives her the house and furniture and plenishings. Her prior right to a monetary provision under section 9 is to £35,000, there being lawful issue of the deceased spouse. The balance available to meet this right is only £30,000, and hence the widow takes the whole of it in satisfaction of her rights. Thus the whole of the deceased's estate has gone to his widow. The son and daughter have a right to legitim in any moveable estate available after the spouse's prior rights have been met and to any free balance of the estate after *jus relictae* and legitim have been deducted. Here, however, the estate is not large enough to reach the stage of calculating

---

[24] *ibid.*, s.9(1) proviso.
[25] *ibid.*, s.9(6)(b).
[26] *ibid.*, s.9(2) and s.9(6)(a).

legal rights, let alone dividing up any free balance under the rules in Part I of the Act. Hence the widow takes the whole estate, and the children get nothing.

Take, however, exactly the same family with exactly the same items of estate, but postulating that the husband had not believed what he had been told about intestate succession, and that he had decided to make sure his widow received his whole estate by saying so in his will. Since he has made a will dealing with his whole estate, his widow has no prior rights.[27] There is, therefore, estate from which legitim is exigible, despite the will. The moveable estate amounts to £50,000 (furniture, etc., plus the net moveable estate) and the legitim fund for division between the children is therefore £16,666. The widow receives the remaining £33,334 of the moveable estate and the house by virtue of the will.

It is therefore possible, by dying intestate, to achieve an exclusion of the children's right to legitim, although it is not possible to achieve this by express testamentary provision. Indeed the children can be better off when their parent makes a will attempting to cut them out of any share in his estate than when he does nothing at all. At first sight it seemed that there might now be situations in which a solicitor would find himself in the position of advising his client not to make a will. This would have been unsatisfactory, since much depends on the precise value of the estate at the intestate's death and ingenious drafting devices were suggested to achieve the best of both worlds.

The simple answer was, however, pointed out by Professor McDonald.[28] If a client seeks to ensure that his widow will receive his whole estate, he should make a will wholly in her favour without a destination over in the event of her failing to take the testamentary gift. If the issue do not claim legitim the will operates whatever the values. If the issue do claim legitim and the estate is above the limit of value at which intestacy ceases to be more beneficial to the widow than testacy, then the widow takes under the will subject to the legitim. If the issue claim legitim and the estate is below that critical value (which is rather above the amount that would pass wholly to the widow by prior rights) the widow simply renounces her benefit under the will. This necessarily results in intestacy, there being no other beneficiary under the will.

The question of whether such a renunciation in fact created an intestacy was closely argued in *Kerr, Petr.*[29] The decision by the sheriff-substitute, affirmed by the sheriff on appeal, was that intestacy did result, so that the widow became entitled to the whole estate by virtue of her prior rights to the total exclusion of her step-daughter. This result was probably inevitable, for the alternative would have been to postulate a species of property which, though not intestate, fell to be divided as if it were, apart from prior rights.

Apportioning the section 9 payment between heritage and moveables

Where the amount of the estate available to meet the monetary payment under section 9 is greater than the amount due to the surviving spouse, section 9(3) provides that the amount concerned "shall be borne by, and paid out of,

---

[27] Prior rights come only from the "intestate estate". ss. 8(1) and 9(1)

[28] (1965) 10 J.L.S. 4.

[29] 1968 S.L.T. (Sh. Ct.) 61. See (1968) 13 J.L.S. 192.

the parts of the intestate estate consisting of heritable and moveable property respectively in proportion to the respective amounts of those parts". Despite the assimilation of heritage and moveables for some purposes of succession, this is necessary because the distinction between heritage and moveables has been kept for the purposes of the legal rights of *jus relicti, jus relictae* and legitim. After the prior rights under sections 8 and 9 have been satisfied, the surviving spouse is entitled to *jus relicti* or *jus relictae* only in the surplus moveables, and issue of the deceased have the right to legitim, also in the surplus moveables. A precise value for moveables must therefore be maintained at the stage of prior rights so that the estate from which legal rights can be taken may be accurately ascertained.

The proportion of the section 9 prior right payable by heritage and by moveables is the proportion which the net capital value of each bears to the net capital value of the whole estate available to meet the monetary payment. As an example, if the net estate after satisfaction of the housing right under section 8 is £40,000, consisting of heritage to the value of £10,000 and moveables to the value of £30,000, heritage represents one-quarter of the estate and bears one-quarter of the payment to the surviving spouse — *i.e.* £5,250 or £8,750 as the case may be. Moveables, representing three-quarters of the estate, bear the remaining three-quarters of the payment. The balance of the moveables is subject to *jus relicti* or *jus relictae*, and to legitim if applicable.[30]

It is not necessary actually to pay the amount due from heritage out of the proceeds of sale of the heritage or to create a security right over the heritage. All that is needed is a notional figure for heritage and moveables for the computation of legal rights. After legal rights have been computed, heritage and moveables are assimilated into one estate and pass under the same rules. No rights are affected if the surviving spouse is actually paid out of available moveable assets or by transfer of heritage to those values.

The surviving spouse is entitled to insist upon the furniture and plenishings and the deceased's interest in the house being transferred in view of the express terms of the statute. However, for other intestate assets the executor has a discretion whether to realise the asset and distribute the proceeds or to distribute *in specie.*[31] The discretion must be exercised in the interest of the estate as a whole, and if distribution is made *in specie* the executor may distribute equally to the beneficiaries (which will normally be appropriate). However circumstances may be such that it is appropriate for the executor to be selective and to transfer different assets to individual beneficiaries.[32]

No representation in prior rights

The rights under sections 8 and 9 are available only to a spouse who does actually survive, and cannot be claimed by issue of a predeceasing spouse as

---

[30] See also Appendix 2, example 2.

[31] *Cochrane's Exrs v. Inland Revenue*, 1975 S.L.T. 6 where the Lord President stated that the executor was not bound to take directions even from a residuary legatee. See *also Murray's J.F. v. Thomas Murray & Sons (Ice Merchants)Ltd*, 1992 S.L.T. 824.

[32] See also *infra*, p.131.

there is no provision for representation in the sections creating prior rights. The scheme of infinite representation set out in sections 5 and 6 applies only to Part I of the Act, dealing with the free estate available after prior rights and legal rights, and the scheme of representation contained in section 11 is limited to representation in legitim.

Previous figures for prior rights

For deaths from September 10, 1964, to May 22, 1973, inclusive:

section 8(1)   —   £ 15,000
section 8(3)   —   £ 5,000
section 9   —   £ 2,500 or £5,000

For deaths from May 23, 1973, to December 30, 1977, inclusive (Succession (Scotland) Act 1973):

section 8(1)   —   £ 30,000
section 8(3)   —   £ 8,000
section 9   —   £ 4,000 or £8,000

For deaths from December 31, 1977, to July 31, 1981, inclusive (S.I. 1977 No. 2110):

section 8(1)   —   £ 30,000
section 8(3)   —   £ 8,000
section 9   —   £ 8,000 or £16,000

For deaths from August 1, 1981, to April 30, 1988, inclusive (S.I. 1981 No. 806):

section 8(1)   —   £ 50,000
section 8(3)   —   £ 10,000
section 9   —   £ 15,000 or £25,000

For deaths from May 1, 1988 to November 25, 1993 inclusive (S.I. 1988 No. 633):

section 8(1)   —   £ 65,000
section 8(3)   —   £ 12,000
section 9   —   £ 21,000 or £35,000

For deaths from November 26, 1993 to April 1, 1999 inclusive (S.I. 1993 No. 2690):

section 8(1)   —   £110,000
section 8(3)   —   £ 20,000
section 9   —   £ 30,000 or £50,000

The current statutory instrument is S.I. 1999 No. 445.

CHAPTER 5

LEGAL RIGHTS OF THE SURVIVING SPOUSE AND OF DESCENDANTS

While the Succession (Scotland) Act 1964 is not a complete restatement of the traditional legal rights of spouses and children, the various particular changes made by the Act were the first substantial alterations in legal rights for some centuries and the following attempts to set out the law as it now exists.

Legal rights no longer applicable on divorce

One of the functions of legal rights used to be to regulate the financial consequences of divorce. The working rule was that legal rights were due on divorce as if the guilty spouse had died but the Succession Act substituted a new discretionary system, subsequently much amended in separate legislation.[1] Thus references to legal rights in marriage contracts which were entered into before September 10, 1964, but which take effect on divorce granted in an action commenced on or after that date are now to be construed as references to rights which the spouse might obtain under the new schemes of financial provision on divorce.[2] Any reference to legal rights in a pre-1964 marriage contract tended to take the form of a renunciation of them by the parties. The result now is that the clause will be treated as a renunciation of any claim for financial provision on divorce. It may also exclude the right to seek a variation of the marriage contract on divorce.[3] The traditional legal rights therefore no longer have any function in dealing with the financial consequences of divorce.

The other functions of legal rights are however still of great importance. One is to act as a family protection device by permitting protected relatives to claim legal rights in place of testamentary provisions of which they disapprove. They have an automatic right to a fixed share without the intervention of a court.[4] Legal rights are automatic rights of succession, and like other rights of succession, vest immediately on the death of the parent or spouse. The use of the terminology of "claiming" legal rights has sometimes caused confusion leading to a suggestion that the rights do not vest until they have actually been paid, but this is clearly wrong. Even an estranged spouse who survives by only one minute has a vested right to *jus relictae* or *relicti*.

---

[1] Succession (Scotland) Act 1964, s.25, repealed and replaced by Divorce (Scotland) Act 1976 (c.39), Sched. 2 and ss. 5 & 6. The basis of the present law is the Family Law (Scotland) Act 1985.
[2] 1964 Act, s.33(2). See Divorce (Scotland) Act 1976, s.5; Matrimonial and Family Proceedings Act 1984 (c.42), s.29 or Family Law (Scotland) Act 1985 (c.37), s.8.
[3] *Thomson v. Thomson*, 1982 S.L.T. 521.
[4] See *infra*, p.101.

The other function is to be one of the three sets of rules of intestate succession, and this function is considered in this chapter.

However one specialty arising from the origin of legal rights is that the right is subject to the long negative prescription of 20 years.[5]

Order of priority of legal rights in intestate succession

In their application to intestate succession, legal rights are exigible from the moveable estate available after any prior rights under sections 8 and 9 of the Succession Act have been satisfied.[6]

If the deceased is survived by a spouse the practical result of the postponement to prior rights may be that legal rights are of no significance. If the composition and size of the deceased's estate are such that the prior rights of the surviving spouse are greater than the value of the estate, the whole estate passes to the surviving spouse and there will be no legal rights.[7] While Scots tend to be proud of the way in which legal rights operate as a bar to capricious disinheritance by a testator, the fact that a child's right to legitim may be defeated if the parent does not make a will, and indeed sometimes even if he does make a will, leaves an interesting jurisprudential question of whether the child can be said to have a right at all if there is no estate on which the right can operate.

The rights available

The legal rights formerly exigible from the heritage of a deceased person are abolished in respect of any deaths occurring on or after September 10, 1964.[8] These were the widow's terce (a right to one third of the income from the heritage) and the widower's courtesy (a right to the income of the whole of the wife's heritage, provided an heir had been born and had been heard to cry). References in any other enactment to courtesy or terce are of no effect.[9] This total abolition of rights which were of very long standing in the law was generally welcomed. Terce, in particular, was of very little value to the recipient in the vast majority of cases and had largely a nuisance value as a trap for unwary conveyancers (if such beings exist!).

However, the opportunity was not taken to extend legal rights to the whole estate. Despite strenuous efforts in Parliament during the consideration of the Succession Bill, the government insisted on retaining the distinction between heritage and moveables for the purposes of legal rights. Consequently the abolition of terce and courtesy means that there are now no legal rights — as opposed to prior rights — in a deceased's heritable property. The legal rights which are now available to the deceased's surviving spouse and to his

---

[5] Prescription and Limitation (Scotland) Act 1973, s.6 and Sched. 1, para. 2(f).
[6] s.10(2).
[7] This is now less often true than it was in 1964, as the values for prior rights have not kept pace with inflation, particularly of house values.
[8] s.10(1). See letter 2001 S.L.T. (News) 318 for a case in which courtesy was still applicable.
[9] Sched. 2, para. 4.

descendants are exigible from his moveable estate only, and the moveable estate in question is that remaining after satisfaction of any prior rights. It is therefore still essential to classify property correctly and to allocate debts to heritage and to moveables.

The surviving wife's right is *jus relictae* while the corresponding right of a husband is *jus relicti*. They are identical in all but name and entitle the surviving spouse to one-third of the deceased's moveable property if the deceased is survived by qualified descendants or to one-half of the moveables if there are no such descendants. The legal right of descendants (not merely immediate children of the deceased as was the case pre-1964) is legitim. If the deceased parent has left a surviving spouse, the descendants share a legitim fund consisting of one-third of the available moveable estate of the deceased parent. If the deceased left no surviving spouse the legitim fund to be shared among the descendants consists of one-half of the moveables.

In other words, when legal rights are involved, there are three possible units of division of the moveable fund from which they are exigible. These units are:

    (1) surviving spouse's share — *jus relicti* or *jus relictae*;

    (2) descendants' share — legitim (bairn's part);

    (3) dead's part — this, along with any heritage not required to meet prior rights, passes on intestacy under the rules of succession to the free estate contained in Part I of the Act.

If the intestate was survived by both spouse and issue, the moveables available to meet legal rights are split into three parts, one part to each of the units of division. If the intestate was survived by a spouse, but not by issue, or conversely was survived by issue but not by a spouse, the available moveables are split into two parts, one being dead's part and the other being the surviving spouse's share or the legitim fund for division among the issue.

Interest on legal rights

Interest is payable on the ascertained amount of the legal rights from the date of death until paid.[10] Although there is little theoretical discussion of the basis for payment of interest, it is well established that it is payable.[11] In only two of the reported cases was interest refused altogether, and in both of these other factors seem to have been taken into account.[12] It may be that interest arises from the same considerations as apply to interest on debts where the general rule is that, apart from contract, interest is payable as a result of a principal sum having been wrongfully withheld and not paid on the date when it ought to have been paid.[13] There is scope for considerable discussion of what that date is,[14] but in the case of legal rights it is established that the relevant

---

[10] No interest was payable on terce or courtesy, they being rights to the income arising from the heritage.

[11] McLaren, *Wills & Succession*, i, 125.

[12] *Wick v. Wick* (1898) 1 F. 199; *Young v. Young*, 1965 S.L.T. (Notes) 95.

[13] See *Kolbin & Sons v. Kinnear & Co.(The Altai)*, 1931 S.C. (H.L.) 128, *per* Lord Atkin at 137.

[14] Wilson. *The Scottish Law of Debt* (2nd ed.), para. 11.7.

date from which interest runs is the date of death.[15] It may seem odd that this should be so, for the law is in the peculiar position of notionally requiring the executor to pay the legal rights on the very day of death while also erecting the principle of vitious intromission against anyone attempting to comply with the requirement. Despite the terms of the decision in *Young v. Young*,[16] interest on legal rights in succession does not depend upon unreasonable delay in payment. In *Kearon v. Thomson's Trs*[17] interest was awarded from the date of death even although it was expressly held by Lord President Cooper that the legitim claim had been promptly complied with by the executors and no objection to their administration had been raised.

The rate of interest is at the discretion of the court,[18] taking account both of prevailing rates and of the interest actually earned by the estate in this period. Factors such as that substantial parts of the estate may not be in a state of productive investment at the time of the deceased's death mean that the rate of interest to be awarded will be somewhat below the current going rate for commercial investments. In practice, the figure of seven per cent, currently specified for the spouse's prior right under section 9, is often acceptable and is commonly recommended by advisers. The Scottish Law Commission has recommended that future legislation should remove the uncertainty of the present discretionary rate by specifying a fixed rate and that in the circumstances then current the same figure of seven per cent should be adopted.

The persons entitled to legal rights

Jus relictae and *jus relicti* are available only to a surviving spouse, there being no representation of a predeceasing spouse at any stage in the division of an intestate estate. The only provisions permitting representation are those in sections 5 and 6 of the Act dealing with the free estate (which expressly do not apply to spouses) and those in section 11 dealing with legitim which is available to issue only.

Legitim was formerly confined to surviving legitimate children related by blood to the deceased, but important changes have now been effected.

Adopted children were given by the Succession Act full rights of succession (including legitim) in the estates of the adopting parent or parents.[19] Adopted children now fall to be treated as legitimate children of the adopter for the calculation of prior and legal rights. This remedied a major anomaly of the older law that adoption had no effect upon rights of succession. Adopted persons retained any rights of succession which they had in the estates of their natural parents but gained none in the estates of the adopting parents. A

---

[15] *Gilchrist v. Gilchrist's Trs* (1889) 16 R. 1118, *per* Lord Fraser at 1120. See also *Russel v. Att.-Gen.*, 1917 S.C. 28; *Sanderson v. Lockhart-Mure*, 1946 S.C. 298; *Kearon v. Thomson's Trs*, 1949 S.C. 287.

[16] 1965 S.L.T. (Notes) 95.

[17] 1949 S.C. 287. The rubric to the report at 1949 S.L.T. 286 is misleading in this respect.

[18] *Kearon v. Thomson's Trs, supra.* There is a comprehensive citation of earlier authority in Lord Cooper's opinion.

[19] s.23(1). Titles of honour etc are however excluded; s.37(1)(a).

belated transitional provision for the case where the adopting parent died before the Succession Act came into force on September 10, 1964, and the natural parent died on or after August 3, 1966, is contained in the Law Reform (Miscellaneous Provisions) (Scotland) Act 1966.[20] In these circumstances, any right to legitim which the child has in the estates of its natural parents is preserved.

Illegitimate children, by an even more far-reaching series of provisions, now have the right to legitim in the estates of both parents. The first step came in the Law Reform (Miscellaneous Provisions) (Scotland) Act 1968[21] which added a new section 10A to the Succession Act. The result then was that in the division of the estates of its parents dying on or after November 25, 1968, an illegitimate child had exactly the same right of legitim as a legitimate child. A decree of affiliation and aliment established paternity for this purpose unless the contrary was proved.[22] There were, however, anomalies even after the 1968 reforms, as a grandchild which was illegitimate could not represent its predeceasing, legitimate, parent to obtain legitim from the estate of a grandparent.[23] The full assimilation of the position of the illegitimate child to that of the legitimate child finally came in the Law Reform (Parent and Child) (Scotland) Act 1986.[24] In the succession to persons dying after the commencement of that Act on December 8, 1986 no distinction is made between legitimate and illegitimate children (except for succession to titles and arms) and in particular, grandchildren will always be able to represent their predeceasing parents for the purposes of legitim in the estates of their grandparents. For practical purposes, illegitimacy has now been abolished. A declarator of parentage (which requires "sufficient evidence") establishes paternity.[25]

The introduction of representation in legitim was another major change effected by the Succession Act. There is no representation of a spouse so as to give that spouse's issue *jus relictae* or *jus relicti*, but legitim is no longer confined to surviving children. This remedies what was widely regarded as one of the major anomalies of the law prior to the Succession Act. In a situation such as the following:

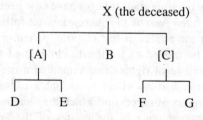

---

[20] (c.19), s.5.

[21] (c.70), s.2.

[22] Law Reform (Miscellaneous Provisions) (Scotland) Act 1968 (c.70), s.11. Repealed by Law Reform (Parent and Child) (Scotland) Act 1986 (c.9), Sched. 2.

[23] The "issue" who could represent their parents were defined by s.36(1) of the Succession Act as lawful issue, however remote, with the result that an illegitimate child could not claim the legitim to which its parent would have been entitled by survivance.

[24] (c.9).

[25] *ibid.*, s.5(3).

B, the surviving child of the intestate, used to take the whole legitim fund to the exclusion of D, E, F and G, the issue of predeceasing children. The lack of representation arose from the wording of the definition of "moveable estate" in section 9 of the Intestate Moveable Succession (Scotland) Act 1855. This provided, inter alia, that "moveable estate" included the "whole free moveable estate on which the deceased, if not subject to any incapacity, might have tested". As the deceased could not in theory test on that proportion of his estate subject to legitim (or *jus relicti* and *jus relictae*), this meant that the proportion of the moveables available for legitim was not part of the "moveable estate" in which a right of representation was created by section 1 of that Act. (Equally it meant that there was no representation in a spouse's rights.) As there was no representation at common law in the division of moveables, the pre-existing position was preserved for legitim and other legal rights in moveables, so that a single surviving child took the whole legitim fund to the exclusion of grandchildren. There was never any doubt that estate subject to legitim was not estate on which the deceased "might have tested." If in fact he made a will dealing with the whole of his estate, it was effective in respect of the property subject to legitim only if the children entitled to claim refrained from doing so.

The Mackintosh Committee on the Law of Succession recommended the introduction of infinite representation in legitim and so far as this was done, it was done by section 11 of the Succession Act. Section 11(1) makes the general provision that where a person dies predeceased by a child who has left issue who survive the deceased, and the child would, if he had survived the deceased, have been entitled to legitim out of the deceased's estate, such issue shall have the like right to legitim as the child would have had if he had survived the deceased. "Child" refers to an immediate child of the deceased, and, in respect of deaths occurring on or after November 25, 1968, includes also an illegitimate child[26], but "issue" was still defined as "lawful" issue. Thus the legitimate children of an illegitimate child could represent it from 1968 onwards, but it was not until 1986 that illegitimate children could actually be the representatives.

In itself, section 11(1) would have the effect of requiring a division of the legitim fund *per stirpes* into as many parts as there were children of the deceased, irrespective of whether any of the children had survived. The division *per stirpes* would always be at the level of immediate children because the right of representation gives the issue "the like right to legitim as the child would have had if he had survived the deceased". However, section 11(1) is stated to be "subject to the next following subsection" which requires the use of the anomalous method of division previously in force in relation to moveable estate rather than the true representation which was applied in heritable succession.[27] Briefly, section 11(2) provides that there is a division *per stirpes* at the level of the class nearest in degree to the deceased of which there are surviving members.

---

[26] See above.

[27] Meston, "Representation in Succession" (1995) 1 Scottish Law & Practice Quarterly 83.

If the deceased's children predecease him, but he is survived by grandchildren, a situation such as the following may arise:

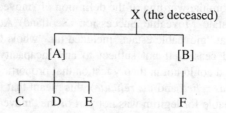

In this situation C, D, E and F are the class nearest in degree to the deceased of which there are surviving members. By virtue of section 11(1) they are entitled to legitim. As they are all of the same degree of relationship to the deceased, the effect of section 11(2)(a) is that the legitim fund is divided among them equally, *i.e.* a *per capita* division. The division is not one-half to A's family and one-half to B's family, but a division into quarters at the level of grandchildren. A's children have benefited substantially by the fact that both A and B predeceased their grandparent X.

However, take a case where the claimants are not all of the same degree of relationship to the deceased, for example:

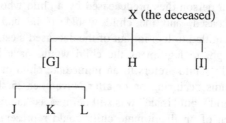

Those entitled to legitim are the child H, and the grandchildren J, K and L. The class nearest in degree to the intestate of which there are surviving members is the class of children, H being the survivor. The division of the legitim fund is therefore *per stirpes* into two parts, there being two children either surviving or represented by surviving issue. Of these parts, H takes one, giving him one-half of the legitim fund, and the other part is divided equally between J, K and L, giving them one-sixth of the fund each.[28] It seems anomalous that the accident of whether or not a member of the previous generation survives should make such a dramatic difference to the shares taken.

Property subject to legal rights

With the abolition of terce and courtesy, there are now no legal rights in heritage. Legal rights are exigible from such of the moveable estate owned by

---

[28] s.11(2)(b).

the deceased at the time of his death as is available after deduction of the appropriate proportion of any surviving spouse's prior rights.

The distinction between heritage and moveables for the purpose of legal rights remains almost completely unaffected.[29] Land, buildings, things annexed to, growing in, or destined for use on, land, and rights having a tract of future time[30] are heritable. Personal rights under contracts for land are heritable. This includes for example, rights under a concluded contract for purchase of land, but also such matters as rights of pre-emption or contracts giving an option to purchase.[31] A rather peculiar case is the position of tenancies at will. Although the special position of the Kindly Tenants of Lochmaben is abolished by section 64 of the Abolition of Feudal Tenure etc. (Scotland) Act 2000[32] there would appear to be no similar abolition of the tenure (if it is a tenure) of tenants at will. It would seem that this form of tenure must also be heritable for the purposes of legal rights.

Things capable of movement and most incorporeal rights are moveable. Assets which have been held to be moveable for the purpose of legal rights include insurance policies on the deceased's own life,[33] or taken out by him on the life of another,[34] the deceased's vested right in the succession to a third party, even where that third party's estate included heritable bonds[35] and certain bonds and debentures issued under statutory powers.[36] An interest in a partnership is moveable, and this can have dramatic effects when farms are involved. If the deceased owned a farm and was in partnership solely for the purpose of working the farm, his interest in the farm itself is clearly heritable and not subject to legal rights. He will normally have granted a lease of the farm to the partnership which includes himself. However if he had conveyed the farm to the partnership as one of its assets, his interest in the partnership is wholly moveable, even if it mainly represents the value of the land which he had conveyed to the firm. He has no direct interest in the individual assets of the partnership.[37] This can make a very big difference to the value of legal rights claims in his estate.

Voluntary acts by a guardian of the deceased do not affect the succession to the deceased's estate. Thus unless the sale of the ward's heritage is completely unavoidable, a merely prudent sale by the guardian does not effect conversion of the heritage into moveables for the purpose of legal rights.[38]

---

[29] See Walker, *Principles of Scottish Private Law* (4th ed.), Vol. III, pp.4–17.

[30] This somewhat esoteric concept refers primarily to regular payments to a creditor although not related to any particular capital sum. An annuity is the standard example. See *Meston's Succession Opinions*, No.35 for an example where an "annuity" was probably not a true annuity qualifying as having a tract of future time.

[31] Baron Hume's Lectures, Vol. IV (Stair Soc. Vol.17) pp.558–559. I am indebted to Professor Paisley for bring this reference to my attention.

[32] (asp 5).

[33] *Muirhead v. Muirhead's Factor* (1867) 6 M. 95.

[34] *Chalmers's Trs* (1882) 9 R. 743. The actuarial value was used.

[35] *Borland's Trs v. Borland*, 1917 S.C. 704.

[36] *Robertson's Trs v. Maxwell*, 1922 S.C. 267.

[37] Gretton, "Who owns partnership property", 1987 J.R. 163.

[38] McLaren, *Wills & Succession*, Vol. I pp.206–208 and 238; *Meston's Succession Opinions*, No.52, p.158.

One perennial problem is whether particular assets were *in bonis* of the deceased at the time of his death, as only such assets are available for legal rights. In *Beveridge v. Beveridge's Exrx*[39] a question arose over a Treasury gratuity paid to the legal representatives of a deceased civil servant. This was held to be part of the moveable estate subject to legal rights, despite the argument that the deceased had no enforceable right to the sum and thus it could not have been *in bonis* of the deceased at his death.

There are also certain points worth notice in connection with bonds. By section 117 of the Titles to Land Consolidation (Scotland) Act 1868,[40] a heritable security is moveable in the general succession of the creditor "except that in relation to the legal rights of the spouse or of the descendants, of the deceased, it shall be heritable estate". As there are now no legal rights in heritage, this means that investment in heritable securities is not subject to legal rights at all. It is strange that the anomaly was not removed when the new standard security was created by the Conveyancing and Feudal Reform (Scotland) Act 1970,[41] and even more strange that it should have been continued by the Abolition of Feudal Tenure etc. (Scotland) Act 2000.[42]

It is surely nonsensical to preserve this classification of a given type of property as heritable for some purposes and moveable for others, the more especially as the distinction between heritage and moveables is abolished for the purpose of succession to the free estate after prior rights and legal rights. The only thing that is achieved by this chameleon-like nature is confusion and uncertainty as to how the executor should deal with a heritable security in allocating funds to meet a surviving spouse's monetary prior right under section 9.[43]

Personal bonds may also be in an anomalous position. At one stage of the Succession Bill's progress it was proposed to repeal the Bonds Act 1661, c.32.[44] That Act made personal bonds moveable in the succession of the creditor, unless they excluded executors or contained an obligation to infeft. When the difficulties which would have arisen from such a repeal were pointed out, the proposal to repeal was dropped and the Act remains in force. The snag is that the part of the Act which should have been repealed, namely the reference to bonds excluding executors, also remains in force. Executors can no longer be excluded, inasmuch as they now administer both heritable and moveable estate, but nonetheless, it would seem that a personal bond which purports to exclude executors still becomes heritable in the creditor's succession, at least after the first term of payment of interest has arrived, and is thus not subject to any legal rights.

The sensible answer would be to apply legal rights to the whole estate, thereby completely abolishing the distinction between heritage and moveables for all purposes of succession. The Scottish Law Commission proposes just

---

[39] 1938 S.C. 160.
[40] As amended by Succession (Scotland) Act 1964, s.34 and Sched. 2 and by the Abolition of Feudal Tenure etc. (Scotland) Act 2000 (asp 5).
[41] (c.35).
[42] (asp 5).
[43] See *supra*, pp.49-50 and Appendix 2, example 4.
[44] A.P.S. c.244.

such a reform in its Report on Succession and it is to be hoped that legislative time will speedily be found for change. The new "legal share" proposed by the Commission will take the form of percentages of the whole estate and this is greatly to be welcomed. It would then be possible to ignore all the oddities of classification of property in the law of succession.

Date of valuation of assets

Legal rights are entitlements to fixed fractions of the value of the moveable estate of the deceased at the time of his death. That value is normally that shown in the Inheritance Tax inventory and in the Confirmation, less the moveable debts of the deceased. However, if the value actually realised after proper administration with due despatch is different from the value in the inventory, it is that realised value which will be used for calculation of legal rights. It is important that the administration has been carried out with all due speed.[45]

Collation *inter liberos*

It should be noted that the necessity under this doctrine of taking account of any "advances" which may have been made to one or more children of the deceased has the result that it is not appropriate simply to divide the whole estate remaining after *jus relictae/ relicti* equally among the children. There may be a different division of the legitim fund from that applicable to the free estate.

This doctrine remains applicable in the division of the legitim fund.[46] As collation *inter haeredes* has been abolished with the abolition of the distinction between heritage and moveables in the succession to the free estate, collation *inter liberos* is now the only form of the doctrine of collation still applicable in the law of succession. The purpose of the doctrine is to preserve equality in the division of the legitim fund when more than one of the persons entitled does in fact claim legitim, and one or more of the claimants has received certain types of advances during the parent's lifetime.

The effect is that if a claimant for legitim has received any advances of the appropriate type during the parent's lifetime, other claimants for legitim may require him to add the amount of the advance to the legitim fund calculated in the ordinary way from the estate owned by the parent at death. The total of the legitim fund plus the advances is then available for distribution among those entitled to legitim. The person who received the advance is required to impute his advance against his rateable share of the combined fund of legitim plus advances.

An example may illustrate the result more clearly. A dies intestate, leaving a widow B and three children, C, D and E.

---

[45] *Russel v. Att.-Gen.*, 1917 S.C. 28; *Alexander v. Alexander's Trs*, 1954 S.C. 436; 1954 S.L.T. 342. In *Alexander* the realised value was so much lower than the original valuation that legal rights calculated on the original figure would have been greater than the whole estate.
[46] s.11(3).

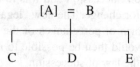

A's net estate amounts to £146,000 in value, consisting of the matrimonial home valued at £80,000, its furniture and plenishings valued at £10,000, and other moveable estate valued at £56,000. By virtue of her prior rights, B, the widow, receives the house and its furniture, etc., plus £35,000. Thus the estate available to meet legal rights is £21,000, all moveable. The legitim fund is therefore £7,000, there being both widow and children.

During his lifetime A had given his child C an advance of £2,000 to enable him to set up in business. This being one of the types of advance covered by the doctrine of collation *inter liberos*, C is required to collate his £2,000 as a condition of claiming legitim. Thus the total value of the fund to be divided among the children as legitim is £9,000, being the £7,000 computed in the ordinary way in the estate owned by the deceased at his death, plus the advance of £2,000. Of this total, C, D and E each are entitled to £3,000 as their share of legitim. In C's case the £2,000 advance already given to him is set against his share of the combined fund, so that he receives only £1,000 from the £7,000 available on A's death, and D and E receive £3,000 each.

If *inter vivos* payments qualifying as advances are large enough the result can be that the beneficiary of the advances will receive nothing from the estate as legitim and could even have to make a payment into the legitim fund if he or she has not renounced the claim for legitim.[47]

There is surprisingly little decided authority on the topic of advances and collation, even although the doctrine is very well established.[48] The advances which must be collated are limited to those which affect the legitim fund.[49] Thus they do not include payments in discharge of a parent's natural duty of maintenance and education of his child,[50] nor do they include payments by way of remuneration for services which arise out of an onerous contract. Loans made to the legitim claimant are not advances to be collated under this doctrine, for they are due to the deceased's executor and form part of the deceased's gross estate from which the legitim fund is computed. Advances made out of the deceased's heritage are not subject to collation *inter liberos*, because they do not directly affect the moveable fund from which legitim is taken, but payments to the child to permit the child to purchase a house or business premises clearly would be included. Testamentary provisions, as distinct from *inter vivos* advances, need not be collated, as they do not affect the legitim fund. Such testamentary provisions, in so far as they are moveable, are paid out of dead's part which is what is left after legal rights and of which

---

[47] See *infra*, p.67. *Meston's Succession Opinions*, No.55, p.174.
[48] See the bemused and somewhat despairing remarks by Lord Cooper in *Galloway's Trs v. Galloway* 1953 S.C. 43.
[49] McLaren, *Wills & Succession*, i, 167–169.
[50] *Elliot's Exrs v. Elliot*, 1953 S.C. 43.

the deceased was completely free to dispose. In any event, if the beneficiary of such a testamentary provision accepts it, he cannot also claim legitim unless there was a partial intestacy, and, if he is not a claimant for legitim, no one can require the collation of advances made to him. Finally, even if *inter vivos* advances of a type otherwise appropriate for the operation of this doctrine have been made, the donor may expressly or impliedly have indicated that the recipient's right to legitim is to be unaffected thereby.

The typical examples of advances which may have to be collated in securing the equitable division of the legitim fund are advances to set the recipient up in trade, for a marriage portion or for settlement in a station in life. The archaic terminology has to be translated into modern terms.

The onus of proof that a particular transfer was an advance may possibly be on the executors, but if so it is a much slighter onus than would be necessary to prove a debt due by the child.[51]

Under the previous law, only surviving children of the deceased could be called upon to collate under this doctrine, because only surviving children were entitled to legitim. Now, however, with the introduction of infinite representation in legitim, provision is made in the Succession Act[52] for the case where remoter descendants are entitled to legitim. The provision is that where any descendant is entitled to legitim by virtue of representation, "he shall be under the like duty to collate any advances made by the deceased to him, and the proportion appropriate to him of any advances so made to any person through whom he derives such entitlement, as if he had been entitled to claim such legitim otherwise than by virtue of" representation.[53]

No standard of appropriateness is laid down by which to determine the share of an advance to his ancestor which a representative claiming legitim must collate. This can give rise to severe difficulties if the only persons entitled to legitim are grandchildren, the immediate children having predeceased, for per capita division means that the share of the legitim fund taken by a grandchild is not the same as the share which his parent — to whom an advance was made — would have taken.[54] The grandchild may be entitled to only, say, one-sixth of the legitim fund where his parent might have been entitled to one-half, but the grandchild may still be debited with the whole of the advance made to the parent. Worse, the parent may have dissipated the advance and the grandchild may have received no benefit from it at all. This is yet another flaw arising from the peculiarity of representation in Scotland.

There must be more than one claimant for legitim before the doctrine of collation *inter liberos* comes into play at all. If, as might arise when the deceased has left a will unfavourable to only one of those entitled to legitim, only one of several possible claimants does actually claim, collation cannot arise. The claimant simply takes his or her rateable share of the legitim fund

---

[51] A comment by L. Gifford in *Welsh v. Welsh's Trs* (1878) 5 R. 542 suggests that the onus, albeit a light one, should rest on the trustees. In *Macphail v. Macphail's Trs* (1906) 13 S.L.T. 879 the trustees were in fact ordained to lead in the proof, but their principal point was that a son was a debtor to his father.

[52] s.11(3).

[53] For an example, see Appendix 2, example 3.

[54] See 1967 S.L.T. (News) 195, 224 and 247.

computed in the estate owned by the deceased at his death and advances are not taken into account at all. Collation is an equitable doctrine for the actual distribution of the legitim fund and can be invoked only by actually competing claimants.[55] Thus if one child has received substantial advances and is subsequently omitted from the parent's will, a situation could arise in which that child could also claim a share of the legitim fund, without collating, if the other children should be happy with the will. This is so even if the size of the advances had been such that if there had been collation, the child with the advances would have had to pay money back to the fund for the other children. Depending on values and the other provisions of the will, the remedy might then be for the other children to reject their testamentary benefits and also claim legitim, whereupon the "advanced" child would be likely to withdraw.

Equally, claimants for legitim cannot require other persons who are entitled to legitim, but are not claiming it, to collate advances made to them. *Coats's Trs*[56] was an unusual case in which the sole claimant for legitim was actively seeking to collate the advances made to her in order to benefit by collation of the much larger advances made to others who were not claiming legitim. The attempt failed.

Legal rights as family protection

As noted above, in addition to their role as part of the regular law of intestate succession, legal rights have the function of acting as forced shares in a system of family protection against disinheritance. The content and characteristics of the rights in this context are exactly the same as in intestate succession.

There have been various arguments as to the true theoretical nature and origin of legal rights in Scotland. They could be classified as debts due by the estate or as rights of succession in the estate. They may be the attenuated remnants of a system of community of property in Scotland. Whatever the origin, two aspects of the nature of legal rights are worth further attention. One is that legal rights are indefeasible without the consent of the person entitled to them and the other that they are, nevertheless, subject to evasion.

It is probably the best-known feature of legal rights in Scotland that they cannot be defeated by any testamentary disposition made by the person from whose estate they are exigible. A testator is technically entitled to test only on that part of his estate remaining after legal rights have been satisfied, and any attempt to go beyond that limitation can be disregarded by those entitled to legal rights. This power to bypass the testator's will is, of course, exercised only when the legal rights are more beneficial than the provisions made in the will. Accordingly, even if a testator directs that his whole estate is to be applied to set up a home for stray dogs, his surviving spouse and descendants are able to claim their legal rights. Only the dead's part need go to the dogs. In this respect, legal rights operate as a limitation on a testator's freedom and as a

---

[55] *Coats's Trs v. Coats*, 1914 S.C. 744.
[56] *ibid.*

bar to capricious disinheritance, thereby ensuring that at least some assets are available for his family.

Before the Succession (Scotland) Act came into force in September 1964 the right to legitim could be defeated without the concurrence of the child otherwise entitled thereto if his parents entered into an ante-nuptial marriage contract in which his right was prospectively discharged. This method of defeating a right to legitim was abolished by section 12 of the 1964 Act and it is now true to say of all legal rights, as it was formerly true of the rights other than legitim, that they cannot be defeated without the consent, express or implied, of the person entitled to them.

However, although the entitlement to legal rights cannot be defeated by unilateral action by the person whose estate is in question, the practical effects of the legal rights can be evaded. The ancestor or spouse is perfectly free to deal with his estate as he sees fit during his lifetime, even if the purpose of his dealings is avowedly to evade legal rights. That, combined with the anomaly that legal rights are due only from part of the estate means that he can reduce the proportion of his estate subject to legal rights. To take advantage of the fact that there are no legal rights in heritage, the moveable part of his estate can be sharply reduced by investing in heritage (including heritable securities). It is true that it is not very convenient to have only heritable assets, as liquidity is then poor. But to the extent that it is suitable in his case, a testator can effectively disinherit his wife and descendants by leaving a will (thereby excluding the surviving spouse's prior rights) and by ensuring that the bulk of his estate consists of heritage. Legal rights would attach only to such portion of his estate as he chose to keep in moveable form. This nonsense will be removed when the Scottish Law Commission's recommendations are eventually enacted.

The result is that legal rights are even more liable to evasion than they were before the 1964 Act came into force, and there remains the even more drastic step by which a person may completely defeat all claims on his estate by transferring the whole of it *inter vivos* to some third party, either as an outright gift or in return for a liferent. Provided the transfer is genuine and irrevocable, this will leave no estate owned by the deceased at his death on which legal rights can operate.[57] All these transactions may be done with the open and expressed intention of evading legal rights, yet no allegations of fraudulent frustration of legal rights will be entertained.[58]

Satisfaction of legal rights

Apart from complete or partial satisfaction of legitim by means of advances which may require to be collated *inter liberos*, legal rights may also be satisfied by testamentary provisions accepted in lieu of the legal rights. The legatee has the choice between the legal right and the testamentary provision, but if the latter is accepted, the legal right is held to be satisfied thereby.

---

[57] *Meston's Succession Opinions*, No.49, p.150 and cases there cited.
[58] *Agnew v. Agnew* (1775) Mor. 8210; *Lashley v. Hog* (1804) 4 Pat. 581.

In the case of testamentary dispositions to which section 13 of the 1964 Act applies, *i.e.* wills actually executed after the commencement of the Act,[59] this will be wholly a question of approbate and reprobate. No person can both accept and reject the same instrument, and thus no person can accept the conventional provisions in his favour in a will and also claim legal rights in such a manner as to be inconsistent with the testator's intentions for the disposal of his estate. This, of course, does not necessarily bar a spouse or descendant of a testator from claiming legal rights in any estate which has fallen into intestacy as well as the conventional provisions in their favour in the will.[60]

Under the pre-1964 law, a claim for legal rights did not automatically involve complete forfeiture of testamentary provisions. Unless there was a provision in the testamentary instrument that the provisions thereby made were in full satisfaction of legal rights, or that a claim for legal rights would involve forfeiture of the provisions, the abstruse doctrine of equitable compensation had the effect that the testamentary provision was not irrevocably forfeited by making a claim for legal rights. Instead it was applied in the first instance to restore what was taken from the estate by way of legal rights, and thereafter it remained available to the spouse or child concerned. The cases usually involved a testamentary liferent, in place of which the beneficiary preferred to have an immediate capital sum by way of a claim for legal rights. The action of claiming legal rights does not necessarily accelerate payment of the fee to the fiar unless the will so provides,[61] and hence the balance of the liferented estate continued to produce income. Once this income had accumulated sufficiently to restore to the estate what it had lost in consequence of the claim for legal rights, the fact that complete compensation had been made to the ultimate fiars usually meant that the liferent again became available to the beneficiary.[62] However a clause in the will declaring that its provisions were in full satisfaction of the legatee's legal rights prevented the beneficiary from relying on equitable compensation. Thus even when full compensation had been made over a period of years, the beneficiary could not then resume his liferent. A full satisfaction clause almost invariably appeared in well-drawn wills.

Section 13 of the 1964 Act reverses this situation. Even if no full satisfaction clause appears in a testamentary disposition executed after the commencement of the Act, it will take effect as if it contained one, unless there is an express provision to the contrary therein. One imagines that there will rarely be such an express provision to the contrary, and the author has never seen such a clause. The result is therefore virtually to abolish the doctrine of equitable compensation in respect of all wills executed after the commencement of the Act. However *Munro's Trs,Petrs* [63] holds that there may

---

[59] s.36(3).
[60] *Naismith v. Boyes* (1899) 1 F. (H.L.) 79; *Petrie's Trs v. Manders's Tr.*, 1954 S.C. 430.
[61] *Muirhead v. Muirhead* (1890) 17 R. (H.L.) 45; *Stair Memorial Encyclopaedia: The Laws of Scotland*, Vol. 25, paras 953 *et seq.*
[62] *Macfarlane's Trs v. Oliver* (1882) 9 R. 1138; *Munro's Trs,Petrs* 1971 S.L.T. 313.
[63] 1971 S.L.T. 313.

still be equitable compensation for other beneficiaries adversely affected by the claim for legal rights.

Testators will sometimes prefer a more stringent type of clause under which the consequence of a claim for legal rights is an express forfeiture of all the beneficiary's rights under the will and sometimes also a forfeiture of the benefits destined to the legatee's issue.[64] Such a forfeiture clause is effective according to its terms, but will be narrowly construed. It is however clearly effective to prevent equitable compensation from being made.

For this purpose, the reference to the date of execution of a will means the date of actual execution, not the date of the testator's death.[65]

Discharge of legal rights

Legal rights may be expressly discharged by the spouse or descendant entitled thereto. Children are capable of granting a discharge from the age of 16 onwards, but as a discharge without full consideration is almost certain to be a prejudicial transaction capable of being set aside by court before the child's 21st birthday, executors would be wise to treat a discharge granted by a 16 or 17-year old with great caution.[66]

It was one of the well-known anomalies of the pre-1964 law that it was possible by ante-nuptial marriage contract for intending spouses to discharge prospectively the legal rights of any children of the marriage. This could not be done after the marriage but the fact that it was possible at all made a severe dent in the protective function of legal rights for children. The children obviously were not parties to the arrangement, and yet their rights might be discharged for them with very little, or even in some cases no, consideration. For example in *Galloway's Trs. v. Galloway*[67] the marriage contract made a provision for children, but the fact that the father appointed the whole of the provision to one of them did not alter the fact that the right of the others to claim legitim was discharged.[68]

Section 12 of the 1964 Act now provides that the right to legitim of a child or of remoter issue cannot be excluded by anything contained in an ante-nuptial marriage contract to which section 12 applies entered into between the parents. Whatever such a marriage contract may provide, the descendant has the election between the provisions in his favour in the marriage contract and his legitim. In other words it is purely a question of satisfaction of legal rights and of approbate and reprobate and no longer one of a prospective discharge of the right to legitim at the instance of third parties.

---

[64] See *Tindall's Trs v. Tindall*, 1933 S.C. 419, where the forfeiture was sufficient to cut out the claimant's issue. See also *MacNaughton v. MacNaughton's Trs*, 1954 S.C. 312 and *Walker v. Orr's Trs*, 1958 S.L.T. 63.

[65] s.36(3).

[66] Age of Legal Capacity (Scotland) Act 1991 (c.50), ss.1, 3.

[67] 1943 S.C. 339.

[68] In *Callander v. Callander's Exr*, 1972 S.L.T. 209 the exclusion of legitim by the marriage contract still stood even although the children had assigned all their interests to their father and thus received nothing under the contract.

Section 12 applies to any ante-nuptial marriage contract actually executed after the commencement of the 1964 Act (*i.e.* on or after September 10, 1964). Older ante-nuptial marriage contracts may well still be coming into operation, and an exclusion of the children's legitim contained in such a contract would still be effective.

With this anomaly removed, it becomes true to say that legal rights cannot be discharged without the consent in some form of the person entitled. A prospective husband and wife can still contract before marriage for renunciation of *jus relicti* or *jus relictae*, but the contract involves mutual agreement. Any person may voluntarily discharge his or her right to *jus relicti*, *jus relictae* or legitim, but it is up to him or her to decide whether or not to do so. There is, however, a difference between the effect of a discharge granted during the lifetime of the deceased and of one granted after his death.

If a discharge is given during the lifetime of the ancestor or spouse from whose estate the rights would have been exigible, the grantor of the discharge is treated as already dead (although not so as to permit the issue of the grantor to claim his share by representation). This therefore increases the share of legitim taken by others.[69]

A discharge of legal rights granted after the death of the ancestor or spouse does not increase the share taken by other claimants for legal rights but benefits the person entitled to the free estate or the residuary legatee as the case may be.

As an illustration, take the case of a man dying, leaving five children and a legitim fund of £5,000. If none of the children has discharged their right to legitim during their father's lifetime, the amount to which any one child is entitled on the father's death is £1,000. This is so even if the others accept testamentary provisions in lieu of legitim, or indeed even if they should now discharge their claims gratuitously. However, if all the others had discharged their claims before their father's death, the one who had not discharged the right would take the whole legitim fund of £5,000. In *Panmure v. Crokat*[70] the discharges were performed by ante-nuptial marriage contract, and the one child not included in the discharge — possibly in error — was held entitled to the whole legitim fund.

Prescription and legal rights

The right to claim jus relictae, jus relicti and legitim is extinguished by the negative prescription if no "relevant claim" has been made within a continuous period of 20 years.[71] Time runs from the date the obligation becomes enforceable, which will usually be the date of death. Any period during which the legal rights creditor was under legal disability is ignored.[72] This seems now

---

[69] *Hog v. Hog* (1791) Mor. 8193.

[70] (1856) 18 D. 703.

[71] Prescription and Limitation (Scotland) Act 1973, s.7, read with Sched. I, para. 2(f). Johnston *Prescription & Limitation* 3.41;6.64 and 7.06. Walker *Prescription and Limitation of Actions* (5th ed.), pp.57, 76.

[72] *ibid.*, s.6(4)(b) read with s.7(2).

to mean that prescription will run from age 16. Under the Age of Legal Capacity (Scotland) Act 1991[73] legal capacity to enter into any transaction is attained at age 16 and any statutory reference to disability by reason of nonage is to be construed as a reference to a person under the age of 16.[74] Unless a claim for legal rights has the effect of reducing the amount received by the claimant as compared with the amount due under the will, executors will be in safety to act upon a claim by a 16-year old. An increased benefit could not be held to be "prejudicial" within the meaning of section 3 of the 1991 Act. Hence it seems highly probable that prescription will now run from age 16.

---

[73] (c.50), s.1.
[74] s.1(2).

CHAPTER 6

SUCCESSION TO THE FREE ESTATE

The rules comprised under this head are mostly stated in Part I (sections 1 to 7) of the Act and deal with the succession to the free estate, heritage and moveables together, after any prior rights and legal rights which are applicable have been deducted.[1] In other words, if the intestate died survived by neither spouse nor issue, these rules apply to the whole estate (apart from the excepted items specified in section 37 of the Act and the effect of section 36(2) on special destinations and powers of appointment). If the intestate is survived by a spouse and/or issue, the appropriate prior rights and legal rights, in that order, are deducted before the rules of Part I come into play as the third set of rules of intestate succession in respect of the balance of the estate. In such cases the provisions in Part I relating to the free estate may apply to only a small proportion of an intestate's estate.

Method of statement in the Act

The pattern of the pre-1964 law was to have a number of common law principles overlaid by specific statutory provisions. This was changed by the Act and there is now a single statutory list of those entitled to succeed. The details of this list are mainly to be found in section 2. While the new list bears a strong resemblance to the previous rules relating to the disposal of moveable estate, the common law concept of the "next of kin" is no longer relevant in finding those entitled to a particular intestate estate.

Section 2 is in the form of a list of specified relations of the intestate but states that it is "Subject to the following provisions of this Part of this Act". The result is that it must be read in conjunction with the scheme of representation applicable to the division of the free estate contained in section 5, and with the rules for division where two or more persons are entitled contained in section 6. For example, section 2 gives a right of succession to "children," but section 5 gives a full right of representation, and in effect converts "children" to "issue," while section 6 deals with the problems of division *per stirpes* or *per capita*.

The list in section 2(1) is in the order in which relatives of the deceased are called to the succession. Those higher up the list are preferred to those lower down. This is achieved by giving a right of succession in each paragraph, and providing in each paragraph other than the first that the right applies only if the deceased was not survived by any "prior relative". That phrase is defined in section 2(2) as a person of any other class who, if he had survived the intestate, would have had right to the free intestate estate or any of it by virtue of an

---

[1] 1964 Act, s.1(2).

earlier paragraph of section 2(1) or by virtue of representation of a person entitled by an earlier paragraph.

Thus, children (and their issue by representation) whose rights are stated in section 2(1)(a) are "prior relatives" and therefore preferred in succession, in a question with brothers and sisters and parents whose rights when representatives of both categories have survived are stated in section 2(1)(b). Similarly, uncles and aunts on either side of the house (and their issue by representation) whose rights are stated in section 2(1)(f) are "prior relatives" in a question with grandparents, whose rights appear in section 2(1)(g).

It may still be relevant to refer to the old law to fill lacunae in the Act, and accordingly, section 1(1)(b) requires the free intestate estate (heritable and moveable) to be subject to the previous law of intestate moveable succession so far as "not inconsistent with" the particular provisions of Part I of the Act.

THE ORDER OF SUCCESSION

(1) Descendants

As before, the category of descendants must first be considered in determining the order of succession to the free estate, as their right is preferable to that of collaterals, spouse or ascendants. The main provision, contained in section 2(1)(a), is "where an intestate is survived by children, they shall have right to the whole of the intestate estate".

It is to be noticed that the "intestate estate" referred to is defined for the purposes of this Part of the Act by section 1(2). Briefly, it means the free estate after satisfaction of prior rights and legal rights. However although children take the whole estate left after the spouse's *jus relictae/ relicti* and it is tempting simply to split everything without calculating the children's legitim, it must be remembered that the division of the legitim fund may be unequal if advances have been made to any of the children.

As already noted, although section 2(1)(a) refers to "children," it does in fact regulate the whole succession of descendants of the intestate when read in conjunction with the scheme of representation contained in section 5(1) and that of distribution contained in section 6.

Adopted children are now treated as lawful children of the adopter or adopters. The position of adopted children was the final cause of the appointment of the Mackintosh Committee on the Law of Succession, and the provisions of Part IV (sections 23 and 24) of the Act remedy a situation which was a major defect in the previous law of succession. For the present purpose of succession to the free estate by descendants on intestacy, the main provisions are contained in section 23(1). So far as here relevant, this provides that "[f]or all purposes relating to — (a) the succession to a deceased person (whether testate or intestate), ... an adopted person shall be treated as the child of the adopter and not as the child of any other person."

A problem might have arisen over the question of what rights are truly rights of "succession". There has, for example, been considerable discussion of the true nature of the traditional legal rights of spouses and children. Views classing them as debts or rights of succession or something in between have been current for some time. Accordingly, for the purposes of section 23(1) it is provided that "succession to a deceased person" is to be construed as including the distribution of any property in consequence of his death and any claim to prior rights or legal rights out of his estate. In other words, an adopted child clearly has a right to legitim out of the estates of his adopting parent or parents as well as his right to share in the free intestate estate and any other property being distributed on the adopter's death, as a lawful child of the adopter.

A natural parent of the adopted child being "any other person" within the meaning of section 23(1), the child's rights of succession in the estates of its natural parents are cut off and replaced by rights in the estates of the adopting parents.

In one situation, however, cutting off the adopted person's rights in the estates of its natural parents had the unfortunate result that the child had no rights in any estate. If the adopting parents died before the Succession Act came into force on September 10, 1964, the child had no rights in their estates. But if the natural parents then died after the commencement of the Succession Act, the child had no rights in their estates either. To remedy this as far as possible, the Law Reform (Miscellaneous Provisions) (Scotland) Act 1966[2] provided that if the adopting parent died before the commencement of the Succession Act and the natural parent died on or after August 3, 1966, the child is to be treated for the purposes of succession to the estate of that natural parent as the child of the natural parent. However, this is only for the purposes of succession to the natural parent. For all other purposes of succession, the adopted child still falls to be regarded as the child of the adopter. If the child was adopted by two spouses jointly, both the adopting parents must have died prior to September 10, 1964, to bring this transitional provision into effect.[3]

The Legitimation (Scotland) Act 1968[4] is still in force although now much less important in view of the virtual abolition of the status of illegitimacy. The effect of the Legitimation Act is that an illegitimate child is always legitimated by the subsequent marriage of its parents instead of only if the parents were free to marry at the time of its conception as was true under the older common law. Since parents whose marriage did not legitimate their child sometimes adopted it, the Act made provision for revocation of such adoption orders on the view that legitimation removed the need for them. However, section 6(2) of the 1968 Act (as amended) preserves succession rights in intestacies which occurred before the revocation.

Illegitimate children were the subject of very limited provisions in the Succession Act itself, but there were radical alterations by the Law Reform

---

[2] (c.19), s.5.
[3] Note however that true adoption did not exist in Scotland before 1930 and that informal "adoptions" which took place before that had no effects on the status of the child.
[4] (c.22).

(Miscellaneous Provisions) (Scotland) Act 1968[5] and by the Law Reform (Parent and Child) (Scotland) Act 1986.[6]

September 10, 1964, to November 24, 1968. The effect of the original section 4 of the Succession Act — applicable in respect of deaths occurring on or after September 10, 1964, up to and including November 24, 1968 — was to give the illegitimate child a right of succession to its mother's free estate when the mother died intestate and without lawful issue. The child had no right to legitim and was postponed to the prior rights and legal rights (calculated on the basis that the mother was not survived by issue) of the mother's husband. It had no rights of succession at all if the mother was survived by lawful issue, and could never have rights in its father's intestate estate.

November 25, 1968, to December 7, 1986. The reforms contained in the 1968 Act applied to the estate of any person dying on or after November 25, 1968, up to and including December 7, 1986. The method used was to substitute a new section 4 in the Succession Act 1964.[7] This conferred on the illegitimate child the right to share in the intestate free estate of both parents on a basis of equality with legitimate children. The right to legitim was separately conferred by a new section 10A of the Succession Act inserted by section 2 of the 1968 Act. The result was that legitimate and illegitimate children were now in a position of formal equality so far as succession to the estates of the parents was concerned. A decree of affiliation and aliment established the paternity of the father for succession purposes unless the contrary was proved.[8]

The one substantial difference which remained between the succession rights of legitimate and illegitimate children was that the illegitimate child could not represent its predeceasing parent in a succession opening after the parent's death. The scheme of representation established by section 5(1) then permitted "issue" to represent their parents but "issue" was defined as lawful issue, so that only legitimate children could represent their parents. This was so even although both legitimate and illegitimate children could succeed to their parents. This was reinforced by the statement in section 4(4) that, except for the specific provisions of section 4 conferring on the child rights in the estates of its parents and the representation provisions of section 5, nothing in Part I of the Act was to be construed as importing any rule of succession through illegitimate relationship. Thus the rights of the illegitimate child in this period were confined to the estates of the persons responsible for its birth.

The result was that an illegitimate grandchild could not represent its predeceasing parent (whether that parent was itself legitimate or illegitimate) in the division of a grandparent's estate, but that a legitimate grandchild could represent its illegitimate parent in the grandparent's estate. In the latter case, the legitimate grandchild, being "issue" of the illegitimate child, could take the share which its parent would have taken by survivance.

However, if the deceased whose estate was being distributed was more remote than a lineal grandparent, the illegitimate person himself would not

---

[5] (c.70).
[6] (c.9).
[7] 1968 Act (c.70), s.1.
[8] *ibid.*, s.11.

have been entitled to a share if he had survived, so that there could be no representation in such an estate even by his legitimate child.

The effect of the valuable improvements in the lot of the illegitimate child was to implement the Report of the Russell Committee on the *Law of Succession in Relation to Illegitimate Persons*[9] in the light of the views expressed by the Scottish Law Commission in its Memorandum *Reform of the Law Relating to legitimation per subsequens matrimonium.*[10]

December 8, 1986, onwards. The present law virtually abolishes the status of illegitimacy.[11] The Law Reform (Parent and Child) (Scotland) Act 1986[12] enacts a general principle of the legal equality of children by the general statement that:

> "The fact that a person's parents are not or have not been married to one another shall be left out of account in establishing the legal relationship between the person and any other person; and accordingly any such relationship shall have effect as if the parents were or had been married to one another."

In its application to succession, this means that whether or not its parents were married to each other a child will have exactly the same rights of succession to its biological parents and also through them by representation. In the older terminology, illegitimate children have full rights of succession.

The general principle is not confined to statutory provisions. Any reference to any relative in any enactment or deed dated after the commencement of the Act is to be construed in accordance with the general principle, unless the contrary intention appears in the enactment or deed.[13] It will, however, be an expression of contrary intention, even in a deed executed after the Act's commencement, to refer to "lawful" or "illegitimate", etc., children.[14] This will mean that a will could still readily exclude any right of a child formerly described as illegitimate to inherit under it. However on intestacy, such a child has exactly the same rights of intestate succession as any other child of the parents. The one exception to future deeds being construed according to the principle of equality is that future grants of titles of honour and coats of arms are not affected by the Act and will not therefore have expressly to exclude succession by illegitimate relatives.[15]

(2) Collaterals

If the category of descendants has been exhausted without finding a survivor entitled to succeed, the category of collaterals of the deceased is next in the line of succession. Subject to the qualification in section 2(1)(b) of the 1964 Act giving the surviving parent or parents of the intestate a right to one-

---

[9] Cmnd. 3051 (1966).
[10] Cmnd. 3223 (1967).
[11] See *supra*, pp.47 and 57.
[12] (c.9).
[13] 1986 Act, s.1(2).
[14] *ibid.*, s.1(4).
[15] *ibid.*, s.9(1)(c).

half of the free estate when the deceased is survived both by collaterals and by a parent or parents, the category of collaterals of the deceased must be exhausted before ancestors or a surviving spouse have any rights of succession to the free estate.

Assume for the moment that the intestate was survived by collaterals, but left no surviving issue and was predeceased by both parents, so that the right of the collaterals is to the whole of the free intestate estate. The statutory basis for their right to succeed is now section 2(1)(c) of the 1964 Act, replacing the previous common law principle that collaterals succeeded next after descendants. Although this paragraph mentions only "brothers and sisters" of the deceased, it must be read along with section 5 (representation) and section 6 (distribution). It is not limited to the case where immediate brothers and sisters of the deceased have survived him.

Half blood. Giving effect to the recommendations of the Mackintosh Committee, section 2(2) and section 3 of the Act deal with the rights of collaterals of the half blood. Where collaterals have rights of succession, collaterals of the whole blood, having the same mother and the same father as the intestate, are preferred to collaterals of the half blood, sharing only one parent with the intestate. This restates the pre-existing law on the subject, and has the effect that if the intestate is survived by any collaterals of the whole blood, or their descendants by representation,[16] collaterals of the half blood and those claiming through them have no rights of succession at all. Those related by the whole blood take the whole amount of the estate falling to collaterals. Take the following example:

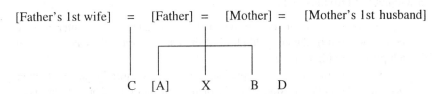

X has died intestate, survived by a full brother B and by two half brothers C and D. In this situation B, the sole surviving collateral of the full blood takes the whole free intestate estate, which, if X left no surviving spouse, is the whole net estate after payment of debts and expenses. C and D, collaterals of the half blood consanguinean and uterine respectively, take no share.

If, however, there are no collaterals of the full blood, so that the right of any collaterals of the half blood emerges, section 3 of the 1964 Act made a radical change from the pre-existing law. Collaterals of the half blood now rank "without distinction as between those related to the intestate ... through their father and those so related through their mother". The words "related through their father" and "related through their mother" were substituted for "consanguinean" and "uterine" in the course of the progress of the Bill through Parliament in the interests of comprehensibility by the layman, but one may wonder whether the same tenderness for the comprehension of the layman

---

[16] *ibid.*, s.3 is expressly made subject to the representation provisions of s.5.

might not also have been applied to the rest of the Act. Before the commencement of the Succession Act 1964 the half blood consanguinean had full rights of succession, postponed only to the full blood, but the half blood uterine had rights limited in all circumstances to one-half of the moveable estate, and even then postponed to the half blood consanguinean and to the parents of the intestate. The general policy of the 1964 Act to remove discrimination between the sexes in the law of succession led to the equation of the positions of the half blood consanguinean and uterine by section 3. Both now have full rights of succession postponed only to the full blood.

Taking the same family as that illustrated above, but this time postulating that both collaterals of the full blood have predeceased, *i.e.* a situation such as the following:

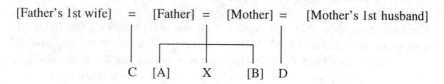

[Father's 1st wife]   =   [Father]   =   [Mother]   =   [Mother's 1st husband]

C   [A]   X   [B]   D

the effect is that C and D share the free intestate estate equally between them as collaterals of the half blood.

Adopted children and collateral succession.

Section 24(1) deals with relationship for the purposes of collateral succession between an adopted child and other children or adopted children of the adopter or adopters. It provides that:

> "[A]n adopted person shall be deemed to be related to any other person, being the child or the adopted child of the adopter or (in the case of a joint adoption) of either of the adopters—
>
> (a) where he or she was adopted by two spouses jointly and that other person is the child or adopted child of both of them, as a brother or sister of the whole blood;
>
> (b) in any other case, as a brother or sister of the half blood."

Thus if a childless couple adopt a child and subsequently have a child of their own, these two children are, for the purposes of succession, related to each other as brothers or sisters of the full blood. Equally a couple's second adopted child is for this purpose a brother or sister of the full blood to the first. But if either party to a marriage had had a child by a previous marriage, or had previously adopted a child, such child or adopted child would be a collateral of the half blood to any child or adopted child of the present marriage.

Certain odd consequences emerge from the provisions of section 24(1). An adopted child can be related as a brother or sister of the full blood to any other person only if he or she has been adopted by two spouses jointly and that other person is the child or adopted child of both of them.[17] In any other case the adopted child is related to any other child or adopted child of the adopter or

---

[17] *ibid.*, s.24(1)(a).

adopters as a brother or sister of the half blood.[18] This means, for example, that if an unmarried woman gives birth to twins and subsequently adopts them in order to get a clear birth certificate for them, these children are related to each other as collaterals of the half blood for the purposes of succession. They cannot be collaterals of the full blood as they do not fall within the provisions of section 24(1)(a) requiring adoption by two spouses jointly. If the mother of the twins subsequently marries someone other than the natural father of the children, and there is a child or adopted child of that marriage, the twins and the subsequent child are all collaterals of the half blood. One twin has no better rights of succession in the other's estate than has the child or adopted child of the subsequent marriage. Until the Law Reform (Parent and Child) (Scotland) Act 1986 came into force it is true that one illegitimate twin was not regarded in law as being in any way related to the other, so that neither had any rights of succession at all in the other's estate without the adoption. However, since 1986, the effect of an adoption by their mother would be to reduce their rights in each other's estate from that of a collateral of the full blood to only half blood status, which might have to be shared with others.

Any question of seniority between collaterals who include an adopted child is resolved by section 24(1A), added by the Children Act 1975. Briefly, an adopted child ranks in seniority as if born on the date of adoption, while two children adopted on the same day take seniority *inter se* according to their actual date of birth.

Illegitimacy and collateral succession

Deaths occurring before December 8, 1986. The position in intestate collateral succession remained as before — namely that illegitimate relationship was no relationship at all. Various provisions deeming illegitimate relationship to be the same as legitimate appeared in the 1968 Act, but only for the construction of deeds. Certain similar provisions now appearing in the Succession Act applied only for the purposes of section 6 and that part of section 11 dealing with the division among those beneficially entitled under sections not having the relationship clause. There was no general rule that illegitimate relationship was the same as legitimate relationship[19] and rights of intestate succession existed only between the illegitimate child and its parents, subject to representation of the child by its issue.

In practice the great improvement of the position of illegitimate children introduced in 1968 was very widely accepted, and it was commonly assumed that reciprocal rights of succession had also been created between the illegitimate child and its "brothers and sisters". In fact the situation was that an illegitimate child did not have, and could not have, brothers and sisters for purposes of succession. There was no right of succession before the Succession Act, and neither it nor the 1968 Act created any rights between

---

[18] *ibid.*, s.24(1)(b).
[19] s.4(4) of the Succession (Scotland) Act originally provided that, apart from specific sections, nothing in Pt I of the Succession (Scotland) Act was to be construed as importing any rule of succession through illegitimate relationship.

collaterals. An illegitimate child could acquire collaterals only by leaving the status of illegitimacy through legitimation or adoption.

Deaths from December 8, 1986. The effect of the Law Reform (Parent and Child) (Scotland) Act 1986 was to complete the partial reform begun in 1968. The assimilation of the positions of legitimate and illegitimate children has the result that in the succession to persons who die after the commencement of the 1986 Act a person formerly described as illegitimate has exactly the same rights as he or she would have had if born legitimate. There are now, *de jure*, brothers and sisters who merely existed de facto before, and the normal rights of succession apply fully. This automatically increases the burden on an executor of establishing that he has identified all the relations. In at least some cases of collateral succession, the problem will be mitigated by the fact that the formerly illegitimate person may rank only as a collateral of the half blood and be postponed to the succession rights of collaterals of the full blood.

(3) Collaterals and parents

As already noted, parents of the intestate are entitled under section 2(1)(b) to one-half of the free intestate estate when the deceased is not survived by any descendants, but is survived by collaterals and by a parent or parents. The remaining one-half is divided among the collaterals. This is in addition to the right of the parent or parents to succeed to the whole free estate when the category of collaterals has been exhausted. Accordingly, if the intestate is survived by brothers or sisters, or their issue by representation under section 5, and by a parent or parents, one-half of the free estate is divided among the collaterals, and one-half falls to the parent or parents, in both cases according to the rules of division specified in section 6.

Although this provision seems very similar to that in the pre-1964 law of moveable succession, it is to be noted that a substantial difference has been made in the position of the mother of the intestate. As part of the general policy of removing discrimination on the ground of sex, the mother is now put upon an equal footing with the father, and shares the one-half falling to parents in this situation equally with the father. Previously the mother's right in moveables was postponed to that of the father, so that effectively she represented the predeceasing father of the intestate, in moveables at least. She had then no rights in heritage. Now she shares equally with the father, and because heritage and moveables are assimilated in the free estate, she shares in both moveables and heritage.

(4) Parents

If the categories of descendants and of collaterals of the intestate have been exhausted without finding a survivor, the surviving parent or parents of the intestate are next in the line of succession, and are entitled to the whole of the free intestate estate (section 2(1)(d)). This right is additional to, and separate from, their right to share along with collaterals when the intestate is survived both by parents and by collaterals.

As in the case of succession under section 2(1)(b) by parents along with collaterals, the mother's right in the case where parents succeed to the whole free estate under section 2(1)(d) has been substantially improved. She now shares equally along with the father of the intestate, instead of being postponed to the father's right. The division between father and mother is equal by virtue of section 6, they being persons "in the same degree of relationship to the intestate" within the meaning of section 6(a).

Parents of illegitimate children

Deaths prior to December 8, 1986. The Succession Act 1964 largely re-enacted earlier legislation by providing rights of succession between the illegitimate child and its mother only. Where an illegitimate person died intestate, and was not survived by lawful issue, or, if the illegitimate person was a woman, by her illegitimate children (or their issue by representation) the surviving mother of the illegitimate person was entitled to the whole of the free intestate estate.

In the division of the estates of persons dying on or after November 25, 1968, the new right of the illegitimate child to share in the estates of both parents equally with legitimate children was counterbalanced by a right of both parents to succeed to the free estate of the child.[20] Where an illegitimate child died intestate, and was not survived by lawful issue or by an illegitimate child or by lawful issue of such a child, the surviving parent or parents had right to the whole free intestate estate.

The paternity of an illegitimate child may well still be uncertain at the time of his death, but there would be no merit in incurring expenditure to prove the paternity of someone who, by definition, had taken no interest in the child till then, in order to present him with a share of the child's estate. It was therefore presumed that an illegitimate person was not survived by his father unless the contrary was shown.[21]

Parents of an illegitimate child ranked immediately after its descendants, there being no collateral succession.

Deaths from December 8, 1986. As the fact that a person's parents were not married to each other is left out of account[22] both of the biological parents of any person continue to have the full rights of parents in succession, irrespective of any question of legitimacy. The presumption that the father of an illegitimate child had predeceased the child was repealed by the Law Reform (Parent and Child) (Scotland) Act 1986, but there is a protection for trustees. This is achieved by adding to section 7 of the Law Reform (Miscellaneous Provisions) (Scotland) Act 1968 a paragraph (c) entitling a trustee or executor to distribute property without having ascertained that no paternal relative of an illegitimate person exists who is or may be entitled to an interest in the property.

---

[20] Law Reform (Miscellaneous Provisions) (Scotland) Act 1968, s.1.
[21] Succession Act, s.4(3) as substituted by Law Reform (Miscellaneous Provisions) (Scotland) Act 1968, s.1.
[22] Law Reform (Parent and Child) (Scotland) Act 1986, s.1(1).

Parents and adopted children

An adopted person being now treated as the child of the adopter and not as the child of any other person,[23] the right of the natural parents to succeed to the child's estate is cut off. In its place arises a right of the adopting parent or parents to succeed. This is unaffected by the transitional provisions in section 5 of the Law Reform (Miscellaneous Provisions) (Scotland) Act 1966.

(5) Surviving spouse

The inclusion of the spouse of the intestate in the list of those entitled to succeed to the free intestate estate was one of the major changes from the pre-1964 law of succession dependent upon blood relationship. Previously a surviving spouse might have certain rights in the predeceaser's estate by way of the extraordinary statutory preference and legal rights, but such a spouse was never in any circumstances the predeceaser's heir,[24] and had no right to share in the free intestate estate after the preference and legal rights had been met. That balance of the intestate estate would have fallen to the Crown as *ultimus haeres* rather than to the spouse. Now, as part of the weakening of the emphasis on direct blood relationship and of the improvement of the position of the surviving spouse, the Succession Act has made a spouse one of the ordinary heirs in intestacy as well as having the various extraordinary rights.

The spouse's right is stated in section 2(1)(e) of the 1964 Act, which allows the surviving spouse to take the free estate in the absence of descendants, brothers and sisters or parents of the intestate. In other words, the surviving spouse is preferred to uncles and aunts and all remoter ancestors of the intestate, and in the situation where this right arises, the surviving spouse will therefore take the whole net estate after payment of debts, partly by virtue of prior rights, partly by virtue of legal rights and the balance under section 2(1)(e).

There is no representation of a spouse under these provisions. Section 5(1) provides representation where a person would have had a right in the intestate's estate "otherwise than as a parent or spouse of the intestate." Thus issue of a predeceasing spouse of the intestate (*i.e.* the intestate's step-children) cannot represent their parent so as to claim the free estate in preference to the intestate's uncles and aunts. Even though the principle of blood relationship has been considerably weakened, it is still felt that the intestate's own uncles and aunts and remoter ancestors have a better claim than his predeceasing wife's children by a previous marriage. Admittedly this may give rise to harsh cases where the step-children have been brought up in his family by the intestate, and find themselves cut off from any share of his estate, but it would be very difficult to frame legislation to cover such cases without including situations where the intestate had no substantial contacts with his step-children. The remedy is to make a will in their favour.

---

[23] Succession (Scotland) Act, s.23(1).
[24] *Brown's Trs v. Brown* (1890) 17 R. 1174.

The lack of representation of a spouse means that all the rights which a spouse may have in the deceased's estate, *i.e.* prior rights, legal rights and rights in the free estate, can be stated as being available to a surviving spouse only.

(6) Ascendants other than parents

When an intestate dies without leaving any survivors in the categories of his or her descendants, collaterals, parents or spouse entitled to succeed under the conditions mentioned previously, the succession to the free estate then opens to the ascendants of the intestate other than his parents. The relevant provisions in the 1964 Act are section 2(1)(f), (g), (h) and (i), dealing respectively with uncles and aunts, grandparents, grandparents' collaterals and remoter ancestors.

The different categories of ascendants and the order in which they are called to the succession remain the same as under the old law of intestate moveable succession, but there is the radical change that relationship through the mother as well as through the father has to be taken into account, thus more than doubling the area of search for those entitled to succeed. There is also the important provision that representation does now apply at this level of succession. From the commencement of the Law Reform (Parent and Child) (Scotland) Act 1986[25] illegitimate relationship has been no bar to rights of inheritance. Relationship is traced through illegitimate relatives in exactly the same way as through the legitimate relationship. This further widens the possible area of investigation of relatives, and could lead a solicitor to ask questions embarrassing to his client.[26]

No question of prior rights or of legal rights arises when the succession opens to ascendants more remote than parents, since, by definition, there is no spouse and there are no descendants to make such claims. Thus the free estate for distribution in this case is the whole net estate after payment of debts and expenses.

The principle remains that direct lineal ascendants of a given degree form a class nearer in degree to the intestate than the brothers and sisters of these lineal ascendants, and that brothers and sisters of lineal ascendants of one degree (or the issue of such brothers and sisters by representation) form a class nearer in degree than lineal ascendants of the next degree.

Thus uncles and aunts of the intestate, whether on the paternal side or on the maternal side, succeed in preference to grandparents (section 2(1)(f)). A typical example of the type of situation which arises under these provisions would be as follows:

---

[25] December 8, 1986.
[26] Meston, "Illegitimacy in Succession" (1986) 31 J.L.S. 358.

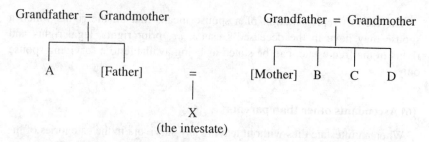

(the intestate)

In this case as the father and mother have both predeceased, A, B, C and D, the uncles and aunts of the intestate, divide the free estate equally between them, and the grandparents have no share. It is to be noted that under section 6 the division is equal between all members of the class entitled to succeed. There is no suggestion of a preference for the paternal side over the maternal or vice versa, nor of an equal division between the paternal and maternal sides. It is a *per capita* division between all the surviving persons in the nearest degree of relationship on either side of the house[27] with representation of any predeceasing members of the class.

Only if the uncles and aunts have also predeceased, without leaving issue to represent them, do the grandparents become entitled to succeed.[28] Again no distinction is made between the paternal and maternal lines. The four grandparents form a class, the surviving members of which share the free estate equally between them when the succession opens at this level.

Failing survivors among the class of grandparents, the brothers and sisters of the grandparents, or their issue by representation, are entitled to the succession.[29] In the absence of any of these, the succession opens to the more remote ancestors of the intestate "generation by generation successively, without distinction between the paternal and maternal lines ... so however that, failing ancestors of any generation, the brothers and sisters of any of those ancestors shall have right thereto before ancestors of the next more remote generation".[30]

Section 2(2) provides that references to brothers and sisters include references to brothers and sisters of the half blood, while section 3 provides, as has already been noted in the case of brothers and sisters of the intestate himself, that collaterals of a parent or other ancestor of an intestate related by the whole blood exclude collaterals of the half blood, but that in the absence of collaterals of the whole blood, collaterals of the half blood are entitled to the succession without distinction as between the half blood consanguinean and the half blood uterine. Note that the existence of issue of a predeceasing uncle of the full blood will exclude any uncles and aunts of the half blood. In a recent example it was found that professional searchers had failed to take account of this fact when identifying beneficiaries.

---

[27] 1964 Act, s.6(a).
[28] *ibid.*, s.2(1)(g).
[29] *ibid.*, s.2(1)(h).
[30] *ibid.*, s.2(1)(i).

Taken together, the principle of infinite search among ancestors specified in section 2(1)(i), the rights of collaterals of the half blood, the removal of the significance of illegitimacy and the availability of representation at all levels, mean that an enormous area of search is opened up when the right of succession appears to open to the remoter ancestors. There may be considerable difficulty in practice in drawing up complete and accurate family trees on both the paternal and maternal sides for possibly several generations back and in tracing all the descendants of every member of the trees. The Mackintosh Committee on the Law of Succession did consider this point, and in paragraph 26 of their report stated that they were much attracted by the principle of limiting succession on intestacy to uncles and aunts and their issue. This was partly because the opening of the succession to maternal relatives should in most cases make further search unnecessary and partly because of the difficulty and expense of further search. However, the Committee made no recommendation as all witnesses to whom they suggested a principle of limitation were strongly against any such idea. The draft Bill which was circulated for comment in 1959 also contained a limitation, the proposal being to exclude relatives more remote than the lineal grandparents, but again objection was taken, mainly on the basis that even if much of the estate might be expended in tracing remoter relatives, this was no justification for increasing the rights of the Crown as *ultimus haeres*. When the Succession Bill was introduced in November 1963, it included a proposal that relatives more remote than lineal grandparents should be excluded from the succession, but the principle of infinite search was restored in Committee in the House of Commons.

The English law of intestate succession does contain an exclusion of relatives more remote than grandparents,[31] but it appears now to be accepted in Scotland that an artificial limit on the circle of relations entitled to succeed on intestacy is repugnant to our system of law. We adhere therefore to the long-standing principle that an infinite search must be made following the principles of the version of the parentelic system which we use.

(7) The Crown

In the absence of any person entitled to succeed to the free estate of an intestate by virtue of the specific provisions of Part I of the Act, the right of the Crown to succeed as *ultimus haeres* is saved by section 7 of the Act. The executor, or anyone holding property for which no valid right of succession can be established, has the duty of transferring it to the Queen's and Lord Treasurer's Remembrancer to be administered on behalf of the Crown. The Queen's and Lord Treasurer's Remembrancer takes possession without the need for confirmation.

There was a suggestion in Parliament in debate on the Bill that the Common Good fund of the local authority for the area of the deceased's last residence

---

[31] Administration of Estates Act 1925 (15 & 16 Geo 5, c23), s.46(1)(v), (vi).

should be substituted for the Crown as *ultimus haeres*, but the principle was not accepted.

The Crown, through the Queen's and Lord Treasurer's Remembrancer, will normally place advertisements in local newspapers to publicise the fact that an estate has fallen to the Crown. If heirs later establish their relationship, the property will be transferred to them. If no heirs come forward, the Crown continues its practice of making grants to persons who have a moral claim on the deceased (as by rendering significant services without payment) or for whom there is evidence to show that the deceased might reasonably have been expected to make provision. Such persons present a Petition for Gift to the Queen's and Lord Treasurer's Remembrancer. At one time the commonest case was that of "relatives" of an illegitimate person who died without issue, but such persons now are treated as full relatives[32] with the result that fewer estates fall to the Crown.

REPRESENTATION IN, AND DIVISION OF, THE FREE ESTATE[33]

In place of the confusingly limited representation in moveables available under the Intestate Moveable Succession (Scotland) Act 1855 there is now a full right of representation of anyone other than a parent or spouse of the intestate who would have been entitled to share in the free estate of the intestate had he survived.[34] The exclusion of representation of the intestate's parents is fairly obvious, for in any event the intestate's own issue and collaterals, who would be the representatives of the parents, would normally take before the parents became entitled to any share. It does, however, also ensure that the intestate's collaterals of the half blood cannot represent the predeceasing common parent to the partial exclusion of collaterals of the whole blood. Take, for example, a situation such as the following:

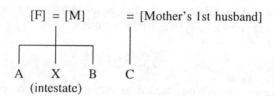

If his mother had survived the intestate, she would have been entitled to one-half of his free estate in preference to A and B under section 2(1)(b). The exclusion of representation of parents means that C, a collateral of the half blood uterine, cannot by representation claim the mother's one-half share of the free estate in a situation where he has otherwise no rights of succession at all.

---

[32] Law Reform (Miscellaneous Provisions) (Scotland) Act 1968, Pt I and Law Reform (Parent and Child) (Scotland) Act 1986, s.1.
[33] See Meston, "Representation in Succession" (1995) 1 Scottish Law & Practice Quarterly, p.83
[34] s.5(1): applying only to the free estate.

The exclusion of representation of a spouse in respect of his or her rights in the free estate is designed to ensure that step-children of the intestate do not acquire rights of succession in his estate. Step-children have no place at all in intestate succession, but if representation of a spouse had been permitted, they could have come in by the back door to the prejudice of uncles and aunts and remoter ancestors of the intestate. Strong arguments were presented in Parliament in debate on the Succession Bill that step-children should have some place in the law of succession, but the attachment to blood relationship as the governing principle, though already weakened, proved too strong to permit this radical change.

Apart from these points, the scheme of representation and division specified in sections 5 and 6 in respect of the free estate is very similar to the separate scheme in section 11 for representation in legitim. As in the case of section 11(1) and (2), section 5(1) might appear to require that division among representatives must always be *per stirpes*, but is stated to be subject to section 6 which specifies the method of division.

This provides that if all the persons entitled to share in the estate are of the same degree of relationship to the intestate the division is made equally among them per capita.[35] Thus, as in the case of the division of legitim,[36] if the intestate is predeceased by his two children but is survived by four grandchildren, three being issue of one child and one of the other, the division is equal, per capita, into quarters.

If, however, those entitled are not all of the same degree of relationship to the intestate, the division is *per stirpes* at the level of the class nearest to the intestate of which there are surviving members — the "nearest surviving relatives".[37]

Since December 8, 1986, the representatives who may take their parent's share are the children of that person without distinction between legitimate and illegitimate children.[38] The former rule that only legitimate issue, however remote, of the predeceaser could represent him now applies only to deaths occurring before December 8, 1986.

Adopted children and representation

The scheme of representation in section 5(1) is in respect of persons entitled to succeed by virtue of the preceding provisions of the Act. The rights of adopted children are specified later in the Act, but in the form that they are to be regarded as children of the adopter for all purposes of succession. This equates them with the "children" mentioned in section 2(1)(a), and therefore

---

[35] 1964 Act, s.6(a).
[36] *supra*, p. 57-58.
[37] s.6(b).
[38] Law Reform (Parent and Child) (Scotland) Act 1986, s.1(1).

they are entitled to represent their adopting parents in successions in which the
adopting parents would have been entitled to share by survivance.

CHAPTER 7

TESTATE SUCCESSION

The Succession (Scotland) Act made only limited alterations to the law affecting succession under a will made by the deceased, but substantial changes have been effected by subsequent legislation. The following is intended to provide a concise account of the law as it now stands and also of the older law which will remain applicable to wills executed when it was in force. The problem of tracing whether a will exists is partly mitigated by the establishment of a National Registry of Wills, which records the location, but not the content, of wills which testators have chosen to register with it.[1]

FORMAL VALIDITY

From August 1, 1995[2]

The rules for the formal validity of written documents, including wills, were radically changed by the Requirements of Writing (Scotland) Act 1995[3] which came into force on August 1, 1995 and which now restates the whole law of execution of deeds.

All wills, testamentary trust dispositions and settlements or codicils must be in writing.[4] The writing must comply with section 2 of the Act which made a radical change in the law by providing that bare validity is achieved merely by the granter subscribing the will without any further formality. Section 2(1) reads: "[n]o document required by section 1(2) of this Act shall be valid in respect of the formalities of execution unless it is subscribed by the granter of it ... but nothing apart from such subscription shall be required for the document to be valid as aforesaid".

Subscription means signature at the end of the last page (excluding any annexations).[5] Thus it no longer matters whether the text of the will is in the testator's handwriting and the concept of the holograph will is no longer relevant. It is no longer necessary that there should be witnesses to the signature by the testator. All that is necessary for minimum validity is the

---

[1] U.K. Wills Record Office, P.O. Box 1771, Salisbury SP1 1UF.
[2] Full details of the present law of execution of deeds of all types is to be found in Halliday *Conveyancing Law and Practice* (2nd ed., 1996), 3-92 to 3-171.
[3] (c.7) implementing most of the recommendations of the Scottish Law Commission's *Report on Requirements of Writing*, Scot. Law. Com. No. 112 (1988). See the Act, annotated as at the date of this edition, in Appendix 3.
[4] Requirements of Writing (Scotland) Act 1995, s.1(2)(c)
[5] *ibid.*, s.7(1)

signature at the end of the document. The result is that many apparently informal documents will be capable of being treated as wills.

However, although the will achieves validity merely by a signature at the end, it does of course remain necessary to establish that the signature is that of the testator. ("Notarial" execution for the testator is dealt with below.)

A presumption that the will was in fact subscribed by the testator arises if, in addition to the subscription at the end, the document bears to have been signed by one witness (aged 16 or over) to the testator's subscription and bears to have been signed by the testator somewhere on each separate sheet of the will.[6] The witness should either see the testator subscribing the will or have the signature acknowledged to him by the testator.[7] The presumption can of course be overcome by such matters as proof of forgery, lack of capacity to act as testator or witness, that the witness did not know the testator or either did not see the subscription or have it acknowledged to him.[8] In the absence of any such proof, the witnessed will is regarded as having self-proving status without further procedure and can immediately be put into effect.

If the will bears to have been subscribed by the testator, but does not qualify for the presumption of subscription by him, it is necessary to take court proceedings under section 4 of the Act. If satisfied that the will was genuinely subscribed by the testator, the Sheriff will normally order the will to be endorsed with a certificate to that effect, but if the will has already been registered in either the sheriff court books or the Books of Council and Session, a decree will be issued. The evidence will normally be led by affidavit.

What constitutes a signature?

Several problems have recently arisen over what constitutes a signature as a subscription of a will. Section 7 of the Requirements of Writing (Scotland) Act 1995 sets out the new statutory requirements. A will is signed if it is signed (a) with the full name by which the testator is described in the will; or (b) with a surname preceded by at least one forename or initial or abbreviation or familiar form of a forename.

So far this has no great difference from the previous rules and most cases will probably fall within category (b). There is, however, an important difference in the third category which is set out verbatim below:

"(c) except for the purposes of section 3(1) to (7) of this Act, with a name (not in accordance with paragraph (a) or (b) above) or description or an initial or mark if it is established that the name, description, initial or mark—
   (i) was his usual method of signing, or his usual method of signing documents or alterations of the type in question; or
   (ii) was intended by him as his signature of the document in question".

---

[6] *ibid.*, s.3(1)(a) and 3(2)
[7] *ibid.*, s.3(7)
[8] *ibid.*, s.3(4)

The reference to section 3(1) to (7) merely ensures that such a non-standard signature would not be sufficient to create a presumption of subscription even if there is also a signature of a witness.

Before the 1995 Act there was a widespread belief that execution of deeds by a mark was not possible in Scotland, even if it was the testator's normal signature. This ignored the fact that early charters were undoubtedly executed by a cross and also that a good many things acceptable as signatures were not legible and were difficult to differentiate from a mark. Indeed in an article on the subject it was suggested that so long as the granter of a deed was not stupid enough to include an express claim that his scrawl was a mark, it would probably be possible to say that it was actually an illegible signature.[9]

The Requirements of Writing Act does, however, now make it clear that a mark can be a valid signature. The important thing is that this is so both if a mark was the normal method of signature and also (even if it was not the normal method) if it was intended as the testator's signature. The word "or" between section 7(2)(c)(i) and (ii) is significant.

In a recent opinion by the author the situation was that a testator was in the last stages of his final illness and had little control of his normal writing hand. He made attempts to sign with that hand, leaving a ragged stroke and rather better attempts at a signature with the other hand. A case could perhaps have been made that these were a signature within the first two categories (even if illegible) but as it was clear that the deceased had intended the penstrokes to be his signature to the will it seemed better to rely on section 7(2)(c)(ii), as at least a mark intended by him to be his signature.

Notarial execution

Although a notary no longer has, as such, any function in execution of wills in Scotland, the term "notarial execution" will no doubt continue to be used. If a testator is blind or unable to write and declares that fact to a "relevant person" the relevant person is entitled to sign the will for the testator after having read it over to the testator (unless the testator expressly declares that he does not wish it read over). A witness is preferable, but like other documents it is not necessary for bare validity. There is nothing to stop a blind person from signing the will, but this alternative is available and is probably to be preferred.

The relevant persons who may sign a will for a testator are a solicitor with a current practising certificate (although the existence or otherwise of a certificate may be difficult to establish many years later), an advocate, a justice of the peace or a sheriff clerk. If documents are signed outwith Scotland a notary public or public officer with appropriate authority in the place of execution may act.

---

[9] Meston and Cusine, *Execution of Deeds by a Mark* (1993) 38 J.L.S. 270; *Meston's Succession Opinions*, No.121, p.399.

Execution of wills before August 1, 1995[10]

Oral Wills

It was possible to make a purely oral will without any writing, provided the words spoken could be vouched by witnesses, but there was a severe practical limitation, in that such an oral will could convey property only up to the value of £100 Scots,[11] which is the equivalent of £8.33 sterling. It was therefore of little practical significance, although an oral legacy of a greater amount was valid up to that sum.

Holograph wills

The holograph will was recognised, and indeed common, in Scotland, although not in England. To be effective, a holograph will had to be wholly in the testator's handwriting and subscribed by him. Such a will was valid without the need for any witnesses, although it might be necessary to obtain affidavits to establish that the writing was in fact that of the deceased. If the body of the text was not in the testator's handwriting, it was sufficient if he wrote, in his own handwriting, the words "adopted as holograph" above his signature at the end of the deed.[12] It was sufficient for a holograph will to be signed on the last page only, although attested wills had to be signed on each page, and there was (and is) no restriction on the type of surface on which it may be written. A will in the North East was accepted as valid when it was written on the back of a painting.

Attested wills

Formal, professionally prepared, wills were invariably attested documents. They were signed on each page by the testator[13] and the testator's signature had to be witnessed on the last page on which there were operative provisions (*i.e.* not merely the testing clause) by two witnesses. The witnesses had to know the testator, but this requirement was not a great restriction, as a mere introduction could suffice. Though highly desirable it was not actually essential that the witnesses should sign immediately after the testator signed or acknowledged his signature to them.[14] As this implies, it was (and is) not necessary that the witnesses should both be present to see the testator sign, as it is acceptable if the testator acknowledges his signature to them. The acknowledgment may be to both witnesses together, or it may be done separately to each witness. Persons of 16 years of age or older could act as witnesses.[15] In the case of attestations occurring before September 25, 1991, the minimum age was 12 for females and 14 for males.

---

[10] A detailed account of the law on execution of deeds before the Requirements of Writing Act is to be found in Halliday *Conveyancing Law and Practice* (2nd ed., 1996), 3-01 to 3-91.

[11] Erskine, Inst., III, ix, 7.

[12] In very special circumstances the court might recognise a typed adoption as holograph. McBeath's *Trs v. McBeath*, 1935 S.L.T. 315. *Cf. Chisholm v. Chisholm*, 1949 S.L.T. 394. Adoption as holograph was rendered wholly superfluous by the Requirements of Writing (Scotland) Act 1995.

[13] The Conveyancing and Feudal Reform (Scotland) Act 1970 (c.35), s.44 which removed this requirement from other deeds, did not apply to wills.

[14] *Walker v. Whitwell*, 1916 S.C. (H.L.) 75.

[15] Age of Legal Capacity (Scotland) Act 1991 (c.50), s.1(1)(a) and s.9.

While it is inadvisable for a beneficiary to act as a witness to the will, this is not in Scotland a ground of invalidity of the will and acting as a witness does not deprive a beneficiary of his rights.

Notarial execution

A system of notarial execution was available for a testator who was blind or unable to write.[16] The procedure involved reading over the will to the testator in the presence of witnesses, obtaining the testator's agreement and then a signature on his behalf by one of the list of persons qualified to act. These were law agents (solicitors) whether or not the solicitor had taken out the annual practising certificate, notaries public, justices of the peace or a parish minister of the Church of Scotland acting within his own parish.

Will substitutes

Various devices are sometimes employed to avoid the necessity of executing a formal will. These include the nominations which are statutorily authorised for some types of small savings asset, now mainly benefits from a friendly society, but formerly including National Savings investments.[17]

The *donatio mortis causa* is also accepted in Scots law, and has fewer restrictions than in some other countries. The classic definition was given by Lord President Inglis in *Morris v. Riddick*[18] in the following terms:

"A conveyance ... so that the property is immediately transferred to the grantee, upon the condition that he shall hold for the grantor so long as he lives, subject to his power of revocation, and failing such revocation, then for the grantee on the death of the grantor."[19]

There must be evidence of an *inter vivos* transfer to the donee, but the gift is not outright, being subject to a double resolutive condition. The gift reverts to the donor (a) if the donee predeceases the donor and (b) if the donor revokes the gift. While it is necessary that the gift should have been made in contemplation of death, it is not necessary that the donor should have been in immediate peril of death, and Scots law differs from many others in that if the gift is in fact made in imminent peril of death, it is not automatically revoked if the donor survives the peril that he envisaged at the time.

However the main device still used as a will substitute, despite its many dangers, is the special destination inserted into the documents of title to certain types of asset, especially land. This will normally take the form of a direction that when there are two owners the predeceaser's share will pass automatically to the survivor. (In Scotland two owners of a single asset are presumed to be owners in common, not joint owners.) Despite what is commonly thought, a survivorship reference in the heading of bank and building society accounts does not amount to a special destination and has of itself no effect upon the

---

[16] Conveyancing (Scotland) Act 1924 (c.27), s.18 and Sched. I.
[17] See for example National Savings Bank Regulations 1972 (S.I. 1972 No. 764).
[18] *Morris v. Riddick* (1867) 5 M. 1036
[19] *ibid.*; *Aiken's Exrs v. Aiken*, 1937 S.L.T. 414.

succession to the money in the account, because a bank passbook or its equivalent is not a document of title to the money in the account.[20]

Although capable of being useful if they are understood and are used properly, special destinations are a relic of a time when it was not technically possible to make a will disposing of heritage and are liable to produce unintended results.[21] They should certainly be abolished and it is unfortunate that the Scottish Law Commission has not been able to recommend their complete abolition, although they will be severely limited when the proposed reforms are brought into effect.

The Succession Act 1964 did make some limited but valuable reforms to the law relating to special destinations. Under section 36(2), proviso (a), heritage owned by the deceased, but subject to a special destination, is not treated for the purposes of the Act as part of his estate unless he could and did evacuate the destination. Section 18(2) creates a restricted vesting in the executor in a case in which the deceased either could not or did not evacuate such a destination, thus providing a method which can, if necessary, be used to transfer the property to the person called as beneficiary in the destination.

However, the law relating to the acts by a testator which will amount to revocation or evacuation of a special destination (assuming he had the power to revoke it) was not entirely clear before the 1964 Act. This was particularly so when the alleged revocation was merely by implication from a subsequent general settlement which made no specific mention of the special destination. Many difficulties arose from the common practice of taking a title to heritage in the names of husband and wife and the survivor, and then subsequently, possibly even on the same day, executing a will which took no account of the survivorship destination. A question of implied revocation frequently arose.

Section 30 of the Act therefore provided that a testamentary disposition executed on or after September 10, 1964 (*i.e.* whose actual date of execution is after the commencement of the Act, irrespective of the testator's date of death)[22] shall not have effect so as to evacuate a special destination unless it contains a specific reference to the destination and a declared intention on the part of the testator to revoke it.[23] All this, of course, assumes that the testator has the power to revoke the destination. If he has no power to revoke, no reference, however specific, and no intention, however well declared, can effect revocation. If he has the power, the revocation must be express and cannot arise merely by implication. Power to revoke will be lost if the special destination is contractual in nature, commonly if both spouses have contributed to the purchase of a house, with the result that inserting a special destination amounts to the creation of an irrevocable will of the house. The effect therefore is that special destinations will normally prevail over contrary

---

[20] Meston, "Survivorship Destinations and Bank Accounts" [1996] 1 Scottish Law and Practice Quarterly, p.315
[21] Meston, "Special Destinations" in *A Scots Conveyancing Miscellany*, ed. Cusine (1987), pp.62–65. *Weir v. J.M. Hodge & Son*, 1990 S.L.T. 266 illustrates a situation in which the existence of the destination was ignored, leading to an action of damages against the solicitor giving negligent advice.
[22] 1964 Act, s.36(3).
[23] *Stirling's Trs*, 1977 S.L.T. 229.

provisions in a will. It is not permissible to go behind a statement in the title deeds about the source of the funds used in the purchase.[24]

Incorporation by reference

It has long been a distinctive feature of Scots law that it is possible to incorporate by reference into a validly executed will not only existing documents which are not in themselves validly executed, but even informal documents which may be created in the future. It is common practice to include in formal wills a clause specifying the nature of future informal writings which are to be accepted and the normal use of the clause is to permit disposal of personal effects although there is nothing in law to prevent the clause from having a much wider effect in validating past or future writings.[25]. Such clauses commonly describe the writing to be incorporated by a phrase such as "writings under my hand" and as this is interpreted as meaning "subscribed"[26] the effect of the Requirements of Writing (Scotland) Act 1995 will be that any such writing would be valid in its own right without the need for incorporation into another will.

It is not entirely clear what the situation now is if the instruction to incorporate a future document does not require the informal document to be subscribed. If the future writing is classified as either a will or a codicil the Act would require it to be in a subscribed document.

Confirmation and the probative character of wills

If confirmation is granted in Scotland to an executor who is acting under a will which disposes of property, the will is treated as valid in respect of the formalities of execution.[27] Whereas the previous procedure merely confirmed the appointment of the executor and made no pronouncement on the validity of the will, the effect now is a judicial statement that the will is validly executed. Hence confirmation now has an important effect in validating a will.

Grants of representation issued in England and Wales or Northern Ireland will have the same effect as confirmation without further formality provided that the deceased was domiciled in the jurisdiction issuing the grant and that fact is specified in it. Grants of representation issued outwith the United Kingdom and to which the Colonial Probates Acts 1892 and 1927 apply also make the will probative once they have been sealed in Scotland under that Act.[28]

REVOCATION OF WILLS

It is one of the fundamental characteristics of a will that the testator is free to revoke it and either substitute another will or let the law of intestacy govern the distribution of his estate. The testator may exercise this power of revocation at any moment up to his death. The fairly minimal level of mental

---

[24] *Gordon-Rogers v. Thomson's Exrs*, 1988 S.L.T. 618.

[25] *Macrorie's Exrs v. McLaren*, 1982 S.L.T. 295 (reversed on a different point 1984 S.L.T. 271).

[26] *Waterson's Trs v. St Giles Boys' Club*, 1943 S.L.T. 295.

[27] 1964 Act, s.32.

[28] *ibid.*, s.32(3)(b).

capacity which is necessary to permit him to execute a will, equally permits him to revoke any existing will, and there are no considerations of public policy which prevent him from changing his mind and altering his will as often as he wishes.

Although delivery of an *inter vivos* conveyance or trust deed may put it beyond the granter's control and make it irrevocable, delivery of a testamentary document to a beneficiary does not make the will irrevocable.[29] In the case of a will it is normally the death of the testator which is equivalent to delivery of an *inter vivos* deed as preventing subsequent revocation, and until that moment he has normally complete freedom to revoke.

The freedom to amend or alter is of the essence of a will. Accordingly, a clause in a will declaring that the will is to be irrevocable does not bind the testator.[30] Thus, it is often said that a will is ambulatory and speaks from the date of death of the testator. Indeed, it is sometimes erroneously said that a will is deemed to have been made at the moment of the testator's death. This formulation has, however, sometimes caused Parliament to define the date of execution of a will when it is important to distinguish that date from the date of the testator's death.[31]

Contract not to revoke.

There may be situations in which a testator loses the power to revoke the will. The main situation is where there has been a contract *inter vivos*. Here the testator has made a valid contract not to revoke his will and thereby has deprived himself of the power to revoke the will so that a purported revocation of the will is ineffective[32] In *Curdy v. Boyd*,[33] for example, Curdy had conveyed his whole property to Boyd in return for an obligation that Boyd would maintain him all the days of his life. Five years later Curdy purported to revoke the disposition. The court held that the disposition was onerous and thus irrevocable in the absence of fraud. The modern view might now be that this was a case of a completed *inter vivos* gift rather than a will. In the *Paterson* case,[34] Mrs Paterson had entered into a formal minute of agreement with her son binding her to execute a settlement of her whole property in his favour. The minute was in consideration of various payments made to her and her husband. She duly made a will as required by the agreement. When she died it was found that she had subsequently made another will revoking the first one and making a different disposal of the estate. The disappointed son raised an action of reduction of the second will. The action was successful on the ground that the onerous contract entered into by his mother bound her both to make the will in his favour and not to revoke it subsequently. The purported revocation was therefore ineffective. The existence of a contract not to revoke

[29] *Clark's Exr v. Clark*, 1943 S.C. 216; 1943 S.L.T. 266. However, if the deed in question is construed as not being testamentary, delivery would bar revocation: see *Duguid v. Caddall's Trs* (1831) 9 S. 844.

[30] *Dougall's Trs v. Dougall* (1789) Mor 15949.

[31] Succession (Scotland) Act 1964, s.36(3). WJD "The date from which a will speaks" 1948 S.L.T. (News) 9.

[32] Stair, Inst., III, 8, 28; Erskine, Inst., III, 9, 6; Bell, Principles, s.1866.

[33] (1775) Mor. 15946.

[34] *Paterson v. Paterson* (1893) 20 R. 484

must be proved in the normal way. In the absence of the appropriate proof of constitution of the contract there will be no restraint upon the testator.[35]

If there is a valid contract not to revoke an existing will, or a contract to make a will in favour of a particular person, the property belongs to the testator during his lifetime. He remains free to use it *inter vivos* as he wishes, even to the extent of dissipating it entirely so that there is nothing left to be conveyed by the obligatory will. Similarly, as the property belongs to the testator at the time of death, it remains subject to claims for legal rights by any issue or surviving spouse, even though this will sharply reduce the value of the benefit taken by the contractual legatee.

Mutual wills.

Much of the litigation over alleged contracts not to revoke wills has been in connection with mutual wills. Particularly when the partners to a mutual will are husband and wife, it is frequently alleged that there is a contract between them which prevents the survivor from altering the will.[36] The onus of proof of contract rests upon the person asserting the existence of the contract,[37] and various factors may be taken into account. The uncertainties created by mutual wills are such that they have now lost much of their former popularity and they tend to be treated as separate wills which happen to be on the same piece of paper.[38] If a contract not to alter is desired, it would be better to enter into an express contract to that effect.

Express Revocation

Express revocation of a will may be carried out either by physical acts of cancellation or destruction of the will itself or by a clause of revocation included in a subsequent deed executed with testamentary formalities. It has long been assumed that the more satisfactory of these two methods is the clause of revocation framed in terms such as to cover the deed being revoked, but decisions on the revival of wills now cast some doubt on this.[39] The result is a considerable increase in the importance of physical destruction or cancellation of wills.

Revocation by destruction or cancellation

The revocation of a will by destruction or cancellation must be effected both *animo et facto*; thus there must be both intention to revoke by destruction and some actual act of destruction. Clearly, if the destruction of the will was accidental, the necessary intention is lacking and the will is not revoked.[40] Similarly, if the testator was insane or otherwise lacked the necessary mental

---

[35] Although proof of a gratuitous promise to make a will in a particular form used to be restricted to the writ or oath of the promiser, *Smith v. Oliver*, 1911 S.C. 103, that form of proof was abolished by the Requirements of Writing (Scotland) Act 1995.
[36] *Corrance's Trs v. Glen* (1903) 5 F. 777
[37] *Garioch's Trs v. Garioch's Exrs*, 1917 S.C. 404; 1917 1 S.L.T. 197.
[38] *Gibson's Trs v. Gibson* (1877) 4 R. 867.
[39] *Bruce's J.F. v. Lord Advocate*, 1969 S.C. 296; 1969 S.L.T. 337; *Scott's J.F. v. Johnston*, 1971 S.L.T. (Notes) 41.
[40] *Cunningham v. Mouat's Trs* (1851) 13 D. 1376.

capacity at the time of the destruction of the will, there would not exist the necessary intention to revoke by destruction and the will would not be revoked. Thus in *Laing v. Bruce*[41] one of the issues was the state of mind of the testatrix at the time her will disappeared.

The onus of proof of intention is liable to be very important because evidence of intention will often be lacking or very thin. In general, it seems that the ordinary rule for proof of facts applies, and thus the onus of proving that acts of destruction were done with intent to revoke lies upon the party founding upon the revocation. In the *Crosbie* case,[42] for example, a testatrix had executed her will in duplicate and the duplicate retained by the testatrix was found in three pieces after her death. The court held that the will was not revoked. This decision was largely based on the absence of proof that the cutting of the will had been carried out by the testatrix but, even if this could have been established, there was also considerable doubt whether it could have been proved to have been done *animo revocandi*. In the *Pattison* case, Lord McLaren expressed this in the first of his four general propositions as follows: "on proof that the cancellation was done by the testator himself ... with the intention of revoking the will, the will is to be held revoked; otherwise it is to be treated as a subsisting will".[43]

The physical acts of destruction or mutilation which revoke a will may take many forms. The obvious actions would be to tear the will into pieces or to burn it. However, it is not necessary that the will be wholly destroyed so long as some positive acts have been performed which are intended by the testator to effect cancellation. Very little by way of physical cancellation will be necessary if the intention of the testator is clear. Thus even a pencil line through a formal deed can suffice, though it has been suggested that writing in pencil is likely to be merely deliberative when written over ink.[44] In the *Nasmyth* case[45] the cancellation consisted of cutting off a seal. Even though the document that remained was *ex facie* probative, being holograph and signed, this was held to amount to revocation. It is sometimes said that this was because the testator had himself prescribed the seal as a formality of execution, but this seems to have been subsidiary to the main point that the mutilation was intended as a symbolic gesture to show that the deed should no longer have effect. In the *Thomson* case[46] very clear evidence of intention, including some holograph writing, indicated that cutting a piece out of a copy of a will should receive effect as a revocation of the part excised. Conversely, if the intention of the testator is less clear, correspondingly stronger evidence of physical cancellation would be necessary to make up the deficiency.

Acts of destruction or mutilation must he carried out either by the testator himself or at his direction. Obviously acts by third parties have no effect, as otherwise any interested party could cancel the whole or any part of a will

---

[41] (1838) 1 D. 59.
[42] *Crosbie v. Wilson* (1865) 3 M. 870.
[43] *Pattison's Tr. v. University of Edinburgh* (1888) 16 R. 73 at 76.
[44] *Cruickshank's Trs v. Glasgow Magistrates* (1887) 14 R. 603.
[45] *Nasmyth v. Hare* (1821) 1 Sh. App. 65.
[46] *Thomson's Trs v. Bowhill Baptist Church*, 1956 S.C. 217; 1956 S.L.T. 302.

merely by running his pen through it. If a will was in the hands of the testator himself, but cannot be found after his death, there arises a presumption that it was destroyed by the testator with intent to revoke.[47] Circumstances may overcome the presumption, but the onus is on the person founding on the will to prove the continued validity of the will by an action of proving the tenor.[48] If the will was in the hands of some person other than the testator, for example a solicitor, and cannot be found, there is no basis for presuming that the testator had intended to revoke it, and so long as there is evidence of what the terms actually were, an action for proving the tenor would be appropriate.

Revocation of a will is equally validly effected by destruction at the testator's directions as by destruction by the testator himself.[49] This is merely an extension of the proposition that the destruction of the will must be both *animo et facto*. If the intention to revoke exists, it does not matter that someone else acts upon the testator's instructions and tears up the will. The mandate to destroy is provable by parole evidence but will not readily be implied.[50] If the agent instructed to destroy the will has not done so at the death of the testator, the act of cancellation is none the less complete on the ground that the testator had done all that was within his power to effect the revocation. The same follows if an intended revocation is frustrated by concealment of the will by an interested party.

Some doubt appears to remain whether the instruction to destroy can properly be carried out after the death of the testator,[51] but if the situation in fact is that the instruction to destroy is equivalent to the destruction itself, it should make no difference whether the will is destroyed before or after the testator's death or indeed whether the will is destroyed at all. Undelivered or unauthenticated instructions to destroy a will do not effect revocation,[52] and obviously destruction which is not in fact authorised by the testator is of no effect.

Assuming power to revoke, a will may also be expressly revoked if the testator declares the revocation in a subsequent deed executed with testamentary formalities. This subsequent deed need not itself contain alternative provisions for disposal of the estate (in which case total or partial intestacy would usually be the result), but it is essential that it be validly executed as a will. No particular form of words is necessary, provided that an intention to revoke former wills can fairly be deduced from the language used. The onus of proving the revocation of an *ex facie* valid will lies upon the person asserting it.[53]

Problems arising from express written revocations tend to resolve themselves into questions as to the interpretation of the language used. If it is intended to revoke all previous wills made by the testator, care has to be taken to ensure that the revocation clause is wide enough to include all of them. For

[47] *Clyde v. Clyde*, 1958 S.C. 343.
[48] *McLernan v. Ash*, 2001 G.W.D. 10-374.
[49] *Bonthrone v. Ireland* (1883) 10 R. 779
[50] *Cullen's Exrx v. Elphinstone*, 1948 S.C. 662; 1949 S.L.T. 228.
[51] *Falconer v. Stephen* (1849) 11 D. 1338.
[52] *France's J.F. v. France's Trs*, 1916 1 S.L.T. 126.
[53] *Hogg's Exrx v. Butcher*, 1947 S.N. 190.

example, in the *Gordon* case[54] the testatrix revoked "two wills ... both of which are recorded in the Books of Session, Edinburgh", but no such wills were to be found. The only will which was known to have existed was not registered. In the circumstances, including the fact that the onus of proof of revocation rests upon the person founding upon it, the court held that the non-registered will was not revoked. Conversely, if the revocation is only partial, care is required to ensure that the wills or parts of wills to be revoked are accurately described.

Implied Revocation

A will may be impliedly revoked in whole or in part without any direct expression of the testator's desire to revoke if there is a subsequent validly executed will containing inconsistent provisions or if the *conditio si testator sine liberis decesserit* applies for the benefit of afterborn children. In Scots law, a will is not revoked by the subsequent marriage of the testator.[55]

Where a later will contains provisions inconsistent with an earlier will, but does not expressly revoke it, there is a revocation to the extent of the inconsistency. The courts endeavour to read the documents together as a single will; and while they will go to some lengths to achieve this harmonisation, if the provisions ultimately conflict it will be assumed that the later document contains the later expression of the testator's wishes, and these will prevail over the inconsistent earlier provisions. Thus, if the later will is a universal settlement clearly dealing with the whole of the deceased's estate, the earlier will is necessarily revoked *in toto*. The universality of the subsequent settlement gives it many of the characteristics of an express clause of revocation of the earlier will. In both cases, even if some of the substantive provisions of the two wills would be capable of standing together, the earlier will is wholly set aside.[56] Universality is not necessarily established merely because a will purports on its face to deal with the testator's whole estate. In *Clark's Executor v. Clark* a will which, apart from a bequest of his coin collection, left the testator's "whole estate, heritable and moveable" to a society and expressly cancelled all previous wills did not revoke a bequest of his stamp collection in a previous testamentary writing.[57]

If the subsequent will is not universal, the implied revocation of earlier wills which it effects is only to the extent of the necessary inconsistency between earlier and later wills[58]. If there can reasonably be found a meaning which permits the apparently conflicting provisions to stand together, then that meaning will be adopted and both the provisions upheld. This has been known to cause some consternation when there have been several home-made wills which do not contain revocation clauses, as it may be that all the bequests have to be paid to the detriment of the residuary beneficiary. The proposed meaning

---

[54] *Gordon's Exr v. Macqueen*, 1907 S.C. 373; 14 S.L.T. 651.
[55] *Westerman's Executor v. Schwab* (1905) 8 F. 132.
[56] *Rutherford's Trs v. Dickie*, 1907 S.C. 1280; 15 S.L.T. 296.
[57] *Clark's Executor v. Clark*, 1943 S.C. 216; 1943 S.L.T. 266.
[58] *Park's Trs v. Park* (1890) 27 S.L.R. 528.

must be a possible interpretation of the testator's wishes and if no reasonable interpretation can reconcile the two provisions, that is if they are necessarily inconsistent, then the later provision must revoke the earlier *pro tanto*.[59]

If one will is to be impliedly revoked in whole or in part by another, it is because the second will is regarded as a later expression of the testator's wishes. It must be established that the second will is in fact a later expression of the testator's intention. In the absence of clear evidence of different intent, separate deeds executed or deemed to have been executed on the same day would usually be regarded as parts of the same deed.[60]

The *conditio si testator sine liberis decesserit* is a method of revocation of wills by operation of law. The Latin nomenclature is traditional and is very firmly established, but it is rather misleading. Read literally, it might be thought that it is concerned with the situation arising should a testator die without children, but it actually deals with the case of a testator who has left children. The principle applies when a testator has made a will which contains no provision for children who may subsequently be born to the testator. If children are born after the date of execution of such a will it is presumed that the testator did not desire his will to remain in effect in the altered circumstances. Thus unless the presumption can be rebutted, the will is revoked and the result is usually intestacy which may not however always be to the child's advantage if a spouse has prior rights.

The *conditio* is a presumption for the benefit of an after-born child and is not a case of automatic revocation of a will by the subsequent birth of children. Thus it has been strongly held that only the after-born child himself may seek to found on the *conditio* for the purpose of revocation of the will.[61] If the after-born child chooses not to contest the will, other heirs in intestacy who may have been passed over cannot improve their share of the estate by having the will revoked on this ground and distribution made on the basis of intestacy. Further, since the rule is only a presumption, it may be rebutted by clear evidence that the testator intended his will to be effective, notwithstanding the subsequent birth of a child.

The clearest case for applying the rule and regarding the will as revoked would be the original one of the posthumous child. However, it will almost certainly also be applied if the testator dies within a short time of the birth of the child without having had a reasonable opportunity of reviewing the provisions of his will. The mere fact that a long time elapses between the birth of a child and date of the testator's death does not overcome the presumption in favour of revocation. In *Milligan's J.F. Milligan*,[62] for example, although ten years had elapsed between the birth of the child and the testator's death, the court held that the will was revoked. Indeed, the opinions in this case suggest that however long a testator may have had to consider whether he wished his will to remain in effect, the court will not accept this by itself as evidence rebutting the presumed intention to revoke.

---

[59] *Ford's Trs v. Ford*, 1940 S.C. 426; 1940 S.L.T. 362.
[60] McLaren, *Wills and Succession* (3rd ed., 1894) 1, para. 749.
[61] *Stevenson's Trs v. Stevenson*, 1932 S.C. 657; 1932 S.L.T. 510.
[62] 1910 S.C. 58; 1909 2 S.L.T. 338.

In effect the presumption that a will not providing for them is revoked by the subsequent birth of children to the testator has become a very strong one and cases in which the presumption has been overcome are rare. One of the few is *Stuart-Gordon*[63] where, although the testatrix's will made no provision for her child born after it was made, there was evidence that she had been considering the will at the time of the child's birth and that she knew the child was well provided for from other sources. Thus it was held that the testatrix did wish the will to apply and the *conditio* was therefore inapplicable.

Conditional revocation, or dependent relative revocation, may exist in Scots law, although the authority is thin.[64] Under this doctrine a revocation of an existing will would not take effect if an intended replacement will turns out not to have been validly executed. It also appears that wills, when revoked other than by physical destruction, may be revived if the revoking will is itself revoked by some method which does not apply to the original will. This unsatisfactory result may be overturned in future legislation.[65]

ESSENTIAL VALIDITY

Capacity to execute a will

Age. For wills actually executed on or after September 25, 1991, the minimum age of testamentary capacity is 12.[66] Prior to that date, full testamentary capacity was attained on attaining majority at 12 for females and 14 for males.[67]

Mental capacity. A purported will executed by someone incapable of understanding the nature and consequences of a will is void on the ground of insanity.[68] Wills obtained from a testator by undue influence used by a person in a position of authority,[69] and wills executed by someone in the state of mental weakness known as "facility" and obtained by improper acts amounting to circumvention,[70] may be set aside by the court.

Intention to test. The deceased must have intended the document to receive effect as his will. Mere lists of names and sums of money may prove not to be more than jottings for what is to be included in a future will.[71] An apparently complete will, sufficiently executed, may however contain qualifications which indicate that it was not intended as a will.[72] The courts may however

---

[63] *Stuart-Gordon v. Stuart-Gordon* (1899) 1 F. 1005.
[64] Meston, "Dependent Relative Revocation in Scots Law", 1977 S.L.T. (News) 77; *France's J.F. v. France's Trs*, 1916 1 S.L.T. 126.
[65] Meston, "Revival by Revocation of the Revoking Will", 1974 S.L.T. (News) 153.
[66] Age of Legal Capacity (Scotland) Act 1991 (c.50), s.2(2).
[67] *Stevenson v. Allans* (1680) Mor. 8949; Succession (Scotland) Act 1964, ss. 28, 38(3).
[68] *Sivewright v. Sivewright's Trs*, 1919 2 S.L.T. 261; The effect of delusions was considered in *Muirden v. Garden's Exrs*, 1981 S.L.T. (Notes) 9.
[69] *MacGilvary v. Gilmartin*, 1986 S.L.T. 89.
[70] *West's Tr. v. West*, 1980 S.L.T.6.; *Anderson v. Beacon Fellowship*, 1992 S.L.T. 111.
[71] *Colvin v. Hutchison* (1885) 12 R. 947; *Jamieson's Exrs*, 1982 S.L.T. (Notes) 198.
[72] *Munro v. Coutts* (1813) Dow's App. 437

now be more ready to accept an apparently informal writing, such as a letter to a daughter signed merely "Mum", as showing completed testamentary intention.[73]

Restrictions on testamentary freedom. Although testators may have a sense of power when disposing of their assets in the knowledge that they will not have personal use for the assets at the crucial time and will not be around to face disappointed relatives, there are significant limits on what they can validly do.[74]

Legal rights. The principal restriction upon the freedom of a testator to do as he wishes with his estate is probably the existence of the legal rights of spouses and descendants. These have been discussed above[75] in their role as one of the three sets of rules involved in a division of an intestate estate. Their other function is to protect the spouse and issue of a testator from disinheritance. Whatever the testator may provide in his will, the surviving spouse and issue have an automatic right to their shares of the moveable estate. In theory, the testator has no power to dispose of these shares in his will and the result is that an automatic fixed share is available to spouse or issue without any necessity for the expense of court application if any of them are dissatisfied with the provisions for them in the will. However they must elect between the will and legal rights and cannot have both. The doctrine of approbate and reprobate prevents a claimant from rejecting part of the will while claiming to apply other parts. There will be substantial changes, including the application to the whole estate of the deceased, when the proposed new "legal share" is substituted for legal rights in accordance with the proposals of the Scottish Law Commission.

Accumulations of income. Other restrictions upon a testator's freedom include the detailed legislation restricting accumulations of income with the capital for excessive periods.[76] Testators sometimes have the miser's dream of imagining their funds growing after their deaths by the power of compound interest without any expenditure having to be met from it. Spectacular sums can be envisaged if income is added to capital for say 100 years and Mr Peter Thellusson is famous for his scheme which eventually led to a prohibition on others attempting to do the same thing.[77]

No accumulation is permitted beyond one of six periods and all directions for accumulation must fall into one of the six. They are:

   (i)   the life of the grantor of the deed;
  (ii) 21 years from the death of the grantor;
 (iii) the minority of any person living or in utero at the testator's death;
 (iv) the minority of any person who would for the time being, if of full age, be entitled to the income directed to be accumulated;
  (v) 21 years from the date of the settlement;

---

[73] *Rhodes v. Peterson & Anr,* 1972 S.L.T. 98.
[74] Meston, "The Power of the Will", 1982 Jur.Rev. 172.
[75] Chap. 5.
[76] Trusts (Scotland) Act 1961 (c.57), s.5 as amended by the Law Reform (Miscellaneous Provisions) (Scotland) Act 1966, s.6
[77] *Thellusson v. Woodford* [1798] 4 Vesey Jr. 227; aff'd House of Lords 11 Vesey 112.

(vi) the minority of any person living or *in utero* at that date.

The commonest example is probably example (ii), so that an accumulation directed in a will normally ceases exactly 21 years from the death of the testator.[78]

Successive liferents. A testator is prevented from achieving effects similar to those of an entail[79] by creating a series of successive liferents. A liferent may be created only in favour of someone alive at the date when the deed creating it came into operation. The draconian sanction is that if anyone born after that date is of full age and becomes entitled to a liferent under the deed, the apparent liferenter becomes the outright fiar and the rights of any fiar nominated in the deed are cancelled.[80]

Repugnancy. This doctrine is not particularly well known, but acts as an important restriction upon the extent to which a testator can impose conditions on the use by the beneficiary of a testamentary gift. It arises when a testator confers an outright gift upon a beneficiary but then proceeds to say that none the less someone else is to look after the property for the beneficiary.

If a beneficiary under a will is of full age and has a vested, unqualified and indefeasible right of fee (all the conditions being important) the beneficiary is entitled to have the provision conveyed to him, notwithstanding any direction to trustees to hold the legacy for him until he attains some age later than majority. The direction is repugnant to the right of fee vested in the beneficiary and is of no effect. Thus a qualifying beneficiary of a will dated from January 1, 1970 on attaining the age of 18 could insist on payment, irrespective of any direction in the will that it was not to be paid until, for example, age 25.[81]

Public policy. The courts have developed a somewhat undefined power to strike down testamentary provisions on the ground of public policy. Most of the cases which have caught the court's attention have involved what are regarded as excessive memorials by the testator for himself.[82] These have ranged from the statues to be placed in the McCaig tower (commonly known as McCaig's Folly) in Oban via a "massive bronze statue of artistic merit" of a testator in Musselburgh to a permanent exhibition of the testatrix's "valuable art collection" in St Andrews. There is nothing to say that further situations may not be included in future, but obviously this type of power to strike down testamentary provisions must be exercised with considerable care.

Power to bequeath a lease

One of significant provisions of the Succession Act was to clarify the law about the effect of a bequest of a lease. When a lease is assignable, the tenant has always been able to bequeath his interest under it to any person whom he chooses. He used to have no power of bequest if there was a condition, express

---

[78] *Campbell's Trs v. Campbell* (1891) 18 R. 992

[79] New entails were prohibited from 1914: Entail (Scotland) Act 1914, s.2.

[80] Law Reform (Miscellaneous Provisions) (Scotland) Act 1968 (c.70), ss. 18, 22(5) in respect of deeds executed on or after November 25, 1968. See *Lord Binning, Petr*, 1984 S.L.T. 18.

[81] Age of Majority (Scotland) Act 1969. The effect of the Age of Legal Capacity Act 1991 may be to reduce the age to 16. See *Barr & Edwards*, 1992 S.L.T. (News) 77.

[82] *McCaig v. University of Glasgow*, 1907 S.C. 231; *Aitken's Trs v. Aitken*, 1927 S.C. 374; *Sutherland's Tr. v. Verschoyle & Ors*, 1968 S.L.T. 43.

or implied, prohibiting assignation. This is still so if there is an express prohibition on assignation, although the deceased's executor may transfer the interest despite an express prohibition.[83] However, if the prohibition on assignation is only an implied one, section 29 gives the tenant a right to bequeath his interest to any one of the persons who, if he had died intestate, would be, or would in any circumstances have been, entitled to succeed to his estate under the Act.

As in the case of an executor's power of transfer of leases, the power of bequest in the face of an implied prohibition on assignation is intended merely to preserve as far as possible in the new circumstances the effect of the prohibition. The purpose of such a prohibition was to ensure that the tenant's heir at law would succeed to the tenancy. That status being now virtually abolished, provision had to be made to ensure that a single tenant could be found to continue the tenancy. This purpose is largely achieved by giving an executor power to transfer the interest to any one person actually entitled to succeed to the deceased's estate on intestacy, irrespective of express or implied prohibitions on assignation.[84] A wider power is, however, given to the tenant himself to select the single tenant to succeed to him from the whole circle of persons who might in any circumstances succeed to the tenancy on intestacy, provided that the prohibition on assignation is no more than an implied one. In effect, transfer by the executor or bequest by the tenant within the circle of relations specified is another method of finding a single "heir at law" to continue the tenancy.

The special provisions relating to bequest of agricultural leases contained in section 16 of the Crofters' Holdings (Scotland) Act 1886, section 11 of the Agricultural Holdings (Scotland) Act 1991 and section 10 of the Crofters (Scotland) Act 1955 are not prejudiced by the power of bequest in the 1964 Act.[85]

Construction of Wills

While every will should ideally be so clear that no question of interpreting or construing the terms used will arise, circumstances do change. Difficult questions can then arise over what the testator really intended in the changed circumstances. In *Couper's J.F. v. Valentine*[86] a testator had made a testamentary provision in favour of "my wife, Mrs Dorothy Couper". He was subsequently divorced a relatively short time before his death but did not alter the will. Was the bequest conditional upon her having the status of his wife at his death — with the name being merely a supplementary description, or was this a gift to the person known as Mrs Dorothy Couper, who happened to be his wife at the time of the will?[87]

---

[83] *infra*, p.128.
[84] The nominee must have a direct entitlement to succeed: *MacLean v. MacLean*, 1988 S.L.T. 626.
[85] 1964 Act, s.29(2).
[86] 1976 S.L.T. 83.
[87] In the circumstances it was paid to the ex wife; see also *Speaker's Exr v. Spicker*, 1969 S.L.T. (Notes) 7; *Stalker's Exrs, Petrs*, 1977 S.L.T. (Notes) 4.

The fundamental rule in establishing the meaning of a will is to read the will, the whole will and in most cases nothing but the will. If, taking account of *all* parts of the will, a meaning can be established, then no artificial rules of interpretation should be allowed to subvert that meaning. Many practical problems could be solved by reading the will carefully and then reading it again. The problems might even be avoided if those drafting wills in the first place had read their drafts in the same way. Wills such as one which required the residue to be divided into nine equal parts and then listed the eleven people each of whom were to get one of the shares could then be avoided. Similarly the wife's will which was found (after her death) to have left the residue of her estate to "my wife" might not have caused so much trouble.[88]

The evidence used to construe a will is to be found solely within the four corners of the will. Extrinsic evidence will rarely be admitted, for the good practical reason that the evidence of witnesses about what the deceased really meant has a tendency to be coloured by what the witnesses think the testator ought to have done. The court is construing the intention which the testator has expressed, not the subjective intention he may have had nor what disappointed beneficiaries would like to believe he intended. Evidence (after the testator's death) of statements during his lifetime are treated as having little evidential value.

Words will be presumed to have their ordinary meaning unless the contrary is shown, *e.g.* if the testator had written in a code.[89] Technical terms will be presumed to have their technical meaning.[90]

The main situation in which extrinsic evidence will be admitted arises if there is a latent ambiguity in the will. The typical example is the description of a legatee in terms which are capable of being applied to two people without fully describing either. The Keiller family of Dundee has been a significant contributor to the law in this area.[91] Provided the ambiguity is latent and not obvious on the face of the will extrinsic evidence may be used to determine the true beneficiary. There must of course actually be an ambiguity. There was no ambiguity in a bequest of two pubs, although the beneficiary claimed that the testator had intended to include the flats above the pubs.[92]

Certainty of beneficiaries

If, despite every effort to make sense of the admissible evidence, the beneficiary of a legacy remains uncertain, the legacy fails from uncertainty.[93]

---

[88] See *Meston's Succession Opinions*, No. 77, p.244.
[89] *Greig's Trs v. Simpson*, 1918 S.C. 321; *Simson's Trs v. Simson*, 1922 S.C. 14; *Lawson's Exr v. Lawson*, 1958 S.L.T. (Notes) 38.
[90] *Macdonald's Trs v. Macdonald* 1974 SLT 87; *Nelson's Trs v. Nelson's C.B.* 1979 SLT 98.
[91] *Keiller v. Thomson's Trs* (1824) 3 S.279 (OE 396) and (1826) 4 S.730 (OE 724).
[92] *Fortunato's J.F. v. Fortunato*, 1981 S.L.T. 277.
[93] *Meston's Succession Opinions*, No. 28 at p.78 and No. 140, p.462.

Vesting[94]

It is very important to understand vesting, as the problem arises quite frequently. If it is not recognised there is a high probability that an estate will be wound up wrongly. The beneficiary who gets less than his or her entitlement because of your failure to notice the correct answer is likely to be disappointed, and to sue. The beneficiary who obtained funds without genuine right will normally have spent it and be unable to repay the amount received.

Vesting can arise in two separate situations. The first, and most simple, is that the whole estate of a deceased person vests for purposes of the administration of the estate in the executor when the executor has obtained confirmation from the court. This is the process equivalent to Probate in England, but unlike England, a Scottish confirmation includes an inventory of the assets of the deceased to which the executor is confirmed. It is the confirmation, not the appointment as executor (whether appointed in the will as an executor-nominate or by the court as an executor-dative) which gives the executor the title to administer the property and transfer it to the correct beneficiaries — after paying the debts due by the estate. For example it gives the executor the formal title to convey heritage to the appropriate person.

More difficulty arises over the concept of vesting in the beneficiary. While the formal administrative right vests in the executor, the beneficial right may also have vested in the appropriate beneficiaries and it is this beneficial vesting which concerns us here. A benefit (*i.e.* a legacy or an intestate share) from the estate of a deceased person is said to vest in the beneficiary when the beneficiary obtains a completed right to it. Once he has a completed right, it is part of his property and he can dispose of it by *inter vivos* or *mortis causa* deed. However it is important to realise that a completed right may be obtained long before the beneficiary can get actual possession of it. This is where difficulties can arise particularly when a liferent is involved.

Vesting problems are not limited to cases where a liferent is conferred by a will, but they are a common example. A typical example, which arose recently, involved a husband who died in 1980. His will conferred a liferent of his whole estate upon his widow, who is still alive. The fee of the estate was given to his two children. The widow is enjoying the liferent, but child B died in 1985. A seems to think that the whole estate is now his, but B's widow has indicated that she expects to receive one half of the estate when the liferent expires on W's death. It is therefore vital to determine when vesting of the fee occurred. If it occurred in 1980 when father died, B had a vested right at the time of his death, and this passed as part of his estate when B subsequently died. If the estate passed to *his* widow then she is entitled to his half when possession is possible. However if vesting was postponed to the expiry of the liferent, then A does collect the lot.

The broad principles on which a decision is made on the date of vesting are as follows:

---

[94] See Henderson, *Vesting* (2nd ed.); Howie, "Vesting" in title Wills & Succession *Laws of Scotland* Vol 25. Gretton, "What is vesting", 1986 J.L.S. 148. See also *Meston's Succession Opinions*, pp.467–499.

Intention of the testator governs. The basic rule when there is a will is that the intention *expressed* by the testator in the will controls the decision about vesting. Hence a well-drafted will usually includes an express statement about the date of vesting and this will normally (that weasel word) settle the question.

Presumption for early vesting. If there is doubt, the court will favour the interpretation which produces the earlier date of vesting. Vesting of shares in the estate of deceased person cannot take place earlier than the date of his death. Hence the presumption is in favour of vesting *a morte testatoris.*

Shares of an intestate estate vest *a morte* immediately on the death of the intestate. Similarly an ordinary legacy with no qualifications vests immediately.

Suspensive conditions postpone vesting. A testator may include a condition in his will that a particular legacy is to vest only if some event occurs. If it is uncertain whether the event will ever happen, such a conditional bequest must necessarily postpone vesting until it can be determined whether the event will in fact happen. Most conditions personal to the legatee will tend to be suspensive conditions of this sort, and the commonest form is a survivorship condition or attaining a particular age. If a will is construed as providing that the legatee is to get his legacy only *if* he attains the age of 18 or survives someone else, typically a liferenter, then vesting has to be postponed until it can be established if he will qualify. These are uncertain events, which may never happen. The legatee may die before the event occurs and would not then qualify. Legacies of this sort are therefore said to vest on a "*dies incertus*" and vesting cannot take place before then.

Great care is therefore necessary in drafting clauses referring to survivorship. It must be clear what it is that the legatee has to survive. Many cases occur in which "survivors" are mentioned without making it clear, and there can often be disputes. Another common form of survivorship clause is a gift to A "whom failing" B. It is essential to make it clear when "failure" is to be determined. Is it at the testator's death or at the liferentrix's death?

Payment postponed to a dies certus *does not postpone vesting.* If there is postponement of *payment* until a day which will certainly happen (a *dies certus*), then vesting of the right is not postponed. No one has yet avoided death, and thus the death of a liferenter is an event which will happen sometime, even if it is not known when. Thus in the typical case of a liferent to A and fee to B, B's right to the fee will vest immediately on the testator's death, because the liferenter will die sometime and there is no uncertainty other than as to the date when the fiar will receive the capital of the sum liferented.

So far so good. It is all quite simple. The whole point is that everyone should know what he or she does or does not own, and can make provision accordingly. A simple legacy vests immediately. A condition postponing payment until a *dies certus* does not prevent immediate vesting, and the beneficiary could always borrow on the security of the inheritance to come in the future. If there is a suspensive condition, however, there is no vesting until it can be determined whether the condition will be purified and the legatee must just wait to find out whether he gets anything. The problem is that there is a concept of resolutive conditions.

Resolutive conditions do not postpone vesting, but may take it away! The courts have introduced in certain cases the concept of vesting subject to defeasance. Even though the whole point of vesting should be to achieve finality and let anyone with a vested right make use of that right even though it has not yet been paid, this doctrine will sometimes allow a court to determine that a right which has vested can be *di*vested or "defeased". Some conditions attached to legacies are held not to be suspensive, but to be resolutive. As such they do not prevent immediate vesting, but if the events specified in the condition do occur, they are "resolutive" of the vesting, and thus bring it to an end. Needless to say this can only be done before the person with the vested right has had a chance to spend the proceeds in the Las Vegas casinos.

While there is no guarantee that further examples may not emerge, three established cases of vesting subject to defeasance are already known. They all involve liferents and the birth of issue. It is to be hoped that no more do emerge!

To A in liferent, A's issue in fee and failing issue of A, then to B in fee. There is little trace of the doctrine before the case of *Taylor v. Gilbert's Trs.*[95] In that case A had no issue at the time when the testator died and B took a vested right to the fee, but subject to defeasance if A subsequently did have issue.

Gift to A with a subsequent direction to hold for A in liferent and his issue in fee. This is really an example of bad drafting and arises from the case of *Tweeddale's Trs v. Tweeddale.*[96] It begins with an outright gift, but later in the will there appears a provision that it is to be a liferent with the fee to the children. To make sense of both provisions this is treated as an outright gift to A, but subject to the resolutive condition that if he subsequently has issue, his right is reduced to a mere liferent with the fee going to his children. If A never has children, he remains outright owner.

To A in liferent and B in fee, but if B predeceases the expiry of the liferent leaving issue, then to the issue in fee. The main case is *Snell's Trs v. Morrison.*[97] The fiar in such a case takes an immediate vested right to the fee, but subject to defeasance in favour of his issue if he predeceases the liferenter, leaving issue, but only in that event.

Conditional Institution and Substitution

This concerns the effect to be given to destinations-over such as "to A, whom failing to B". In that situation A is called the "institute", *i.e.* he is the person primarily called or "instituted" as the heir. The question is the position of B and this depends upon the construction to be given to the terms of the will. There are no hard rules about construction; everything depends on a

---

[95] (1878) 5 R. (H.L.) 217.
[96] (1905) 8 F. 264.
[97] (1877) 4 R. 709.

detailed examination of the whole of the will. B may be a "conditional institute" or a "substitute".[98]

If he is only a conditional institute, the effect is that if A survives the testator he acquires the legacy and B's right permanently disappears. B gets the legacy only if A predeceases the testator.

If, however, he is a "substitute", the difference is that even if A does survive to obtain the legacy, B will inherit it after A dies — unless the substitution is defeated by A during his lifetime either by transferring it to someone else or by dealing specifically with it in his will.

Every substitution includes a conditional institution, but not vice versa. There is a presumption in favour of substitution when the subjects are heritage, but against substitution when the subjects are moveables — moveables would be likely to be difficult to trace once mixed in A's other property, but heritage usually remains identifiable.

Adopted persons and construction of wills[99]

Adopted persons are defined (section 23(5)) for the purposes of the Succession (Scotland) Act 1964 as persons adopted in pursuance of a formal adoption order which has the same meaning as in section 38 of the Adoption (Scotland) Act 1978, whether the order took effect before or after the commencement of the Succession Act.

The general policy of the Act was to remove the anomalies of the previous law in relation to adopted persons. The effect of Part IV of the Act is therefore that they are treated for all purposes, whether of succession or of entitlement under an *inter vivos* deed, as children of the adopter or adopters.[1] This is reinforced by section 39(1) of the Adoption (Scotland) Act 1978[2] which declares, *inter alia*, that a child who is the subject of an adoption order is to be treated in law as if he had been born as a legitimate child of the adopter or adopters. Section 24(1) of the Succession Act specifies the relationship adopted children are to be deemed to have to other children or adopted children of the adopter. The provisions of the Adoption Act 1958 which formerly prevented an adopted child from acquiring any rights of intestate succession or legal rights in the adopter's estate are repealed.[3]

The details of the reciprocal rights of succession between an adopted child and its adopting parents have already been considered in chapters 5 and 6, along with the place of adopted persons in collateral succession. Briefly, the adopted person's rights either in the estates of its natural parents or through them by representation are cut off, subject to the transitional provisions of the Law Reform (Miscellaneous Provisions) (Scotland) Act 1966.[4] In substitution the adopted person has full rights as a child in the estates of its adopting parents and through them by representation.[5] A person adopted by two spouses

[98] *Meston's Succession Opinions*, No.21, p.54.
[99] See Wilkinson & Norrie, *Parent and Child* (2nd ed.), para. 4.16.
[1] s.23(1).
[2] (c.28). In force September 1, 1984 (S.I. 1984 No. 1050).
[3] Succession (Scotland) Act, s.24(4).
[4] (c.19), s.5.
[5] 1964 Act, s.23(1).

jointly has rights of succession as a brother or sister of the whole blood to any other child or adopted child of both spouses. In any other case, however, the adopted person has rights of succession to any other person being the adopted child of the adopter or of either of the adopters as a brother or sister of the half blood.[6] Equally, since adopted persons are deemed to be related to collaterals in these capacities, they have rights of succession through the collaterals by representation.

There are also provisions in the Act relating to the construction of deeds when adopted children exist. Some confusion has existed over the commencement of these provisions in view of the complex relationship between sections 23(2), 23(4) and 36(3).

Section 23(4) states that nothing in section 23 "shall affect any deed executed ... before the commencement of this Act". The effect is that wills actually executed[7] before September 10, 1964, have the same meaning as they had then. In other words, references in such wills to "children" or "issue" are presumed not to include adopted children. It is presumed that the testator was aware of the state of the law at the time and that by not mentioning adopted children he intended not to include them. Such children will, of course, now be entitled to legitim irrespective of the terms of the adopter's will if the adopting parent died after the commencement of the Succession Act. The intention in this, as in other parts of the Act, was to avoid the necessity of disturbing existing arrangements.[8]

Section 23(2) therefore means that in wills executed on or after September 10, 1964, a general reference to "children" or "issue" will, unless the contrary intention appears, include adopted children. The point of the proviso (that for the purposes of section 23(2) a deed taking effect on the death of any person is to be deemed to have been executed on the date of death of that person) is that if a will is executed *after the commencement of the Act* referring to "children", or "issue," and subsequently the testator adopts a child, that child is included. The beginning of section 23(2) refers to deeds executed after the making of an adoption order, but the proviso ensures that the will is regarded as being executed at the date of the testator's death and hence after the adoption order, so that the adopted child is included in the term "children".

Similarly a deed executed after the commencement of the Succession Act and taking effect on the death of some person other than the grantor of the deed will be deemed, for the purposes of section 23(2), to have been executed on the date of death of that person, and therefore after the adoption of any child who by then had been adopted.

The general policy that an adopted person is to be treated as the child of the adopter is specifically applied to the construction of the terms used in wills and of *inter vivos* deeds disposing of property by section 23(1)(a) and (b). This is subject only to the special transitional provision that if the adopting parent died before September 10, 1964, and the natural parent died on or after August 3,

---

[6] *ibid.*, s.24(1).
[7] *ibid.*, s.36(3).
[8] "Class Terms in the Construction of Deeds" (1969) 14 J.L.S. 204.

1966, the child is treated as the child of the natural parent for purposes of succession to that parent.[9]

The general policy is made more specific by section 23(2). In deeds executed after the making of an adoption order (deeds taking effect on the death of any person being deemed to have been executed on the date of his death), any express or implied reference to the child or children of the adopter is to be construed as including a reference to the adopted person. References in any deed to the children of the adopted person's natural parents are to be construed as not including a reference to the adopted person, and references to a person related to the adopted person in any particular degree are to be construed as references to a person who would be related to him in that degree if he were the child of the adopter. As examples of these situations, a legacy to the "children" of X includes X's adopted children, but a legacy to the "children" of the natural parents of a person who has been adopted by a third party does not include the adopted person. A legacy by an adopted person to, say, his "nephews" is payable to the issue of other children adopted by, or born to, the adopters of the adopted person himself and not to his nephews by natural relationship. The latter aspect of construction in collateral succession is also stated in section 24(1) and similar situations can be envisaged for *inter vivos* conveyances. For so long as it continues to exist it would seem that the *conditio si testator sine liberis decesserit* would be available to a child adopted after the date of a will for whom no provision is made in it. The proviso to section 23(2) of the Succession Act is only for the purposes of that subsection, which deals with references to children in deeds.

A question was thought to arise whether a bequest to "the issue of any of my children who fail to survive me" would include the predeceasing child's adopted child. In the view of the present writer, there is no doubt upon the matter. Such an adopted child would be included as a beneficiary. It is, of course, open to a testator to make such provision as he wishes, but if he used a phrase such as that quoted above, the whole purpose of the Act is to ensure that its meaning includes the adopted child. In the vigorous correspondence on this topic[10] the most convincing argument was that presented by Professor Clive at page 182 (January 1981), and this is the view which should be acted upon. It will be reinforced by the new section 39A of the Adoption (Scotland) Act 1978 which will be enacted when the Scottish Law Commission's draft Bill in its *Report on Succession*[11] is eventually enacted.

One of the major difficulties preventing the introduction of full rights of succession for adopted children at an earlier date was the existence of the rules of primogeniture and preference of males in the succession to heritage. While these rules have now largely disappeared, they are still relevant in the case of titles and some other items to which the Act does not apply.[12] Adopted children have no rights of succession to these items, in so far as included in the estate of the adopter. Accordingly, where the terms of any deed provide that any

---

[9] Law Reform (Miscellaneous Provisions) (Scotland) Act 1966 (c.19), s.5.
[10] 1981 J.L.S. (Workshop) pp.159, 165, 172, 182, 191 and 206.
[11] Scot. Law Com. No. 124.
[12] 1964 Act, s.37(1).

property or interest in property is to devolve along with a title, honour or dignity, nothing in section 23 of the Succession Act 1964 or in the Children Act 1975 or in the Adoption (Scotland) Act 1978 is to prevent that devolution.[13]

If a person has been adopted more than once, in effect only the last adoption is reckoned for the purposes of succession, of establishing relationships and of construction of deeds executed after the last adoption order.[14]

An adoption order may be revoked in various circumstances, *e.g.* when a child who had previously been adopted by his parents is legitimated by virtue of the Legitimation (Scotland) Act 1968. However section 6 of that Act provides that revocation of an adoption order is not to affect an intestacy which occurred, or a deed which came into operation, before the revocation.

Illegitimate persons in the construction of wills

The radical improvements in the direct rights of succession of illegitimate children have already been noted in Chapters 5 and 6. However these reforms of the law of intestate succession, even taking into account the right to legitim, by no means exhausted the problem.

At common law there was very serious discrimination against the illegitimate child in the construction of deeds. The rule of construction amounted to a very strong presumption that terms such as "children" or "issue" referred to the legitimate relationship only. This stemmed from the general rule that an illegitimate child is *filius nullius* and the ultimate logic of this rule was well expressed by Lord Watson in *Clarke v. Carfin Coal Co.*[15] when he said that "at common law the mother is as much as the father, an utter stranger in blood to her child". With this somewhat nonsensical proposition built into the law it is not surprising to find that it could be authoritatively stated[16] that "the mere fact that there were no legitimate children answering the description could scarcely be regarded as a sufficient reason for giving to a designative bequest a construction which would admit persons who in law are regarded as strangers".

In other words, it seemed to be assumed that no testator in his senses would intend to include illegitimate children in the benefits of a bequest to the "children" of a particular person. Thus that construction was avoided unless it was completely impossible to do so — and sometimes even then. For example, in *Mitchell's Trs v. Cables*[17] a testator made a gift to his son "and his lawful children" whom failing to his daughter "and to the whole children procreated or that may yet be procreated of her body". At the date of the will, the daughter had an illegitimate child who was known to and indeed lived with the testator, and one might have thought that the difference in the wording of the two provisions indicated as clearly as humanly possible that the illegitimate child was intended to be a beneficiary. Nonetheless that construction was rejected.

---

[13] *ibid.*, s.23(3).
[14] *ibid.*, s.24(3).
[15] (1891) 18 R. (H.L.) 63 p.70.
[16] McLaren, *Wills & Succession*, I, 694.
[17] (1893) 1 S.L.T. 156.

In the interpretation of deeds executed on or after November 25, 1968, this position was reversed by section 5 of the Law Reform (Miscellaneous Provisions) (Scotland) Act 1968.[18] This provides that in deducing any relationship for the purpose of ascertaining beneficiaries under a deed, the persons concerned are to be taken to be related to each other notwithstanding that the relationship was an illegitimate one only. It is interesting that this part of the 1968 reforms affecting illegitimate children was much wider in scope than the reform of their direct rights of intestate succession. The changed rules of interpretation apply to all deeds creating benefits, not just to deeds by the parents of an illegitimate child, with the result that the further reform in the Law Reform (Parent and Child) (Scotland) Act 1986 was of less significance for the construction of wills than in the creation of rights of succession. The rule of construction contained in the 1968 Act was already a general one, and the main further change effected in 1986 was to apply the principle of equality to most statutes as well as to private deeds.

The main qualification is that the grantor of the deed may express a contrary intention, probably by using such terms as "lawful children" and such a contrary intention will receive effect.[19] Others are that the new rule did not apply to the construction of enactments until 1986 and that it still does not affect the succession to titles, honours or dignities.[20] However the provision in the 1968 Act that the new rule of construction did not prevent property from devolving along with a title does not appear in the 1986 Act. Since 1986 it may therefore be that while a title may pass to the heir at law, property destined along with it may pass to an illegitimate child instead.

Subject to all the same qualifications, section 6 of the 1968 Act also provides that illegitimacy is no longer to prevent the operation of *the conditio si testator sine liberis decesserit*, the *conditio si institutus sine liberis decesserit*, or the principle of accretion. Previously a number of cases had established that the children of a predeceasing illegitimate child for whom a testamentary provision had been made could not invoke the *conditio si institutus*.[21] There was no question of an after-born illegitimate child invoking the *conditio si testator* to set aside a will since it had no ordinary rights of succession to protect, and there was no accretion in a gift to illegitimate children as a class.[22]

Accretion

This problem of interpretation arises when a single legacy has been left to two or more persons, but one of them has died without having acquired a vested right, normally by predeceasing the testator. Do the others share the whole legacy or does the predeceaser's share fall into residue or intestacy?

If the legacy is left jointly without any words suggesting separate shares, there is accretion in favour of the survivor, who takes the whole legacy. But if

---

[18] Deeds exercising a power of appointment are treated as having the date of the deed which created the power: 1968 Act, s.5(3).
[19] Law Reform (Parent and Child) (Scotland) Act 1986, s.1(4)(c).
[20] 1968 Act, s.5(5)(b) and 1986 Act, s.9(1)(c).
[21] *Farquharson v. Kelly* (1900) 7 S.L.T. 442.
[22] McLaren, *Wills & Succession*, I, 695.

there are words of severance such as "equally between them" there is no accretion and the survivor is entitled only to his or her own share.[23] There is a further qualification that, if the gift is to a class of persons (the definition of "class" being obscure), words of severance do not prevent accretion to the survivor.[24]

Conditio si institutus sine liberis decesserit

This is a rule of construction of wills and applies solely to testamentary writings.[25] The normal rule is that a legacy to a specified person simply fails if that person fails to survive the testator, but when the *conditio si institutus* applies it adds to the legacy an implied condition that the legatee's issue may take the legacy instead. Only the issue of certain close relatives of the testator can benefit. These are the testator's own descendants (including since 1968 any who are illegitimate[26] but not step-children) and the issue of the testator's nephews and nieces. Since the decision in *Hall v. Hall*[27] it does not apply to the nephews and nieces themselves if the gift was to brothers and sisters of the testator. The doctrine is said to apply to gifts to nephews and nieces only if the testator had placed himself *in loco parentis* to them, but this test appears to be easily satisfied.

The *conditio* is only a presumption on the basis that the omission of the issue was an oversight, and can be rebutted.[28] The onus is on a challenger to prove that this was not so and recent cases have tended to uphold the *conditio* when it has been challenged.[29]

Special legacies

A special legacy is a gift of a particular asset which can be identified as a specific item of the deceased's estate, as distinguished from a general legacy out of the general assets of the estate, a residuary legacy of what is left after other legacies have been met or the rare demonstrative legacy.[30]

A special legacy has many of the features of an assignation to the legatee, who can assert a real right to the particular asset from the moment of death unlike other beneficiaries. However a special legacy is also adeemed (or cancelled) if the object of it is no longer part of the deceased's estate at the time of his death. There is no question of compensation for its value from other sources, and a purely technical decision will be made on whether the object was or was not part of the estate at death. If missives have been concluded for sale of heritage, but no actual conveyance has yet occurred, the heritage remains part of the estate at the crucial time.[31]

---

[23] *Paxton's Trs v. Cowie* (1886) 13 R. 1191
[24] *Roberts' Trs v. Roberts* (1903) 5 F. 541; *Fraser's Trs v. Fraser & Ors*, 1980 S.L.T. 211.
[25] *Spalding v. Spalding's Curator ad Litem*, 1963 S.C. 141.
[26] Law Reform (Miscellaneous Provisions) (Scotland) Act 1968, s.6.
[27] (1891) 18 R. 690.
[28] *McNab v. Brown's Trs*, 1926 S.C. 387.
[29] *Reid's Trs v. Reid*, 1960 S.C. 46; *MacGregor's Trs v. Gray*, 1969 S.L.T. 355.
[30] *Meston's Succession Opinions*, No. 19, p.45.
[31] *Pollock's Trs v. Anderson* (1902) 4 F. 455; see also *Ballantyne's Trs v. Ballantyne's Trs*, 1941 S.C. 35.

Because of their "special" nature, special legacies are the last to suffer abatement if the estate is not large enough to meet all the legacies provided by the will. Other types of legacy (residuary, general and demonstrative) may not have funds to meet them, but the special legacy will be effective if the asset remains in the estate and the debts of the estate can be satisfied without disposing of it.

Cumulative and Substitutional legacies

It sometimes happens that there are multiple testamentary writings but that none of them revoke previous writings. If the writings include multiple legacies to the same person, the question arises whether the writings should be construed as giving all the legacies to that person or whether only one was intended. The results often cause surprise to those who do not get multiple legacies!

Everything depends upon a detailed examination of the will. The working principles will be that if the same amount is given twice to the same person in the same deed, the legatee gets only one of the gifts, but that if the same amount is given in different deeds or different amounts are given in the same deed the presumption will be that they are cumulative.[32]

---

[32] The classic case is *Royal Infirmary of Edinburgh v. Muir's Trs* (1881) 9 R. 352. However the circumstances in *Gillies v. Glasgow Royal Infirmary*, 1961 S.L.T. 93 were such that two separate legacies of the same amount in the same deed were treated as cumulative.

CHAPTER 8

EXECUTORS AND THE ADMINISTRATION OF ESTATES

The Succession Act had a profound effect upon the law affecting executors in the administration of estates. The relevant provisions are mainly contained in Part III of the Act and apply to the administration of the estates of persons dying on or after September 10, 1964.[1] What follows does not purport to be a full account of the position of executors or of the details of administration of estates, but instead an account of the changes effected by the Act.[2]

The general effect was to make the executor, as such, a much more significant figure than he had previously been. Prior to the Act the functions of an executor were confined to the moveable estate of the deceased. In his capacity as executor, he had no concern with the deceased's heritage. Thus while his function was to ingather and distribute moveables after paying moveable debts, the heritage passed on intestacy directly to the heir at law without the intervention of a middleman. The administrative provisions of the Act were designed to extend the executor's competence to the whole estate of the deceased — other than titles of honour, coats of arms, and property falling within the provisos to section 36(2) of the Succession Act. The general policy is put into effect by section 14(1) and the modification of existing statutes.[3] The executor thus became the key figure in the transfer of property on death and a number of difficulties, especially in connection with methods of completion of title to heritage, had to be faced.

Right to the office of executor

The effect of the Succession Act on the order of preference of claims to the office was not entirely clear. In practice there may not be much likelihood of competition for the office, but the principles of the order of preference remain somewhat difficult to determine.

What is clear is that the person entitled to the office of executor in preference to all others is the executor nominated by the deceased. Nothing is said in the 1964 Act about those entitled to office as executors-nominate. Accordingly, the position remains that an executor-nominate may be a person expressly or impliedly appointed by the deceased or one placed in that position by construction under section 3 of the Executors (Scotland) Act 1900.[4]

The normal, and simplest, case is that of the express appointment of an executor, e.g. "I appoint X to be my executor". Equally, it is the practice to

---

[1] 1964 Act, s.37(1)(d).
[2] Full accounts are given in Wilson & Duncan, *Trusts, Trustees and Executors* (2nd ed.) and especially by Eilidh Scobbie in *Currie on Confirmation of Executors* (8th ed.).
[3] 1964 Act, Sched. 2, especially para. 3.
[4] (63 & 64 Vict. c.55).

treat as executors-nominate any persons on whom the deceased has conferred the powers of an executor, even although he may not have used the term "executor". For example, in *Martin v. Ferguson's Trustees*,[5] where the expression used was "I wish my estate to be managed" by specified persons, those persons were to be regarded as executors-nominate.

Constructive appointment as executor-nominate arises under section 3 of the Executors (Scotland) Act 1900 as amended.[6] This provides:

> "Where a testator has not appointed any person to act as his executor, or failing any person so appointed, the testamentary trustees of such testator, original or assumed, or appointed by the Supreme Court or the sheriff court (if any), failing whom any general disponee or universal legatory or residuary legatee appointed by such testator, shall be held to be his executor nominate and entitled to confirmation in that character."

This is a fairly comprehensive coverage of persons whom the deceased might possibly have wished to act as his executor, and it is to be noted that assumed trustees, even if the original trustees have resigned immediately after the assumption, are still entitled to confirmation as executors-nominate.

Provided that it is clear from the whole tenor of the deceased's will, or from the terms of an appointment of trustees by the court, that there is not intended to be any bar to the persons in question taking up office as executors, they will be entitled to that office in preference to all others whose claim is merely through relationship.

It is when the deceased has not appointed executors, either through dying intestate or by not making a nomination in his will, that the rules of preference are less clear. The only provisions in the 1964 Act regulating the right to appointment by the court as executor-dative appear in sections 9(4) and 5(2), and they do not appear to cover the whole situation.

Section 9(4), restating the corresponding provisions in the Intestate Husband's Estate (Scotland) Acts, provides that where a surviving spouse's monetary prior right exhausts the deceased spouse's estate, so that the survivor is entitled to the whole estate, that survivor has the right to be appointed executor. This right is exclusive of all other claimants to the office, the surviving spouse being the only person beneficially interested in the estate.

The other provision in the 1964 Act is that in section 5(2). This also bears a relationship to one of the few previous statutory enactments on the subject — namely, the last part of section 1 of the Intestate Moveable Succession (Scotland) Act 1855.[7] That provided that, in a competition for the office of executor, surviving next of kin were to be preferred to the representatives of predeceasing next of kin, who were given a right of succession for the first time by section 1 of the 1855 Act. Section 5(2) of the 1964 Act provides that the right of representatives to the office of executor is postponed to the right of

---

[5] (1892) 19 R. 474.
[6] (63 & 64 Vict. c.55), s.3, amended Law Reform (Miscellaneous Provisions) (Scotland) Act 1980 (c.55), Sched. 2.
[7] (18 & 19 Vict. c.23).

surviving members of the class, predeceasing members of which they are representing.

In settling the order of preference of rights to the office of executor, the pre-1964 position was that the next of kin (ascertained according to the common law) were primarily entitled to the office. Failing them, at common law the widow as creditor in respect of her jus relictae was entitled to office, followed by other creditors and special legatees. The various statutory amendments to the common law of intestate moveable succession, particularly the Intestate Moveable Succession (Scotland) Act 1855, had the effect of giving the various statutory beneficiaries rights to the office of executor either along with, or postponed to, the next of kin. For example, the right of succession conferred on a mother by section 4 of the 1855 Act gave her also a right to the office of executor-dative *qua* mother, probably even along with the next of kin if they competed. However, the whole order of preference in the office of executor, as also the order of succession, hinged on the next of kin under the common law rules, with possible additions in respect of statutory beneficiaries.

Under the 1964 Act, however, the common law concept of next of kin is no longer relevant in determining the order of the beneficial succession to the estate of a deceased person. Instead there is a statutory list of those entitled to succeed, mainly specified in section 2. A question therefore arose whether the concept of the next of kin is still relevant in competitions for the office of executor-dative or whether there is now a new basic concept that the right to be executor depends on the existence of a right of beneficial succession under the 1964 Act.

There is no inherent improbability in the existence of a different method of establishing the right to the executorship from that employed in settling the beneficial succession, and it would seem that it is still correct to appoint an executor *qua* next of kin if he falls within the common law category, even though his right of succession may be by a different title under the 1964 Act. There is nothing in the Act to alter the previous rule under which the next of kin had the pre-eminent right.[x] This is fortified by the provisions of Schedules 1 and 2 of the Act of Sederunt (Confirmation of Executors) 1964 which continue to provide for decerniture of an executor-dative *qua* next of kin.

At common law the class nearest in degree to the deceased in which there were surviving members was the class of next of kin, the spouse, mother and maternal relatives not being counted for this purpose. In other words, the order was children and remoter descendants, then brothers and sisters german and their descendants, then brothers and sisters of the half blood consanguinean and their descendants, then the father, then his collaterals and ascendants on the same principles.

On the analogy of the treatment of the purely statutory beneficiaries under the previous law, those who have a right of succession under the 1964 Act, though not being in the category of next of kin, would seem to be entitled in a competition to be executors along with the next of kin. It seems doubtful whether the next of kin could be completely ousted by a statutory beneficiary,

---

[x] *Bennett v. Rennie*, 1988 S.C.L.R. 307. See *Currie on Confirmation* (8th ed.), paras 6.07–6.13

although there can be cases where the next of kin have no rights of beneficial succession. For example, a deceased might be survived by a spouse and by a paternal uncle. Even if the estate were large enough to leave a surplus after the surviving spouse's prior rights, the free estate after deduction of legal rights would not fall to the uncle, who is the next of kin, but to the surviving spouse under section 2(1)(e). Admittedly, the uncle would be unlikely to take active steps to seek the office of executor in these circumstances, but it seems very doubtful whether, if he made one, his claim could be rejected in favour of that of the spouse. The more probable course would seem to be to make two appointments, one *qua* next of kin and one *qua* surviving spouse. The surviving spouse's exclusive right under section 9(4) would not apply here, being limited to cases where the survivor takes the whole estate by virtue of the monetary prior right.

The situation which seems to have arisen most frequently in practice since the Succession Act is that of an elderly surviving spouse who is either *incapax* or unwilling to act as executor and a son who is willing to act. In these circumstances, it would seem to be perfectly competent to appoint the son executor in his capacity as next of kin, possibly coupled with a declinature by the spouse if the spouse is the sole beneficiary.

Apart from this type of situation, it is probably true that only those who have beneficial rights of succession under the 1964 Act will seek to be appointed executors. The office is usually regarded as a burden rather than as a benefit to be actively sought. But the result would seem to be that those of the statutory beneficiaries who apply and who are also next of kin should be appointed and confirmed in the character of next of kin. Any statutory beneficiary who is not one of the next of kin should be appointed and confirmed in his statutory character. Thus a mother would be confirmed *qua* mother, never being one of the next of kin, while the father would be confirmed *qua* father when there were also brothers and sisters, so that his right of succession was purely statutory, but *qua* next of kin when there were no brothers and sisters. Similarly, when the succession has opened to collaterals of the half blood, there is now no distinction between the half blood consanguinean and the half blood uterine. But only the half blood consanguinean could be next of kin at common law. Hence, if two persons sought appointment as executor, one in each category of collateral of the half blood, the half blood consanguinean would be confirmed *qua* next of kin but the half blood uterine would be confirmed qua brother or sister of the half blood "related through their mother" in the words of section 3.

To talk of "competition" for the office of executor can sometimes be misleading, for it is not the case that the number who may be executors is limited or that only those at the head of the order of preference may be appointed. Anyone who is directly entitled to share in the succession may be appointed without special intimation to other persons having an equal or even a preferable claim to the office. All applicants having the same or an equal right in the order of preference are entitled to be conjoined.

Duties of an executor

The executor's first responsibility is to ingather the whole estate of the deceased with due dispatch. The mere nomination, or even judicial appointment, of an executor does not of itself give him the authority to do this. Once his right to the office has been established in this way, he then requires confirmation by the appropriate Commissary Court before he has a title to intromit with the estate, and it is this confirmation which saves him from the penalties applicable to a vitious intromitter. However, confirmation purges the vitiosity of prior intromissions, so he is not debarred from taking interim measures of administration in connection with the estate.

The second major function of the executor is to use the estate so ingathered to meet the liabilities of the estate. No change was made in this position by the Succession Act so that, as before, the executor acts independently of both creditors and beneficiaries, and subject to the limitation of his liability to the value of the deceased's estate, he is *eadem persona cum defuncto.* If he discovers, or should have discovered, that the estate is absolutely insolvent, an executor has the duty to petition for sequestration of the estate or the appointment of a judicial factor. The sanction is that any intromissions after that date render him liable to the penalties of vitious intromission even although he has obtained confirmation from the court.[9]

An executor cannot be compelled to pay any debts (other than privileged debts) before the expiry of a period of six months within which creditors may claim equal ranking. Although the Succession Act does bring both heritage and moveables under his control, it has not entirely assimilated heritage and moveables for the purposes of succession rights. Thus, in order to permit an accurate value to be struck for the moveables subject to legal rights, the executor must still allocate debts between heritage and moveables, and section 14(3) specifically preserves the rules relating to the incidence of liability for debts. The incidence of inheritance tax on heritage and moveables differs from the former rules for estate duty, so that a specific legacy of a house does not now bear the burden of the tax applicable to the house.[10] There is no longer an heir to contrast with the executor, so that the division "as between heir and executor" has now become a division "as between heritage and moveables". Indeed references in any enactment to "heirs" now include a reference to executors.[11]

Finally, having satisfied the debts, the executor is under a duty to account for the balance of the estate to those entitled to it. This means that the primary responsibility for determining who is entitled to it falls upon him, although the courts may be invoked by requiring a claimant to establish his claim or by raising a special case or multiplepoinding. In the ordinary case, however, the matter will be settled by the executor and there is some onus on him, possibly only in the interests of self-protection, to search out beneficiaries. It would be at least advisable for him in an intestacy to investigate the family tree

---

[9] Bankruptcy (Scotland) Act 1985 (c.66), s.8(4).
[10] *Cowie's Trs, Petrs*, 1982 S.L.T. 326 and Inheritance Tax Act 1984, s.211.
[11] Sched. 2, para. 2(b).

sufficiently to establish that there are no relatives closer to the deceased than those of whose claims he has notice.

However, in view of the practical difficulties which would arise when an illegitimate person is, or might be, involved, the Law Reform (Miscellaneous Provisions) (Scotland) Act 1968[12] gives the executor some protection. Section 7 absolves him of the necessity to establish that there is no illegitimate person who has a right of succession or whose existence would affect rights of succession. In addition the executor is not required to establish that there is no paternal relative of an illegitimate person.[13] He is exempted from personal liability to any person whose claim depends on illegitimacy if he had no notice of the claim at the time of distribution. The claimant's right is not barred and he may take any steps open to him to recover property from those holding it, but the executor's personal liability to him is avoided.

If express claims by illegitimate persons (or which depend on the existence of illegitimate persons) are presented to the executor, he will decide on their validity in the usual way, and in cases of doubt will require the claimant to prove his relationship. This proof may now take the form of a declarator of parentage, which gives rise to a general presumption (*i.e.* one not limited in effect to the parties to the declarator) to the same effect as the declarator.[14]

Similarly, section 24(2) of the Succession Act provides that an executor or trustee may distribute the deceased's estate without ascertaining that no adoption order has been made by virtue of which any person is or may be entitled to an interest therein. An intolerable burden would be placed on an executor if he had to ensure not only that the deceased himself had never adopted a child, but also that his parents, or either of them, or indeed any other relative had never adopted a child. He is therefore freed from liability to any such person of whose claim he had no notice.

For carrying out his extended functions, an executor-dative is given by section 20 all the powers, privileges and immunities of a gratuitous trustee and is subject to all the restrictions on such a trustee. This includes, for example, the duty to avoid acting as *auctor in rem suam*.[15] The term "trustee" in the Trusts (Scotland) Acts 1921 and 1961 now includes executors-dative. This does not, however, exempt an executor-dative from finding caution for his intromissions, nor does it give him any power to resign or to assume new trustees.

A problem which has been the subject of some discussion is whether an executor has a duty to tell a spouse or descendant of the possibility of claiming legal rights instead of accepting the provisions of the deceased's will. It can be argued that an executor has the usual duty of a trustee to uphold the trust and thus to carry out the terms of the will, so that any advice to beneficiaries on how to defeat the trust purposes would be contrary to his duty. In practice, however, an executor will often take the view that some information should be

---

[12] (c.70).
[13] Law Reform (Miscellaneous Provisions) (Scotland) Act 1968, s.7(c) added by the Law Reform (Parent and Child) (Scotland) Act 1986 to replace s.4(3) of the Succession (Scotland) Act 1964.
[14] Law Reform (Parent and Child) (Scotland) Act 1986 (c.9), ss. 7 and 5(3).
[15] *Inglis v. Inglis*, 1983 S.L.T. 437.

given, possibly in a guarded form suggesting separate advice, and this compromise would seem to be a sound course of action.

Obtaining confirmation

Before obtaining confirmation an executor-dative (but not normally an executor-nominate) must find caution for his administration of the estate.[16] The amount of caution, unless judicially restricted, is the full gross amount of the deceased's estate and is usually provided by means of a bond of caution from an insurance company. There is, however, considerable doubt whether the rules relating to caution serve a useful purpose. When the executor is also the sole beneficiary there is no need to protect the beneficiary against the possibility that as executor he might defraud himself. The cost of a bond in such circumstances is useless expenditure, and there is now a provision that if an intestate's spouse is executor-dative and is also entitled to the whole estate by virtue of prior rights, there is no requirement to find caution. A serious gap in the protection afforded by bonds of caution arises when items such as civil service gratuities are involved. Such gratuities will not normally be included in the estate confirmed to, and if the executor should fail to account to the beneficiaries for the amount of the gratuity, caution may not protect the true beneficiary.[17]

As a consequence of the assimilation of heritage and moveables, and of the extension to heritage of the executor's authority, confirmation is now granted to the heritage as well as the moveables. Before the Succession Act came into force, an executor, *qua* executor, had authority over moveable estate only and was confirmed only to the moveable estate. He did prepare an inventory which included details of heritage, but that was for taxation purposes. For purposes of confirmation, the inventory was solely of moveable property. Now, however, the inventory reproduced in the confirmation includes the whole estate, heritable and moveable, and the bond of caution is for the same amount.

The inclusion of heritage in the confirmation is provided for by section 14(2) of the Succession Act, and a general power of regulation of procedure is conferred on the Court of Session by section 22. Section 22(1) provides that the court shall have power "to regulate the procedure to be followed, and to prescribe the form and content of any petition, writ or other document to be used, in connection with the confirmation of executors in cases where, by virtue of this Act, heritable property devolves upon the executor".

In virtue of these and other powers, the Act of Sederunt (Confirmation of Executors) 1964 as amended by the Act of Sederunt (Confirmation of Executors Amendment) 1966 provides that the inventory embodied in a confirmation must include such a description of heritage "as will be sufficient to identify the property or interest therein as a separate item in the deceased

---

[16] 1964 Act, s.20, proviso.

[17] See (1967) 12 J.L.S. 258, and the remarkable case of *Harrison v. Butters*, 1969 S.L.T. 183 in which a divorced wife represented herself as the widow and obtained confirmation with the backing of a bond of caution. When the true widow appeared, it seems that the caution provided no protection as it would have been void from essential error as to identity.

person's estate". The intention is that something less than a full conveyancing description will be adequate, so that, for instance, a mere statement of the street name and number would be acceptable.

Vesting of estate in an executor

Here one is concerned solely with vesting of property in the executor and not with the separate issue of completion of title through the executor. As a consequence of the general extension of the executor's functions to include heritage, section 14(1) provides that:

> "[O]n the death of any person (whether testate or intestate) every part of his estate (whether consisting of moveable property or heritable property) falling to be administered under the law of Scotland shall, by virtue of confirmation thereto, vest for the purposes of administration in the executor thereby confirmed and shall be administered and disposed of according to law by such executor."

The whole estate to which he has confirmed thus vests in the executor. The heritage which previously vested directly in the heir at law in cases of intestacy or in a trustee (who might of course be the executor) if one was appointed, now vests directly in the executor qua executor by virtue of confirmation. As such, the executor may exercise all the powers arising from a vested right, including completion of title.[18] The executor, unless he is an executor-creditor, must confirm to the whole estate, including agricultural leases and interests therein.[19] If any part of the deceased's estate should prove to have been omitted from the confirmation, it is necessary for the executor to expede an eik to his confirmation in order to vest the omitted property in him. It is only estate to which he has confirmed which vests in the executor.

Supplementary provisions about the effect of confirmation in estates including entailed property and special destinations appear in section 18(1) and (2). Despite the prohibition on the creation of new entails which has existed since 1914[20] there are apparently about 1,000 entails still in existence in Scotland, justifying special provisions. Section 18(1) provides that, on the death of an heir of entail in possession, the entailed property, though not regarded as part of the deceased's estate, nevertheless vests by confirmation in the executor in order that it may be conveyed to the person next entitled to it under the entail. The vesting in the executor is for that purpose only and, apparently, if no such conveyance to the next person entitled is necessary, there is no vesting in the executor at all.

Section 18(2) makes very similar provisions in respect of heritage subject to a special destination.[21] On the death of a person entitled to property which is

---

[18] *Robertson, Petr*, 1978 S.L.T. (Sh.Ct.) 30; *Garvie's Trs v. Garvie's Tutors*, 1975 S.L.T. 94. This may possibly mean that the spouse of a single executor could have occupancy rights under the Matrimonial Homes (Family Protection) (Scotland) Act 1981.
[19] *Cormack v. McIldowie's Exrs*, 1975 S.L.T. 214; *Rotherwick's Trs v. Hope*, 1975 S.L.T. 187.
[20] Entail (Scotland) Act 1914 (4 & 5 Geo. 5 c.43), s.2.
[21] One definition of a "special destination" appears in *Cormack v. McIldowie's Exrs*, 1975 S.L.T. 214, *per* L.J.-C. Wheatley at 218. The definition may not cover all types.

subject to a special destination in favour of a third party, provided the deceased had either no power to revoke the destination or has in fact not revoked it, the property in question vests by confirmation in the executor solely for the purpose of conveyance to the person next entitled to it, if such conveyance is necessary.

The basis for this seemingly odd provision is that property subject to an unrevoked special destination is not part of the deceased's estate for the purposes of the Succession Act.[22] Thus the executor could not normally confirm to it at all. However, in most cases the person called in the destination requires to have a title formally conferred on him, and the function of section 18(2) is to permit a limited vesting in the executor to enable him to grant that title. Thus it is only when the substitute requires a title that confirmation vests the property in the executor, and there is no vesting (indeed it is probably incompetent to confirm) if the substitute does not require a title.

The ordinary survivorship destination is the main example of the situation in which no title is required. Thus in these cases, it appears that his executor should not confirm to the predeceaser's *pro indiviso* share and that a purported confirmation would be ineffective.[23] Of course, if the deceased had validly revoked the destination, the property is part of the deceased's estate and vests fully in the executor by virtue of section 14(1).

If there has been restricted vesting in an executor of property subject to a destination, the docket procedure for transfer is available and the protection given by section 17 applies.[24]

Completion of title to heritage

Various points in connection with the completion of title to heritage arise out of the provisions of the Succession Act. The basic proposition, contained in section 15(1), is that confirmation is of itself a valid title in the executor to heritage included in the confirmation and which has vested in him by virtue of section 14. This result is achieved by the clumsy device of providing that references to heritable securities in section 5(2) of the Conveyancing (Scotland) Act 1924 are to be construed as including a reference to any interest in heritage which has vested in an executor. That section of the 1924 Act made confirmation a valid title to heritable securities included in the confirmation and therefore now gives a title to any heritage included in the confirmation.

However, a proviso to section 15(1) requires that for this purpose an appropriate description of the heritage must be included in the confirmation. This meant that, although property might vest in the executor without a description being included at all (*e.g.* in the case of an English probate certified in Scotland) or where the description which did exist was defective (*e.g.* when under the original Act of Sederunt of 1964 a full conveyancing description may have been called for), he had no title in these cases. Any need for the description to be a full and formal one was removed by the Act of Sederunt

---

[22] 1964 Act, s.36(2)(a).
[23] McDonald (1965) 10 J.L.S. at 73.
[24] 1964 Act, s.18(4).

(Confirmation of Executors Amendment) 1966, but the problem over English probates or letters of administration — which contain no details of the particular items of property in the estate — remained until 1968. Even though the process of certification in Scotland gave them the status of implied confirmation it seemed that the proviso to section 15(1) prevented them from being used as links in title. The difficulty was eventually resolved retrospectively by section 19 of the Law Reform (Miscellaneous Provisions) (Scotland) Act 1968. Section 15(1) is deemed always to have had effect as if the proviso requiring a description applied only to confirmations other than implied confirmations. The result is that English probates and letters of administration are now just as valid as links in title as Scottish confirmations. As between England and Wales, Scotland and Northern Ireland, certification and resealing are no longer necessary[25] but this change does not alter the validity of probates as links in title.

Another problem which arose shortly after the Succession Act came into force concerned the continued competency of using the procedure of section 10 of the Conveyancing (Scotland) Act 1874. That section, together with the whole provisions relating to services and petitions by persons having only personal rights, was repealed by the Succession Act. However, the Succession Act is not retrospective, and section 37(1)(d) specifies that nothing in the Act is to "affect the administration, winding up or distribution of or the making up of title to any part of the estate of any person who died before the commencement" of the Act. Hence it was readily accepted that a living person might still have himself served heir to someone who died before September 10, 1964, and indeed the Act itself contemplates this in section 35 by giving authority for rearranging the jurisdiction over services. In section 10 cases the issue was clouded by the fact that there was usually a second, post-Succession Act, death of the person who had only a personal right. However, despite this death, the question still is one of completion of title to the estate of the last infeft proprietor, who died before the Act, and petitions may still be presented under section 10 of the 1874 Act.[26] However it will be noted that if the proprietor with only a personal right died on or after September 10, 1964, his heirs entitled to petition will be those with rights of succession under the Succession Act.[27]

The effect of the abolition of the process of service of heirs in the case of deaths after the commencement of the Succession Act was that there was no longer any machinery by which an heir of a last surviving trustee, called as heir of provision could establish that he was the heir. His entitlement to office was preserved, but he had no means of proving it. For some time after 1964 the problem had been masked by the fact that title was usually being made up to the estate of a person who died before the commencement of the Succession Act so that service of heirs remained competent under section 37(1)(d).

---

[25] Administration of Estates Act 1971 (c.25). See also *infra.*, pp.139-140.
[26] *Duthie's Trs, Petrs*, 1966 S.L.T. (Sh.Ct.) 24; *Robertson, Petr*, 1978 S.L.T. (Sh.Ct.) 30; Allan, "Completion of Title" (1978) 23 J.L.S. 438.
[27] *Findlay, Petr*, 1975 S.L.T. (Sh.Ct.) 46.

However there was no answer if the last surviving trustee died after the commencement of the Act.[28]

The Law Reform (Miscellaneous Provisions) (Scotland) Act 1980, section 6 provided a remedy by the remarkable process of reviving the sections of the Titles to Land Consolidation (Scotland) Act 1868 dealing with service of heirs. The revival is for the limited purpose of providing machinery for heirs at law to establish that they were the heirs of provision and for that purpose only.

The provisions of the Succession Act making confirmation a link in the title to heritage opened up a new stream of title through the executor. It was not immediately obvious what effect this had upon the alternative method of completion of title through the deceased's will in cases where he left one, and even yet the position is somewhat clouded on certain points. It seems likely that the intention was to make the confirmation the only valid link in title, but this was not in fact done.

The position seems to be that in all cases where a will contains a general conveyance to testamentary trustees or executors-nominate, title may be completed or deduced by using the will as a link. There is, however, grave doubt whether it is competent for a special legatee to whom a direct bequest of heritage is made to complete or deduce his title by use of the will.[29] Difficulties can be avoided by following the strong recommendation of the Professors that the confirmation should be used in preference to the will. It will be noted that use of the confirmation permits the use of the simplified docket procedure for transfer and gives the protection of section 17, which would not seem to apply if title is taken through the will.

Section 15(2) made a very valuable innovation by permitting an executor to transfer heritage to beneficiaries by means of the simplified docket procedure. Where heritage has vested in him *qua* executor and "it is necessary for him in distributing the estate to transfer that property —

(a) to any person in satisfaction of a claim to legal rights or the prior rights of a surviving spouse out of the estate, or
(b) to any person entitled to share in the estate by virtue of this Act, or
(c) to any person entitled to take the said property under any testamentary disposition of the deceased",

the executor may effect the transfer merely by endorsing a docket in the form specified in Schedule 1 either on the confirmation itself or on a separate certificate of confirmation relating to the particular item of heritage in question. The docket specifies the title of the executor and beneficiary, identifies the property transferred, and is subscribed by the executor. There should preferably also be one witness. In view of its simplicity the procedure is widely used, usually by docketing a certificate of confirmation to avoid including the details of the whole of the deceased's estate among the titles.

The docketed confirmation cannot be recorded *de plano* in the Register of Sasines, and therefore acts only as a midcouple or link in title. Section 15(2)

---

[28] *Skinner, Petr*, 1976 S.L.T. 60 and *Browning, Petr*, 1976 S.L.T. (Sh.Ct.) 87.
[29] Opinion of the Professors of Conveyancing (1965) 10 J.L.S. 153 and notes issued by the Law Society (1966) 11 J.L.S. 84.

specifically envisages its use in this way. It will therefore be necessary to register it for preservation to avoid the possibility of it being lost or mislaid. However, it is a transfer to the beneficiary, not merely a statement of who at the deceased's death was entitled to the heritage, so that it would be incompetent to execute a docket in his favour after the beneficiary's death.[30]

Other methods of transfer are not excluded by the existence of the docket procedure, so that a beneficiary who anticipates no change in his title over a substantial period may choose either to take and record a full conveyance from the executor or to expede and record a notice of title specifying the docket as a midcouple.

Taking advantage of the confirmation as vesting estate in an executor also permits the completion of title in cases where heritage has been sold but not conveyed. It would be possible to proceed through the will if there has been a general trust conveyance, but in any event confirmation to the heritage would give the appropriate executor a title.

Similarly, a method of completing title to heritage in a lapsed trust now exists via the executor of the last surviving trustee. The Executors (Scotland) Act 1900, section 6 as amended by Schedule 2 to the Succession Act, provides that:

> "When any sole or last surviving trustee ... has died with any property (whether heritable or moveable) in Scotland vested in him as trustee ... confirmation by his executors (if any) to the proper estate of such trustee ... shall ... be valid, and available to such executors for recovering such property and for assigning and transferring the same ... directly to the beneficiaries entitled thereto ... provided always that a note or statement of such property shall have been appended to any inventory or additional inventory of the estate of such deceased trustee ... given up by his executors in Scotland, and duly confirmed."[31]

A very valuable measure of protection is given to those acquiring property from an executor. Supplementing the previous provisions protecting those who acquire moveable property from an executor, section 17 protects those who in good faith and for value have acquired title to any interest in, or security over, heritable property vested in the executor. If the title was acquired directly or indirectly from the executor or from a person deriving title directly from the executor, no challenge to the acquirer's title may be made on the ground that the executor's confirmation was reducible or even that it has been reduced. Equally, where the title was acquired from a person who himself derived title directly from the executor, it is not a competent ground of challenge that the executor should not have transferred the property to him. This means that there is no need for third parties to investigate the validity of a confirmation.

---

[30] (1966) 11 J.L.S. 36.
[31] *Currie on Confirmation* (8th ed.), para. 16.04. See *supra*, pp.125-126 for service as heir of provision in a trust.

Leases

The right of a tenant of land is heritable, and thus it is an asset of the estate to which the tenant's executor is required to confirm. Section 16 of the Succession Act expressly confers on an executor certain powers over leases or tenancies included in the estate and to which he has confirmed. Leases cannot, however, be included in the deceased's estate if they were "liferent leases" expiring on his death. Section 36(2) includes in the definition of estate only cases "where the deceased immediately before his death held the interest of a tenant under a tenancy or lease which was not expressed to expire on his death". The reference to expiring on the deceased's death qualifies the nouns "tenancy" and "lease" (and not the "interest") so that, if a lease carries on or is capable of being carried on past the death of the tenant, the fact that the tenant's interest ceased at his death does not prevent the lease from being part of his estate.[32]

It is essential that executors should confirm to the tenant's interest in a lease. It is true that they have not always in the past done so, presumably because the right of a tenant has not always had a measurable value which could be transferred. However, the importance of confirmation was emphasised in *Rotherwick's Trustees v. Hope & Others.*[33] The executors had not confirmed to the deceased's lease of a farm. The lease had therefore not vested in the executors of the tenant, who therefore did not have the powers conferred by section 16. As they had not disposed of the lease within one year,[34] the lease had terminated and decree of removing was granted. Agricultural and crofting tenancies do have a value which is part of the estate (even if the principles of valuation are not always very clear) and must be confirmed to.[35]

The first of the particular powers granted to executors by section 16 concerns the transfer of the lease or tenancy. Section 16(2) provides that where the deceased has not made a valid bequest of his lease,[36] or, such a bequest having been made, it is either not accepted by the legatee[37] or is null and void under the statutory provisions relating to agricultural leases, the executor is entitled to transfer the lease to any person entitled to succeed on intestacy. This is so even if there is in the lease a condition either express or implied prohibiting assignation (if there is no prohibition on assignation, the executor has no need to rely on this statutory power). If the executor does have to rely on the statutory power *i.e.* when there is a prohibition on assignation he cannot transfer the lease to any person other than one of those with rights of intestate

---

[32] *Cormack v. McIldowie's Exrs*, 1975 S.L.T. 214 at 217.

[33] 1975 S.L.T. 187.

[34] s.16(3)(b).

[35] In *Inglis v. Inglis*, 1983 S.L.T. 437 the assignee of a farm lease was able to obtain a settlement of £35,000 plus a lease of a smaller area from the landlord. This was held to be part of the deceased's estate in a settlement with the other heirs.

[36] as to which see section 29 and p.103, supra.

[37] If the bequest is accepted (even without timeous notification) an intestate transfer is no longer possible: *Coats v. Logan*, 1985 S.L.T. 221.

succession without the landlord's consent. However, section 16 does not apply where there is a valid destination in the lease itself.[38]

It was pointed out in debate in the House of Commons that these provisions give the executor greater powers over the lease than the deceased himself had. The power of bequest of leases specified in section 29 applies only in the face of an implied prohibition on assignation and is not exercisable in face of an express prohibition. The executor's power of transfer transcends both express and implied prohibitions on assignation in the lease. The apparent anomaly can, however, be explained by considering the purpose of prohibitions on assignation. This used to be to ensure that the tenant's heir at law would succeed to the tenancy. In consequence of the virtual abolition of the status of heir at law, provision had to be made to ensure that a single tenant would be found to continue the tenancy. A landlord could not reasonably be required to accept fragmentation of the tenancy. All heritage now vests in the executor, and therefore there has to be some form of assignation by him if the tenancy is to continue at all. Thus he is given power to transfer the lease, irrespective of the prohibition, to a single member of the class entitled to share in the deceased's estate. In effect this is another method of finding an "heir at law," but it does have the merit that the executor may be able to find a person who is genuinely interested in continuing the tenancy, which was not always the case under the old rules for selection of the heir at law. The different conditions which apply when the question is one of bequest by the tenant himself would seem to justify a different approach there.

Among the consequential modifications to existing statutes specified in Schedule 2 are provisions taking account of the powers of an executor to transfer leases. For example section 21 of the Agricultural Holdings (Scotland) Act 1949, which dealt with the landlord's right to object to the heir at law of the tenant succeeding to the holding, was replaced by a new section 21, which now appears as section 12 of the Agricultural Holdings (Scotland) Act 1991.[39] This deals with the landlord's right to object to the acquirer of a lease. The provisions, although similar to those of the original section 21, are amended to meet the new situation. Thus the first step is now for the acquirer to notify the landlord of his acquisition of the holding within 21 days of the acquisition or as soon as possible thereafter.[40] Previously the landlord could always find out who was the tenant's heir at law, but he must now be told who is to acquire the lease. Thereafter it is up to the landlord to set the procedure of objection in motion by serving a counter-notice within one month. It will be noted that the landlord may have to possess his soul in patience for a very long time, for at least a year may elapse from the death of the tenant before the landlord can find out who the acquirer of the lease is to be.

Section 16(3) and (4) of the 1964 Act provide for termination of the lease, irrespective of its provisions or of any statutory or other provisions, either by the executor or by the landlord, if the executor is satisfied that he cannot

---

[38] *Reid's Trs v. Macpherson*, 1975 S.L.T. 101.
[39] (c.55).
[40] *Garvie's Trs v. Garvie's Tutors*, 1975 S.L.T. 94: *Coats v. Logan*, 1985 S.L.T. 221: Gill, *The Law of Agricultural Holdings in Scotland* (2nd ed.), Chap. 34.

dispose of the lease to an acquirer or if he has in fact not disposed of it within the time limit specified. Note that if the executor simply delays in disposal of the lease, it is liable to be lost to the beneficiaries. Only he can dispose of it, but if he fails to do so within the time limit, the lease may be terminated.[41] Beneficiaries will have to be vigilant to protect their rights.

The time limit is normally one year from the date of death of the deceased, but in the case of an agricultural lease which is the subject of a petition to the Land Court under the Crofters' Holdings (Scotland) Act 1886, section 16, or an application thereto under the Agricultural Holdings (Scotland) Act 1991, the period of one year runs from the date of the determination or withdrawal of the petition or application. These statutory provisions relate to the situation when the landlord seeks to object to the legatee of a lease as his tenant. Similar provisions are now made for crofts also. The one-year time limit within which the lease must be transferred may be extended by agreement between landlord and executor or, failing agreement, by the sheriff on summary application by the executor.[42] However, it is the executor who must seek the extension. It would seem that the beneficiaries could not prevent an executor from procrastinating until the year was up, thereby permitting the landlord to terminate the lease.

Due notice must be given of any such termination by the landlord or executor. For agricultural leases it is such period as may be agreed or, failing agreement, the familiar period of not less than one year nor more than two years ending with such term of Whitsunday or Martinmas as may be specified in the notice.[43] In the case of any other lease, the maximum period of notice for this purpose is six months, without prejudice to any statutory provision prescribing a shorter period of notice for the lease in question.[44] The period of notice required to terminate a lease of an ordinary dwelling-house would normally be substantially less than six months.

The fact that executor and landlord may have a power to terminate a lease does not prejudice any claim by either party to the lease for compensation or damages in respect of the termination. However, to preserve the limitation of the liability of the executor, any award of compensation or damages in respect of a termination by the executor is enforceable only against the estate of the deceased and not against the executor personally.[45]

The special provisions of section 16(6) and (7) take account of the fact that a lease is vested in an executor only qua executor in considering questions based on breaches of the conditions of a lease. In the case of agricultural leases the Land Court is not to make an order for removal under section 3 of the Small Landholders and Agricultural Holdings (Scotland) Act 1931 or section 13 of the Crofters (Scotland) Act 1955, and the arbiter is not to make an order in favour of the landlord in a question under section 22(2)(e) of the

---

[41] *Sproat v. South West Services (Galloway) Ltd*, 2000 G.W.D. 37-1416; *Lord Rotherwick's Trs v. Hope*, 1975 S.L.T. 187; *Gifford v. Buchanan*, 1983 S.L.T. 613.
[42] The application must be made within the year and is not competent after the landlord has given notice of termination: *Gifford v. Buchanan, supra.*
[43] 1964 Act, s.16(4)(a).
[44] *ibid.*, s.16(4)(b) and proviso.
[45] *ibid.*, s.16(5).

Agricultural Holdings (Scotland) Act 1991 unless the court or arbiter is satisfied that it is reasonable, having regard to the fact that the interest is vested in the executor in his capacity as executor, that it should be made.

In the case of non-agricultural leases, the court is not to grant decree in an action of removing based on a breach of a condition of the lease unless it is satisfied that the condition alleged to have been breached is one which it is reasonable to expect the executor to have observed, having regard to the fact that the interest is vested in him in his capacity as an executor.

Finally it is provided that the detailed provisions relating to bequest of agricultural leases specified in the Crofters' Holdings (Scotland) Act 1886, the Agricultural Holdings (Scotland) Act 1991 and the Crofters (Scotland) Act 1955, as amended, are to have effect notwithstanding that the lease, or the deceased's interest therein, has vested in the executor for purposes of administration.[46]

One particular difficulty facing executors in connection with agricultural leases shows up in acute form a general problem of Scots law. It is not at all clear in Scotland who owns a deceased's property between the date of his death and the appointment and confirmation of his executor. As there is no longer an heir at law to succeed automatically to heritage, this means that a landlord may encounter severe difficulties in attempting to serve a notice to quit if the tenant's executor has not yet been appointed. If the tenant dies shortly before a term of Whitsunday or Martinmas, the landlord may be at least delayed in exercising his right to obtain possession by being unable to find someone on whom to serve notice before the term. Various suggestions for methods of coping with this problem have been put forward and the Scottish Law Commission has recommended that any notice to be given under a lease should continue to be addressed to the deceased party to the lease as if he were still alive. That notice would be effective.[47]

Satisfaction of legacies in kind

One of the perennial problems facing an executor arises when it is desired to satisfy legacies in kind rather than in cash. In that situation there seem to be unending disputes about the allocation of particular assets and the values to be attached to them.[48] The only real answer is to make proper provision in the will for the transfer of assets *in specie*.

If there is a true special legacy, it operates as an assignation of the particular subject of the gift, and the executor has no discretion about how to satisfy the legacy. He simply transfers the property specially identified. However, apart from special legacies, and the special element of demonstrative legacies, an executor is free to convey any asset to any beneficiary in full or part

---

[46] *ibid.*, s.16(8).
[47] *Report on Recovery of Possession of Heritable Property*, Scot. Law Com. No. 118 (1989), recommendation 69. This does not appear to have been adopted in the Agricultural Holdings (Scotland) Act 1991. For the similar problem in crofting law, see MacCuish and Flyn, *Crofting Law*, para. 7.05.
[48] See for example *Coats's Trs v. Coats*, 1914 S.C. 723.

satisfaction of his share. The choice is that of the executor and not of the beneficiary.

A particularly significant decision is *Cochrane's Exrs v. Inland Revenue.*[49] In this case the executors were held liable for capital gains tax even though the residuary legatee, with a vested right to the whole residue, was not so liable. The legatee argued that he was entitled to the whole assets from the moment of the deceased's death and was entitled to call for delivery of the assets. The successful position of the Revenue was that a residuary legatee is entitled to what is left after the executor has exercised his discretionary powers and cannot give directions to the executor about particular assets. It was even emphasised that executors are not bound to consider the views of a residuary beneficiary before realising any part of the estate.

This illustrates that no general beneficiary has any right to any particular asset, with the result that the executor is free to allocate the whole of a shareholding to one beneficiary and is not bound to divide it equally between them all. The important proviso is that a proper valuation of the shares must be used, and the valuation for purposes of division must be that at the date of the distribution, not the date of death values in the inventory. Pecuniary legatees are entitled only to assets which, at the date of transfer to them, amount to the value of their legacy.

---

[49] 1975 S.L.T. 6.

CHAPTER 9

PRIVATE INTERNATIONAL LAW

Problems of private international law arise in practice far more frequently than is usually thought, especially in the field of succession. Every Scottish estate of any size tends to include shares in English companies and therefore involves some aspect of private international law, even if it is no more than the question of the validity of a Scottish confirmation in England. The oil industry is international in its personnel, and problems frequently arise about wills and rights of inheritance under different legal systems. The authoritative and essential work is Anton, *Private International Law*.[1] There is very useful material concerning administration of estates with a foreign element in *Currie on Confirmation*.[2] What follows is no more than an attempt to set out the broad principles as they apply to the law of succession in Scotland and reference should be made to these authorities for detailed consideration of problems.

The Succession Act does not purport to affect or alter the rules of private international law. Section 37(2) expressly preserves the pre-existing law by providing that "[n]othing in this Act shall be construed as affecting the operation of any rule of law applicable immediately before the commencement of this Act to the choice of the system of law governing the administration, winding up or distribution of the estate, or part of the estate, of any deceased person".

Intestate succession

Put very briefly, the result is that the Scots law of intestate succession governs the succession to the moveable estate of a person whose last domicile was in Scotland, irrespective of where the property may be situated (subject always to a different view being taken by the legal system having control over the property).[3] It also means that Scots law governs the devolution of immoveable property situated in Scotland, irrespective of the owner's domicile. These follow as aspects of the twin propositions that succession to moveables is governed by the *lex domicilii* of the deceased whereas succession to immoveables is governed by the *lex situs* of the property.

The classification of particular items as moveable or immoveable falls to be performed by the *lex situs* of the property and is not necessarily identical with any classification used by that system for its own internal purposes. In

---

[1] 2nd ed., 1990, esp. Chaps. 26 & 27. See also Maher, "Private International Law", *Cases and Materials* and Stair Memorial Encyclopaedia: The Laws of Scotland, Vol. 25, under "Wills and Succession" and Vol. 17, under "Private International Law".
[2] Edited by E.M. Scobbie (8th ed.). Major works primarily from the English standpoint include Cheshire & North, *Private International Law* (13th ed., 1999)and Dicey & Morris, *Conflict of Laws* (13th ed., 2000).
[3] *Bruce v. Bruce* (1790) 3 Pat. 163.

particular, it is not identical with the classification as heritable or moveable in Scotland or as real or personal in England.[4] Some items may be heritable (*e.g.* by destination) for the purposes of Scots private law, but still moveable as opposed to immoveable for the purposes of private international law. In every case, the classification must be performed so that the appropriate system of law may be determined.

However while it is clear that this is the present state of the law, it is by no means so clear that it ought to be the law. Virtually every country in the world has abolished any special rules for the succession to land so that for its own internal purposes no distinction is made between moveable and immoveable property. The distinction is no longer felt to serve a meaningful social purpose, and yet, despite the virtually unanimous international opinion to this effect, Scots law persists with the distinction as if it separated significantly different categories for purposes of choice of law. This can produce bizarre variations in the result in a particular case depending upon where particular items of the estate happen to be situated. Even within the United Kingdom, where Northern Ireland, England and Scotland seek to achieve similar results on intestacy but by very different methods, the present rules for the choice of the appropriate system of law can produce remarkable and quite unjustifiable variations in the amount that a widow will receive depending on the situation of the property.[5] It is submitted that all property ought to devolve according to the law of the deceased's last domicile and that the role of the *lex situs* should disappear.[6] If this were carried out, there would, of course, be difficulties in administering systems of title to land, for rights of a type unknown to the law of the country where the land is situated might have to be catered for and documents of unusual types accepted. However these problems would not be insuperable, and indeed are no more serious than those which already exist, and are already overcome, in our present rules of private international law. It is to be hoped that future legislation will effect this reform.

In the application of the existing rules to the scheme of succession set out in the Succession (Scotland) Act, some points are worth special notice.

Prior rights

The surviving spouse's prior right under section 8 to the deceased's interest in the dwelling-house is clearly a right in immoveable property and is governed by the *lex situs*. Thus the Scottish rule applies to houses situated in Scotland, irrespective of the owner's domicile, provided the conditions of section 8 are met. For example a wife living apart from her English husband in a house belonging to him in Scotland, would have a prior right to the house on his death.

---

[4] *Macdonald v. Macdonald*, 1932 S.C. (H.L.) 79.
[5] See *Morris* (1969) 85 L.Q.R. 339.
[6] The Scottish Law Commission had proposed that both moveables and immoveables should devolve on intestacy according to the law of the last domicile, but made no formal recommendation to this effect in its *Report on Succession*, Scot. Law Com. No. 124, in view of the existence of a draft Convention prepared by the Hague Conference on Private International Law.

In the situation to which section 8(2) applies (*i.e.* farmhouses and other business premises including a house)[7] a surviving spouse receives a "sum equal to the value of the relevant interest" held by the deceased. It is fairly easy to regard this cash sum as a kind of surrogatum for the immoveable itself, since it is equated with the interest which the survivor would otherwise have received. Hence there can be little doubt that this right to a cash sum is also to be treated as an interest in an immoveable falling to be governed by the *lex situs*, so that it also could be due out of houses situated in Scotland, irrespective of the domicile of the owner.

However, there is greater difficulty in knowing how to classify the surviving spouse's right to a fixed sum when the value of the house is greater than the maximum limit. Under section 8(1)(b), where the value of the deceased's "relevant interest" exceeds £130,000, the survivor is entitled to "the sum of £130,000" without any words classifying this sum as a surrogatum for the house itself. An argument can therefore be presented that the right is an interest in moveables, and therefore applicable only to domiciled Scots, and is not due when a house in Scotland is owned by someone domiciled elsewhere. However, the better view would seem to be that the right to the cash sum is in lieu of the house itself. The purpose of the provision is merely to put an upper limit on the benefit to a surviving spouse of the housing right, and it is an integral part of the right to the house, however it may be expressed. Thus it is suggested that if an appropriate house worth more than £130,000 is situated in Scotland, the surviving spouse will be entitled to the cash sum even if the deceased was domiciled outwith Scotland, on the basis that the right is part of the succession to immoveables. Conversely, the survivor will not be entitled to the cash sum if the house is situated outside Scotland, even if the deceased's domicile was Scottish, but would be entitled to any comparable right granted by the law of the country where the house is situated.[8]

The prior right to furniture and plenishings conferred by section 8(3) is clearly moveable. Hence this right applies only when the deceased was domiciled in Scotland. It would seem, therefore, that the reference in section 8(5) to a deceased who was domiciled furth of Scotland is inept so far as concerns the furniture and plenishings. If the deceased was not a domiciled Scot, the surviving spouse is not entitled to the furniture and plenishings under the Succession Act, and there is little point in having an arbiter of their value appointed by the sheriff. (The main purpose of this subsection is, of course, to provide means for obtaining a valuation of the house itself, and for this purpose it is perfectly effective.)

The prior right under section 9 of the Succession Act might at first sight seem to be purely moveable and thus applicable only when the deceased was domiciled in Scotland. This would, however, be a mistaken view, for the sum is required to be "borne by, and paid out of, the parts of the intestate estate consisting of heritable and moveable property respectively".[9] It is thus part of the Scots law affecting succession to immoveable property (being in effect a

---

[7] See *supra*, pp.42-43.
[8] Leslie, "Prior Rights in Succession", 1988 S.L.T. (News) 105.
[9] 1964 Act, s.9(3)

charge upon heritage in Scotland) as well as part of the Scots law of moveable succession.

The result is that if the deceased was domiciled in Scotland, the financial right is due from his moveables, wherever situated, and from his immoveable property in Scotland. No account is taken of any immoveable property situated outside Scotland. However, even if the deceased was domiciled outside Scotland, the fact that the section 9 right is part of the Scots law of succession to immoveable property means that the surviving spouse is entitled to £35,000 or to £58,000 as the case may be out of any immoveable property situated in Scotland. The full amount is payable under Scots law to the surviving spouse irrespective of the amount or value of any other estate owned by the deceased, and irrespective of any rights which the surviving spouse may have under any other system.[10]

Legal rights

Legal rights in Scots law now exist only in the moveable estate belonging to the deceased at the time of his death and are classified as rights of succession despite their origin in a form of community of property between husband and wife. As rules governing moveable succession they apply only when the deceased was domiciled in Scotland and affect his moveable property wherever situated. The fact that a foreign system of law may treat land for the purposes of succession as if it were moveable or personal property does not, however, give the widow and children of a Scottish domiciliary legal rights in that land.[11] Any comparable forced share provisions affecting moveables in a foreign system of law would be applied in Scotland in the succession to a deceased who was domiciled in that country.

There are no longer any Scottish legal rights in immoveable property. As succession to immoveables is governed by the *lex situs*, this means that immoveable property situated in Scotland is immune from all legal rights or their equivalents, Scottish or foreign. Equally, there are no Scottish rights to attempt to enforce against foreign immoveable property and any equivalents to Scottish legal rights which may exist will be those granted by that foreign system. It will be noted, however, that the English equivalent under the Inheritance (Provision for Family and Dependants) Act 1975 applies only in cases where the deceased died domiciled in England and Wales.[12] It cannot therefore be invoked by the dependants of a deceased who dies domiciled in Scotland, but who owned immoveable property in England. The (English) Law Commission has so far rejected proposals for rectification of this anomaly.

Free estate

In the distribution of the free estate, the general rules that moveables are governed by the *lex domicilii* of the deceased and immoveables by the *lex situs* of the property operate with full force. The preservation of these rules for this Part of the Succession Act is reinforced by the provision in section 1(1) that it

---

[10] (1967) 12 J.L.S. 401.
[11] *Macdonald v. Macdonald, supra.*
[12] s.1(1).

applies to "estate the succession to which falls to be regulated by the law of Scotland".

The Crown as ultimus haeres

The property of anyone dying without heirs or testate beneficiaries passes to the Crown as *ultimus haeres*. The estate is received and administered by the Queen's and Lord Treasurer's Remembrancer. There are serious doubts about the theoretical nature of this right of the Crown[13] but in practice the Crown claims the moveable property in Scotland of foreign domiciliaries and does not claim moveable property abroad belonging to Scottish domiciliaries.[14]

Testate succession

The questions of capacity to make a will, of formal validity of the will, of essential validity of the will and of construction of the terms used in a will give rise to different considerations of private international law.

In Scotland, capacity to make a will is now attained at the age of 12.[15] Below that age, there is no legal capacity to make a will, and other legal systems impose restrictions on different categories of persons. The rule appears to be that capacity to make a will of moveable estate is referred to the law of the testator's domicile at the date of execution of the will while a will dealing with immoveables would be referred to the lex situs. The Scottish Law Commission has recommended that capacity should in all cases be referred to the domestic law of the country of the deceased's domicile at the time of making (or revoking) the will.[16]

Formal validity

Formal validity is now governed primarily by the Wills Act 1963.[17] A will is validly executed if it is properly executed according to the internal law of the country of the testator's domicile, nationality or habitual residence either at the date of execution or at the date of death. In addition it is validly executed if it conforms to the law of the place of execution or to the law with which a ship or aeroplane is most closely connected if the testator is travelling in it. A will dealing only with immoveable property may employ the formalities of the lex situs of the immoveable property.

Applying this to the Scottish solicitor, he may therefore properly use the Scottish formalities whenever a will is executed in this country, whenever the testator qualifies by reason of domicile, nationality or habitual residence, and whenever the will deals solely with Scottish immoveables. What he must not do is to send a will abroad for signature without considering the Wills Act. There are numerous cases in which people with some family connection with Scotland (often an interest in a Scottish trust) seek to make a will dealing only

---

[13] Anton, *Private International Law* (2nd ed., 1990), pp.678–680.
[14] As between Scotland and England, see Law Reform (Miscellaneous Provisions) (Scotland) Act 1940 (3 & 4 Geo. 6, c.42), s.6.
[15] Age of Legal Capacity (Scotland) Act 1991 (c.50), s.2(2).
[16] Report on Succession, recommendation 67.
[17] (c.44).

with their Scottish estate although they are no longer domiciled or resident here and have another nationality. Unless the will deals solely with Scottish heritage, the formalities will have to be those pointed out by the Wills Act. It is not the case that the ordinary Scottish attested will, either signed before two witnesses under the older law, or complying with the Requirements of Writing (Scotland) Act 1995, is acceptable everywhere. For example, several of the United States require three witnesses, and South African law requires the witnesses to sign on each page. Several countries (*e.g.* Germany) simply do not have the concept of the attested will and may require either a holograph will or a formal notarial act. This has recently caused difficulty in a will sent for signature to Germany when the testator was domiciled and resident there, and had German nationality. Fortunately the testator also had British nationality, which saved the validity.

Since domicile, residence and nationality can all be difficult concepts, and may be difficult to prove many years after the relevant date, it will often be wise to ensure that a will sent out from Scotland should be taken to a local lawyer for execution according to the formalities of the place of execution. That place should easily be identified and virtually every legal system will accept the formalities of the place of execution.

When the provisions of the Administration of Justice Act 1982[18] are eventually brought into force, there will be a new form of "international will" which will automatically be accepted as formally valid in all contracting countries if it complies with the formalities specified in the Act, irrespective of any contrary requirements in the local law.

Essential validity

This is governed by different considerations, as the content of a will may not be acceptable even if the formalities of execution have been properly observed. Questions of public policy may arise, or there may be statutory provisions such as the Scottish rules prohibiting successive liferents, entails or accumulations. For these purposes the governing law is the law of the domicile at the time of death for moveable property and the *lex situs* for immoveable property.[19]

Construction of the terms used in wills depends upon the testator's intention, but there is rarely an express statement of intention. In the absence of express intentions or of unambiguous directions there will be some presumption that a will of moveable property will be construed according to the law of the domicile and a will of immoveable property by the law of the *situs*. The domicile in question is probably the domicile at the time of execution of the will.[20]

---

[18] (c.53), ss.27, 28, Sched. 2.
[19] *Ommanney v. Bingham* (1796) 3 Pat. 448; *Brown's Trs v. Gregson*, 1920 S.C. (H.L.) 87.
[20] Anton, *Private International Law* (2nd ed., 1990), pp.686–687. *Meston's Succession Opinions*, No. 37, p.106, and No. 75, p.236.

Administration of estates

Quite apart from questions of beneficial right to the property of a deceased person, many problems may arise in the administration of the property if there is a foreign element. For example, the general rule in Scotland is that the right to be executor is determined by the law of the deceased's domicile so that confirmation will be issued to the foreign executor. Indeed if the deceased was domiciled abroad, a petition for confirmation in Scotland would be rejected if based on Scottish internal law. However, some legal systems (*e.g.* Germany) do not provide for the appointment of executors in our sense, and hold that deceased's property vests directly and immediately in the heirs without any intervention or formality. In these cases, confirmation will be granted on evidence from a qualified person as to who is entitled under the law of the domicile to administer the estate.[21]

A clear distinction is made between the right to administer the property and the title or authority to do so. As indicated above, the fact that the right to the office of executor is determined by the law of the deceased's domicile does not absolve him from the necessity of further procedure where the property is situated. He must still obtain authority to deal with the property, and for considerations of effectiveness of control, this authority must be conferred by the *lex situs* of the property. Thus a foreign executor must still obtain confirmation from the Scottish courts to be entitled to uplift property here and conversely a Scottish executor of a person dying domiciled in Scotland requires to obtain the appropriate authority under the law of the country where the property is situated. Even a formal grant of powers and title to an executor in one country does not of itself give the executor any authority over property subject to another legal system. Hence in principle it is necessary to obtain a separate grant of authority under each legal system having control over any of the deceased's property. At one time, for example, this meant that a Scottish executor had to obtain a separate grant of probate or letters of administration in England, and vice versa.

The Confirmation of Executors (Scotland) Act 1858[22] established a more convenient procedure commonly known as "resealing", under which an English grant of representation could be certified, and thus given full effect in Scotland, while comparable provisions permitted the resealing of Scottish confirmations in England (latterly the Supreme Court of Judicature (Consolidation) Act 1925). Despite a strong attachment to the procedure in some quarters, resealing was a rather farcical process over which the courts nominally granting authority could and did exercise little control.

Substantial reform was eventually achieved by the Administration of Estates Act 1971.[23] This Act ended the need for resealing or certification as between the courts of England and Wales, Scotland and Northern Ireland. There is now automatic recognition in each of these jurisdictions of confirmations or grants of representation issued by any of the others, subject to

---

[21] *Meston's Succession Opinions*, No.76, p.239.
[22] (21 & 22 Vict. c.56).
[23] (c.25).

the important proviso that the deceased died domiciled in the jurisdiction issuing the confirmation or grant to be recognised.[24] Oddly enough, there seems not to be any special procedure for grants of representation in the Channel Islands or Isle of Man.

Outwith the United Kingdom jurisdictions, there is not as yet any system of automatic recognition of the title of executors appointed elsewhere. Special reciprocal provisions do exist between Scotland and most other Commonwealth and colonial systems in a special relationship with the United Kingdom under the Colonial Probates Acts of 1892 and 1927.[25]

Where no reciprocal arrangements exist, the basic rule still applies, so that the foreign executor requires confirmation in Scotland and vice versa. However progress is being made in the development of a Hague Convention for the international recognition of the title of executors, and it is to be hoped that this will speedily reach fruition without too many nationalistic obstacles being put in its path.

---

[24] ss.1(1), 2(2) and 3(1).
[25] Lists of the territories are set out in the Colonial Probates Act Application Orders 1965 (S.I. 1965 No. 1530) and 1976 (S.I. 1976 No. 579). See Anton, *Private International Law* (2nd ed., 1990), pp.658–659. For procedure, see *Currie on Confirmation* (8th ed.), Chap. 15 — which includes the current list at 15.03.

CHAPTER 10

THE SCOTTISH LAW COMMISSION'S PROPOSALS FOR REFORM

The Scottish Law Commission published three consultative memoranda on the law of succession in 1986.[1] Following on the comments received in response to the memoranda, the Commission in 1990 published its *Report on Succession.*[2] This Report proposes major changes in the law of intestate succession and a number of reforms in other parts of the law of succession, which will make valuable improvements in the law. The detailed consideration of the existing law, and of the need for reform, set out in the consultative memoranda will remain valuable sources as well as the final recommendations in the Report. The draft Bill included with the Report would form the basis of the legislation which will replace the Succession (Scotland) Act 1964, although there may well be alteration of particular details. It is not known when the government will find time in the legislative programme for the new Succession Bill, but with diminishing confidence in view of the lapse of time, it is hoped that the history of delay before the passing of the 1964 Act referred to in Chapter One will not be repeated with its successor.

This chapter sets out the broad scheme of the reforms proposed by the Scottish Law Commission. It does not purport to be a detailed analysis of the text of the draft Bill, as that is likely to be subject to amendment both before being submitted to Parliament and in the course of its eventual progress through Parliament, but some comment is offered on points where difficulty may arise or where contrary views may be pressed on Parliament.

Private international law

The Commission proposes only relatively small alterations.[3] The existing rules will continue in force subject to two provisions. One is that capacity to make or revoke a will should be determined by the law of the domicile at the time of making or revoking the will, irrespective of whether it deals with moveables or with immoveables.[4] The other is a very valuable attempt to clear up some of the confusion surrounding survivorship destinations. Special destinations create unnecessary problems even in internal Scots law, but these are compounded if more than one system is involved. Particular problems have arisen over the working rule of English law that a title taken in the name of two persons implies a survivorship destination, and the cases have not given a

---

[1] *Intestate Succession and Legal Rights* (No. 69); *The Making and Revocation of Wills* (No. 70); *Some Miscellaneous Topics in the Law of Succession* (No. 71).
[2] Scot. Law Com. No. 124 (1990).
[3] Draft Bill, cl.32.
[4] *supra*, p.137.

clear lead on the system of law to be applied. Hence the Commission proposes that the question of whether the terms of a title to moveable property should pass the property on the owner's death should be determined by the law of the deceased's domicile at his death.

Proof of survivorship

The practical consequences of two members of a family dying within a short time of each other are the same as those when they die in the same incident without it being possible to prove that one survived the other. The present law treats proved survival for one second in the same way as survival for a period of years although it is clearly not appropriate to do so. In addition, the words of a will which purports to deal with the potential problems will be scrutinised and analysed with very precise logic, whether or not that seems sensible in the circumstances.[5]

The Commission therefore proposes a general rule that mere survivorship should not be sufficient to qualify a beneficiary to inherit or to succeed under a special destination.[6] Instead it would be necessary to survive for a period to be specified by Parliament. The Commission suggests five days, counting from the beginning of the day on which the deceased died, but longer periods up to 30 days are often specified in wills and a period longer than five days may eventually be chosen. The general principle is very welcome. Where a problem still arises in which it is uncertain whether either person survived for the five days, the estate of each of them would be distributed as if the other had failed to survive. Such a provision has already been enacted in England, although the concept causes considerable surprise on the continent.

A very valuable provision in clause 28(3) of the proposed Bill would remove the difficulty when the word "predeceasing" is used in a will. At present a third party whose right depends on the predecease of someone else will be unable to prove the predecease in the event of a common calamity even if the other person cannot be proved to have survived. When the Bill is enacted, anyone who has failed to survive for the requisite period will be regarded for the purposes of the succession rights of other persons as having predeceased the deceased. Thus a destination-over which depends on a beneficiary "predeceasing" will come into effect if he cannot be proved to have survived for the specified period after the deceased's death.

The unworthy heir

The Commission's recommendations appear as clauses 19 and 20 of the proposed Bill. The aim is to rationalise the existing mixture of statutory provisions and common law rules of doubtful effect. The Parricide Act 1594 would be repealed and the whole law restated. Unfortunately the Commission

---

[5] See *Re Rowland* [1963] Ch. 1 where a provision in the event of the testator's wife's death "coinciding" with his own was held not to include the case where they both perished without proof of survivorship when a ship sank.

[6] cl.28.

proceeded on the assumption that the existing common law was based on the principle that no one can invoke the law to obtain a benefit from his or her own crime. That this is not so is demonstrated by the fact that many crimes exist which would not act as disqualification (*e.g.* death caused in an accident which amounted to only careless driving) and a version of the disqualification does exist even where there is no crime (*e.g.* suicide, which prevents the deceased's estate from receiving the proceeds of his life insurance).

The proposal is that only a specified and limited list of crimes would bring about disqualification. Final conviction of murder, culpable homicide or manslaughter or convictions elsewhere of crimes which would amount to these crimes in Britain would automatically result in forfeiture of rights of succession. The specification of a list of crimes may well make the law clearer, but it is a serious mistake to make the disqualification also depend upon conviction by a court. One of the reasons why the Parricide Act was never invoked was precisely that it required conviction by an assize. If that could not be shown, for example if the killer merely disappeared without conviction, then there was no disqualification.[7] The benefit of certainty in the statutory rule would be offset by the ability to avoid the disqualification by disappearance, and even if the common law rule is, as suggested, to be retained along with the statutory rule, the suicide of a murderer would prevent the disqualification from coming into effect. It is to be hoped that this provision will be improved when the Bill is before Parliament.

The proposal is that any person who has incurred forfeiture would be deemed to have failed to survive the victim, but this may be modified in the light of the decision in *Hunter's Exrs, Petrs.*[8]

The Forfeiture Act 1982 would be repealed and replaced with a more carefully drafted provision in clause 20. Apart from cases where the killer has been convicted of murder, it will be possible to apply to the court for relief, in whole or in part, from the forfeiture.

Special destinations

Special destinations will be defined in the Bill and will be treated as rights of succession for purposes of the new legal share and the surviving spouse's right to have the matrimonial home allocated as part of his or her share. All special destinations except the common survivorship destination will be abolished for deeds executed after the commencement of the new Act.[9]

Although it is unfortunate that the Commission did not find itself able to recommend the total abolition of special destinations (which have been unnecessary and a source of continual trouble since 1868) the recommendations do at least go some way towards mitigating their worst effects. In the remaining survivorship destinations, there will no longer be any restriction on either party such as to prevent them from evacuating the destination either *inter vivos* or *mortis causa*. It will not matter which party

---

[7] *Yeaman v. Oliphant* (1663) Mor. 4773 and *Oliphant v. Oliphant* (1674) Mor. 3429.
[8] 1992 S.L.T. 1141.
[9] cl.29.

provided the money for the purchase, as either will be able to confer a good title to his half either by *inter vivos* transfer or by will. Evacuation of the destination by will would still require express reference to the destination and a declared intention to revoke it.

However, if there is a contract not to revoke the destination, there could be a claim for damages against the person who has revoked it, based on the contract. This would not affect the validity of the evacuation. It will also be made clear that anyone succeeding to property by virtue of a destination will be liable for the debts of the deceased. This will remove any effect which the decision in *Barclay's Bank v. McGreish*[10] may have had. It will be the person succeeding to the property who will be liable for the debts up to the value of the property, but he may have a right of relief against the executors, and could in any event always renounce the succession.

Intestate succession

The Commission's proposals would produce a major simplification of the law which is greatly to be welcomed, even if teachers of law will thereby lose a fertile source of knotty examination questions. They will also further increase the preference given to the surviving spouse over the deceased's children or other relatives.

The distinction between heritage and moveables will genuinely disappear, apart from the preservation of the old rules of intestate heritable succession for titles of honour.[11] The estate to be divided on death will be treated as a single cash figure, being the total of the values of all the items of the estate, less the debts. It will not be necessary to keep the values of heritage and moveables separate, and neither will it be necessary to calculate apportionments between them.

The present complex method of working through three sets of rules, themselves subdivided, in order to work out the division of an intestate estate will be abolished. In its place there will be a single Part of the new Act, consisting of a mere four sections, which will cover the whole of the rules of intestate succession.

Broadly, the surviving spouse will receive the first £100,000[12] of the net estate. If there is issue of the intestate, they would be entitled to share only when the estate exceeds that figure, when they would be entitled to one half of the surplus over £100,000. The remaining half of the surplus would go to the spouse.[13] If there is no issue of the intestate, the surviving spouse would take the whole estate, irrespective of its size, in preference to any other relatives. In any circumstances, the spouse would be entitled to require the executor to transfer the matrimonial home as part of his or her share of the estate.[14]

---

[10] 1983 S.L.T. 344.
[11] cl.36(4).
[12] The figure used in the Act, when passed, would be subject to alteration by the Secretary of State by statutory instrument.
[13] cl.1(2).
[14] cl.23.

If there is no surviving spouse, the order of succession to the whole estate would be very like the present rules in the Succession (Scotland) Act 1964 for the division of the free estate, except of course that the spouse is not included.[15] However, one significant difference will be that collaterals of the half blood will share equally with collaterals of the full blood instead of being postponed to them as at present.[16]

Representation will apply on the same basis as in sections 5 and 6 of the 1964 Act[17] and the Bill therefore repeats the error made in 1964 of commencing representation only at the level of the nearest class to the deceased in which a survivor is found. Despite the fact that clause 2 states a general principle of representation, this is immediately contradicted by clause 3 and the anomalous variations which arise from the chance of survival of one member of intervening generations will be perpetuated. It is to be hoped that Parliament will rectify this anomaly.

Legal share and legal rights

The time-hallowed legal rights of *jus relictae*, *jus relicti* and legitim, and their various functions, will disappear from the law when the new Act is passed, being expressly abolished by clause 5(6). Collation *inter liberos* will disappear along with them. In their place will be a new right, to be called legal share, based on an entirely new concept. They will no longer be part of the law of intestate succession and the old authorities will no longer be relevant.

The new legal share will be solely a protection against disinheritance and will be claimable whenever the surviving spouse or the issue of the deceased are dissatisfied with their provisions (or lack of provisions) in the deceased's will. It will be a right to a fixed share and not a mere right to apply to the court for a discretionary award. It will not vest automatically as it will have to be expressly claimed by the beneficiary within two years of the deceased's death.[18] If a spouse or child does not claim legal share within the time limit, there will be no share.

The protection is primarily for a surviving spouse, although the Commission, after some hesitation, does recommend that issue should also have some protection. If one assumes that both spouse and issue are completely cut out of the deceased's will, the spouse's legal share will be 30 per cent, of the first £200,000 of the net estate, plus 10 per cent, of the estate above £200,000. The slicing principle recognises that above a certain figure, the argument for protection becomes less strong. If there is no surviving spouse, the legal share of the issue will be the same as that of the spouse.

If the deceased was survived by both spouse and by issue, the spouse's share remains the same, but to avoid excessive interference with testamentary freedom (especially as heritage will now be included in the estate subject to legal share) and recognising that the claim of children is less strong, the legal

---

[15] cl.1(3).
[16] cl.1(4).
[17] cl.2 and 3.
[18] cl.6(1).

share of issue will be one half of the spouse's share, *i.e.* 15 per cent, and five per cent, respectively.[19] However, there is a very opaque provision, the meaning of which should be spelt out more clearly. Clause 5(3) of the draft Bill states that, for the purpose of calculating the amount of any claim by surviving issue under clause 7, the net estate of the deceased will not include the first £100,000 of the net estate to the fee of which the spouse succeeds otherwise than by virtue of a claim for legal share by the spouse. This fairly clearly means that the first £100,000 to which a spouse succeeds by testamentary succession (including special destinations) will be excluded in calculating the legal share of the issue, so that in most such cases the children will have no legal share at all in competition with a bequest to a spouse. Their right would be to 15 per cent, of the estate from £100,000 to £300,000 and five per cent, thereafter, but nothing from the estate below £100,000. This means that the spouse will always receive the first £100,000 and the *Kerr, Petr* problem of intestacy being more profitable than a will should cease to exist.

However, it is not entirely clear whether the right of the issue will still be postponed to the spouse's first £100,000 if both spouse and issue are excluded from benefit under the will. It would seem not, in view of the fact that clause 5(3) excludes from the issue only property to which the spouse "succeeds otherwise than by virtue of a claim by the spouse under this Part of this Act" but the result might be more clearly expressed. If this is correct, the total legal share when both spouse and issue are ignored in the will would amount to 45 per cent, of the first £200,000 and 15 per cent, thereafter. There are very welcome provisions clarifying the incidence of legal shares and liability for expenses and provision for payment to be made in instalments over 10 years when the estate includes agricultural property[20] and interest will be payable on legal share at seven per cent.

A very significant provision appears in clause 8. If a claim for legal share is carried through to payment, the claimant is deemed to have failed to survive the deceased and forfeits all rights of succession to the deceased's estate other than the legal share.

Validation of wills

Cases arise in which there is no doubt that a purported will was genuinely intended to operate as a will, but where the will has to be declared invalid through failure to comply with the appropriate formalities. This is especially true when several different legal systems might possibly be involved and the formalities in fact employed do not meet the requirements of the system or systems pointed out by private international law. However other problems can arise, such as the one pointed out by the Law Commission of both husband and wife having mirror-image wills but signing each other's will by mistake. Clause 12 of the draft Bill would give the court power to declare the will to be genuine, whereupon it would receive effect as if it were formally valid. This is

---

[19] cl.7.
[20] cl.9–11.

an important power for the limited number of cases which are likely to arise, and may indeed help to reduce litigation, for anyone who might now present a purely technical objection to the validity of the execution of a will in order to benefit on intestacy would realise that the court would probably uphold the will.

Rectification of wills

The Commission proposes in clause 13 that the court (including both the Court of Session and the sheriff court) should be given power to rectify errors in the expression of a will, but only where the will was drawn up by someone other than the testator, and the will as signed did not in fact carry out the testator's instructions. This means that there would have to have been instructions, the existence of which can be proved, which the person preparing the will failed to implement. Applications for rectification would have to be presented within six months of the granting of confirmation to the deceased's estate. There is some opposition to this power being created, but the vast majority of consultees supported it, and it will in any event be of rare occurrence.

Revocation of wills

The Commission proposes that on divorce, the former spouse of the testator should be treated as having failed to survive the testator for the purposes of the testator's will. The effect will be a revocation of the provisions in favour of the spouse. It is not recommended that wills should be automatically revoked by the subsequent marriage of the testator. The *conditio si testator sine liberis decesserit*, which permits a will to be revoked at the instance of an after-born child who is not provided for in the will, is to be abolished.[21]

The confused state of the law on the revival of wills which have been revoked is much improved by clause 16. A will which has been expressly revoked by a later will (but not one which was merely impliedly revoked by it) will no longer be revived by the revocation of the later will. The unsatisfactory decisions in *Bruce's J.F. v. Lord Advocate*[22] and *Scott's J.F. v. Johnston*[23] will be reversed and the law will return to the distinction proposed in *Nicolson v. Nicolson's Tutrix*.[24]

Conditio si institutus sine liberis decesserit

Clause 17 of the proposed Bill would retain the substance of this doctrine, but in a modified form and under the description of "Beneficiary predeceasing leaving issue." It will be interesting to see if the old name remains in general use or whether the more bland terminology of the Bill is adopted. Effectively

---

[21] cl.14 and 15.

[22] 1969 S.L.T. 337.

[23] 1971 S.L.T. (Notes) 41.

[24] 1922 S.C. 649.

the doctrine remains in force for gifts to direct descendants. Any such gift will impliedly include a provision in favour of the beneficiary's issue in the event of the beneficiary predeceasing the testator. However the doctrine will no longer apply to gifts to nephews and nieces. The present law has the anomalous result that a gift to brothers or sisters does not include an implied benefit for nephews and nieces in the event of the predecease of the brother or sister, but does impliedly include the beneficiary's issue if the gift is directly to a nephew or niece. This clearly had to be tidied up in one direction or the other, and the Commission has recommended that it be done by complete removal of the implied provision in the case of collaterals and their issue. It may be that this will not meet with general approval.

Administration of estates

A number of provisions affecting the administration of estates is included in Part V of the proposed Bill. These are mainly minor matters of tidying up the procedure and powers of executors, such as the provision removing the provision of the common law preventing an executor from transferring to himself the deceased's interest in a lease.[25] There are provisions for the valuation of the estate of a deceased person, and some long-standing rules of little practical importance, such as the right to aliment and temporary aliment from the estate will be abolished.

---

[25] *Inglis v. Inglis*, 1983 S.L.T. 437.

PART II

SUCCESSION (SCOTLAND) ACT 1964

(1964 c.41)

An Act to assimilate and amend the law of Scotland with respect to the succession to the heritable and moveable property of deceased persons; to amend the law in relation to the legal and other prior rights exigible out of such property, to the administration of deceased persons' estates and other property passing on death, to the capacity of minors to test, and to the presumption of survivorship; to provide for certain testamentary dispositions to be probative; to provide for adopted persons to be treated for certain purposes as children of their adopters; to make new provision as to the financial rights and obligations of the parties on the dissolution of a marriage; and for purposes connected with the matters aforesaid

[June 10, 1964]

INTRODUCTION AND GENERAL NOTE

When it was passed in 1964 the Succession (Scotland) Act was a long overdue reform of much of the law of intestate succession in Scotland, together with a number of other reforms to aspects of testate succession and administration of estates. From September 10, 1964 the radically improved position, especially the position of surviving spouses, has been generally accepted, and there is now no trace whatever of the case (still being advanced in 1964) for the eldest son to inherit all the land. However further reform is now badly needed, and it is hoped that it will be along the lines of the Scottish Law Commission's *Report on Succession* published in 1990 (Scot Law Com. No. 124).

The Act is not a complete code of the Scots law of succession. Parts I and II do deal with most of the law of intestate succession, but contain only modifications to legal rights which (in addition to their protective functions) are part of the rules of intestate succession. The current pattern of intestate succession is very complex, as it involves three separate sets of rules—prior rights, legal rights and free estate—which have to be considered in their proper order and independently of each other. This produces odd results and it is possible for the amounts received by two surviving spouses to vary substantially even although the values of the estates are identical. This is primarily because the nature and the form of financing of the housing arrangements are not taken into account in establishing the value of the other rights of the survivor. Matters will be much clearer when the Scottish Law Commission's proposals are enacted.

Part III makes a number of important changes in the administration and winding-up of estates, most of the changes being consequential upon the assimilation of heritage and moveables in the distribution of the free estate.

The Act applies to Scotland only and came into force on September 10, 1964.

PARLIAMENTARY DEBATES

Scottish Grand Committee, Nov. 26, 1963: Scottish Standing Committee, Dec. 12, 17 and 19, 1963, Jan. 16, 21, 23, 28 and 30, 1964: H.L. Vol. 256, cols.551, 582, 1043 and 1062: Vol. 257, col. 352: H.C. Vol. 689, col. 1211; Vol. 695, col. 125.

PART I

INTESTATE SUCCESSION

Assimilation of heritage to moveables for purpose of devolution on intestacy

1.—(1) The whole of the intestate estate of any person dying after the commencement of this Act (so far as it is estate the succession to which falls to

149

be regulated by the law of Scotland) shall devolve, without distinction as between heritable and moveable property, in accordance with—

(a) the provisions of this Part in this Act; and

(b) any enactment or rule of law in force immediately before the commencement of this Act which is not inconsistent with those provisions and which, apart from this section, would apply to that person's moveable intestate estate, if any;

and, subject to section 37 of this Act, any enactment or rule of law in force immediately before the commencement of this Act with respect to the succession to intestate estates shall, in so far as it is inconsistent with the provisions of this Part of this Act, cease to have effect.

(2) Nothing in this Part of this Act shall affect legal rights or the prior rights of a surviving spouse; and accordingly any reference in this Part of this Act to an intestate estate shall be construed as a reference to so much of the net intestate estate as remains after the satisfaction of those rights, or the proportion thereof properly attributable to the intestate estate.

DEFINITION

"intestate estate": ss.1(2), and 36(1) and (2). See also s.37(1)(a) and (b).

GENERAL NOTE

This section deals only with the "intestate estate" which, for the purposes of Pt I of the Act, is the free estate remaining after the prior rights of any surviving spouse and the legal rights of spouse and descendants have been satisfied. In relation to that free estate (though not in respect of prior and legal rights) s.1 abolishes the distinction between heritage and moveables. The whole free estate is a single fund for division among those entitled. The privileged position of the heir-at-law therefore vanished from the law, except in respect of the items excepted from the operation of the Act by s.37.

The whole free estate is divided on the principles set out in Pt I of the Act together with such of the previous law of intestate *moveable* succession as is "not inconsistent with" the Act. The Act is not a complete code, but there could be scope for doubt about how much of the previous law can still be in force as a result of this provision.

Rights of succession to intestate estate

2.—(1) Subject to the following provisions of this Part of this Act—

(a) where an intestate is survived by children, they shall have right to the whole of the intestate estate;

(b) where an intestate is survived by either of, or both, his parents and is also survived by brothers or sisters, but is not survived by any prior relative, the surviving parent or parents shall have right to one half of the intestate estate and the surviving brothers and sisters to the other half thereof;

(c) where an intestate is survived by brothers or sisters, but is not survived by any prior relative, the surviving brothers and sisters shall have right to the whole of the intestate estate;

(d) where an intestate is survived by either of, or both, his parents, but is not survived by any prior relative, the surviving parent or parents shall have right to the whole of the intestate estate;

(e) where an intestate is survived by a husband or a wife, but is not survived by any prior relative, the surviving spouse shall have right to the whole of the intestate estate;

(f) where an intestate is survived by uncles or aunts (being brothers or sisters of either parent of the intestate), but is not survived by any prior relative, the surviving uncles and aunts shall have right to the whole of the intestate estate;

(g) where an intestate is survived by a grandparent or grandparents (being a parent or parents of either parent of the intestate), but is not survived by any prior relative, the surviving grandparent or grandparents shall have right to the whole of the intestate estate;

(h) where an intestate is survived by brothers or sisters of any of his grandparents (being a parent or parents of either parent of the intestate), but is not survived by any prior relative, those surviving brothers and sisters shall have right to the whole of the intestate estate;

(i) where an intestate is not survived by any prior relative, the ancestors of the intestate (being remoter than grandparents) generation by generation successively, without distinction between the paternal and maternal lines, shall have right to the whole of the intestate estate; so however that, failing ancestors of any generation, the brothers and sisters of any of those ancestors shall have right thereto before ancestors of the next more remote generation.

(2) References in the foregoing subsection to brothers or sisters include respectively brothers and sisters of the half blood as well as of the whole blood; and in the said subsection "prior relative", in relation to any class of person mentioned in any paragraph of that subsection, means a person of any other class who, if he had survived the intestate, would have had right to the intestate estate or any of it by virtue of an earlier paragraph of that subsection or by virtue of any such paragraph and section 5 of this Act.

DEFINITIONS

"intestate estate": ss.1(2) and 36(1) and (2). See also s.37(1)(a) and (b) and note to s.1.

"children": include adopted children (ss.23 and 24) and illegitimate children (Law Reform (Parent and Child) (Scotland) Act 1986).

"brothers or sisters": s.2(2) and 3.

"prior relative": s.2(2).

GENERAL NOTE

This section provides the new statutory order of succession to the free estate. The order is established from the order of the paragraphs of s.2(1). Those claiming under an earlier paragraph take in preference to those claiming under a later paragraph by virtue of the use of the term "prior relative" as defined in s.2(2). Parents and brothers and sisters have rights under s.2(1)(b) when both categories survive, while brothers and sisters have rights under s.2(1)(c) and parents under s.2 (1)(d). To meet the difficulty in claims under s.2(1)(c) or (d) that parents and brothers and sisters would be their own "prior relatives" by virtue of their rights under s.2(1)(b), the definition in s.2(2) mentions "a person of any *other* class" who would have been entitled under an earlier paragraph.

The general pattern of the order of succession is similar to the previous law of intestate moveable succession, with the succession opening first to descendants, then to collaterals and then to ascendants, with the qualification that when parents and collaterals both survive, each category takes one-half of the estate.

Despite the similarity, there are, however, important modifications to the pre-existing law. As the existence of a right to succeed is now purely statutory, the common law concept of the "next-of-kin" is no longer relevant in the process of finding the persons entitled to succeed, although it is still relevant in competitions for appointment as executor-dative. An equalisation of the sexes was carried out, so that "ancestors" for the purposes of succession are no longer limited to the paternal line but include the maternal line as well. Thus the mother's right of succession is to an equal share along with the father when the succession opens to parents, instead of the previous right arising only when the father predeceased. The mother's brothers and sisters have equal rights with the father's brothers and sisters, and similarly at all levels in an infinite search among ancestors. Thus an enormous area of search has now been opened up when the succession opens to ancestors, and it is less likely that the Crown will succeed as *ultimus haeres*.

Another important change made by the Act was that the deceased's spouse has now full rights of succession to the free estate, and thus in appropriate circumstances can receive the whole of the deceased spouse's estate. In order of preference, s.2(1)(e) places the surviving spouse after children, collaterals and parents of the deceased, but before uncles and aunts and remoter ancestors. The situation can never now arise in which a surviving spouse will see part of the deceased's estate passing to the Crown.

The list of specified relatives must be read along with the scheme of representation contained in s.5 and that of division in s.6. Thus although s.2(1)(a) mentions only "children" it in fact regulates the rights of succession to the free estate of the whole category of descendants of the deceased.

Similarly "brothers or sisters" must be read in the light of ss.5 and 6, and also of s.2(2) and s.3 dealing with the position of collaterals of the half blood.

Succession of collaterals

3. Subject to section 5 of this Act, where brothers and sisters of an intestate or of an ancestor of an intestate (in this section referred to as "collaterals") have right to the whole, or, in a case to which subsection (1)(*b*) of the last foregoing section applies, to a half, of the intestate estate, the collaterals of the whole blood shall be entitled to succeed thereto in preference to the collaterals of the half blood; but where the collaterals of the half blood have right as aforesaid they shall rank without distinction as between those related to the intestate, or, as the case may be, the ancestor, through their father and those so related through their mother.

DEFINITION
"intestate estate": ss.1(2) and 36(1) and (2). See also s.37(1)(a) and (b).

GENERAL NOTE
This section made one of the changes which were then regarded as radical, namely equalisation of the position of collaterals of the half blood, whether uterine or consanguinean. The whole category of collaterals of the half blood is postponed to the full blood (including their issue by representation) but if the succession does open to the half blood there is no distinction between those related through the mother and those related through the father.

4. [*Repealed by the Law Reform (Parent and Child) (Scotland) Act 1986 (c.9), Sched.2.*]

Representation

5.—(1) Subject to section 6 of this Act, where a person who, if he had survived an intestate, would, by virtue of any of the foregoing provisions of this Part of this Act, have had right (otherwise than as a parent or spouse of the intestate) to the whole or to any part of the intestate estate has predeceased the intestate, but has left issue who survive the intestate, such issue shall have the like right to the whole or to that part of the intestate estate as the said person would have had if he had survived the intestate.

(2) The right of any issue entitled to share in an intestate estate by virtue of the foregoing subsection to be appointed to the office of executor on the intestate estate shall be postponed to the right thereto of any person who succeeds to the whole or part of the intestate estate by virtue of the foregoing provisions of this Act apart from this section and who applies for appointment to that office.

DEFINITIONS
"intestate estate": ss.1(2) and 36(1) and (2). See also s.37(1)(a) and (b).
"issue": s.36(1).

GENERAL NOTE
Being in Pt I of the Act, this section applies only to the free estate. Section 5(1) provides a scheme of infinite representation in all degrees of relationship, apart from parents and spouses, who cannot be represented. The fact that there is no representation of a predeceasing spouse means that step-children are completely excluded from the succession, and that collaterals of the half blood cannot increase their rights by claiming to represent their parent.

The provision that the representative takes the share that his ancestor would have taken by survivance might appear to involve a division *per stirpes* in all circumstances. However, s.5(1) is stated to be "subject to s.6" which specifies the nature of the division.

Subsection (2) is one of the few provisions in the Act dealing with the right to the office of executor. It bears a relationship to the former provision in s.1 of the Intestate Moveable Succession (Scotland) Act 1855 (18 & 19 Vict. c.23), and provides that if there is a competition for office, the right of representatives to the office of executor is postponed to the right of surviving members of the class which they are representing.

Division of intestate estate among those having right thereto

6. If, by virtue of the foregoing provisions of this Part of this Act, there are two or more persons having right among them to the whole, or, in a case to which section 2(1)(*b*) of this Act relates, to a half, of an intestate estate, then the said estate, or, as the case may be, that half thereof, shall—

(a) if all of those persons are in the same degree of relationship to the intestate, be divided among them equally; and

(b) in any other case, be divided equally into a number of parts equal to the aggregate of—

(i) those of the said persons who are nearest in degree of relationship to the intestate (in this section referred to as "the nearest surviving relatives"), and

(ii) any other persons who were related to the intestate in that degree, but who have predeceased him leaving issue who survive him;

and, of those parts, one shall be taken by each of the nearest surviving relatives, and one shall be taken *per stirpes* by the issue of each of the said predeceased persons.[1]

NOTE

[1]Further sentence added by the Law Reform (Miscellaneous Provisions) (Scotland) Act 1968 (c.70), Sched.1 (estate of any person dying after the commencement of that Act), and repealed by the Law Reform (Parent and Child) (Scotland) Act 1986 (c.9), Sched.2.

DEFINITION

"intestate estate": ss.1(2) and 36(1) and (2). See also s.37(1)(a) and (b).

GENERAL NOTE

This is one of the least satisfactory provisions in the Act. It alters the general rule of infinite representation set out in s.5 by substituting special rules for the division of the free estate. For detailed criticism of the effects of this section see "Representation in Succession" (1995) 1 *Scottish Law and Practice Quarterly,* pp. 83–92. The effect can be to produce great variations of succession rights depending upon the accident of the order of deaths.

It must be noted that this section (and s.5) apply only to the free estate, and not to prior rights or to legal rights. Similar provision for the division of the legitim fund appears in s.11. If all the persons entitled to share in the free estate are of the same degree of relationship to the deceased, the division is equally among them, *per capita.* Thus if the succession opens to uncles and aunts, it is available to brothers and sisters of both mother and father, and all members of that category share equally, irrespective of how many are on the paternal side and how many on the maternal side. However it also means that if the deceased's two children both predecease, leaving one and five grandchildren respectively, the division will be into sixths, with the result that one family takes five-sixths and the other only one-sixth.

If the persons entitled are not all of the same degree of relationship to the deceased, the division is made *per stirpes* at the level of the class nearest to the deceased in which there are members who actually survive. One part is taken by each of the surviving members of that class and one part by the representatives of each predeceasing member who has left issue.

Saving of right of Crown as ultimus haeres

7. Nothing in this Part of this Act shall be held to affect the right of the Crown as *ultimus haeres* to any estate to which no person is entitled by virtue of this Act to succeed.

PART II

NOTE
[1] See the Finance Act 1985 (c.54), s.84(5) and (6).

Prior rights of surviving spouse, on intestacy, in dwelling house and furniture

[1]**8.**—(1) Where a person dies intestate leaving a spouse, and the intestate estate includes a relevant interest in a dwelling house to which this section applies, the surviving spouse shall be entitled to receive out of the intestate estate—

(a) where the value of the relevant interest does not exceed £130,000[2] or such larger amount as may from time to time be fixed by order of the Secretary of State—

   (i) if subsection (2) of this section does not apply, the relevant interest;

   (ii) if the said subsection (2) applies, a sum equal to the value of the relevant interest;

(b) in any other case, the sum of £130,000[2] or such larger amount as may from time to time be fixed by order of the Secretary of State:

Provided that, if the intestate estate comprises a relevant interest in two or more dwelling houses to which this section applies, this subsection shall have effect only in relation to such one of them as the surviving spouse may elect for the purposes of this subsection within six months of the date of death of the intestate.

(2) This subsection shall apply for the purposes of paragraph (*a*) of the foregoing subsection if—

(a) the dwelling house forms part only of the subjects comprised in one tenancy or lease under which the intestate was the tenant; or

(b) the dwelling house forms the whole or part of subjects an interest in which is comprised in the intestate estate and which were used by the intestate for carrying on a trade, profession or occupation, and the value of the estate as a whole would be likely to be substantially diminished if the dwelling house were disposed of otherwise than with the assets of the trade, profession or occupation.

(3) Where a person dies intestate leaving a spouse, and the intestate estate includes the furniture and plenishings of a dwelling house to which this section applies (whether or not the dwelling house is comprised in the intestate estate), the surviving spouse shall be entitled to receive out of the intestate estate—

(a) where the value of the furniture and plenishings does not exceed £22,000[3] or such larger amount as may from time to time be fixed by order of the Secretary of State, the whole thereof;

(b) in any other case, such part of the furniture and plenishings, to a value not exceeding £22,000[3] or such larger amount as may from time to time be fixed by order of the Secretary of State, as may be chosen by the surviving spouse:

Provided that, if the intestate estate comprises the furniture and plenishings of two or more such dwelling houses, this subsection shall have effect only in relation to the furniture and plenishings of such one of them as the surviving spouse may elect for the purposes of this subsection within six months of the date of death of the intestate.

(4) This section applies, in the case of any intestate, to any dwelling house in which the surviving spouse of the intestate was ordinarily resident at the date of death of the intestate.

⁴(5)Where any question arises as to the value of any furniture or plenishings, or of any interest in a dwelling house, for the purposes of any provision of this section the question shall be determined by arbitration by a single arbiter appointed, in default of agreement, by the sheriff of the sheriffdom in which the intestate was domiciled at the date of his death or, if that sheriffdom is uncertain or the intestate was domiciled furth of Scotland, the sheriff of Lothian and Peebles at Edinburgh.

(6) In this section—

(a) "dwelling house" includes a part of a building occupied (at the date of death of the intestate) as a separate dwelling; and any reference to a dwelling house shall be construed as including any garden or portion of ground attached to, and usually occupied with, the dwelling house or otherwise required for the amenity or convenience of the dwelling house;

(b) "furniture and plenishings" includes garden effects, domestic animals, plate, plated articles, linen, china, glass, books, pictures, prints, articles of household use and consumable stores; but does not include any article or animal used at the date of death of the intestate for business purposes, or money or securities for money, or any heirloom;

(c) "heirloom", in relation to an intestate estate, means any article which has associations with the intestate's family of such nature and extent that it ought to pass to some member of that family other than the surviving spouse of the intestate;

(d) "relevant interest", in relation to a dwelling house, means the interest therein of an owner, or the interest therein of a tenant, subject in either case to any heritable debt secured over the interest; and for the purposes of this definition "tenant" means a tenant under a tenancy or lease (whether of the dwelling house alone or of the dwelling house together with other subjects) which is not a tenancy to which the Rent Acts 1971–74 apply.

NOTES

¹As amended by S.I. 1993 No. 2690, in the case of a person dying on or after 26th November 1993 and S.I. 1999 No. 445 in the case of deaths on or after April 2, 1999. Saved by the Prescription and Limitation (Scotland) Act 1973 (c.52), Sched.1, para. 2(f).

²As amended by S.I. 1999 No. 445. Earlier values: September 10, 1964 to May 22, 1973— £15,000: May 22, 1973 to July 31, 1981—£30,000; August 1, 1981 to April 30, 1988—£50,000; May 1, 1988 to November 25, 1993—£65,000; November 26, 1993 to April 1, 1999—£110,000.

³As amended by S.I. 1999 No. 445. Earlier values: September 10, 1964 to May 22, 1973— £5,000; May 22, 1973 to July 31, 1981—£8,000; August 1, 1981 to April 30, 1988—£10,000; May 1, 1988 to November 25, 1993—£12,000; November 26, 1993 to April 1, 1999—£20,000.

⁴Amended by the Sheriff Courts (Scotland) Act 1971, Sched.1, para. 1. For interpretation of the term "sheriff," see *ibid.* s.4(2) and the Interpretation Act 1978, Sched.1.

DEFINITIONS

"intestate": s.36(1).
"intestate estate": s.36(1) and (2). See also s.37(1)(a) and (b).
"relevant interest": s.8(6)(d).
"dwelling-house": s.8(6)(a).
"furniture and plenishings": s.8(6)(b).
"heirloom": s.8(6)(c).

GENERAL NOTE

Section 8 is probably the most important section in the whole Act, as the "prior right" which it creates is the most important single improvement in the position of a surviving spouse. The general purpose is to ensure that a surviving spouse (with a widow principally in mind) can live undisturbed in the house which he or she has been occupying, and can retain the furniture and plenishings of that house.

As s.8 is in Pt II of the Act, the "intestate estate" from which the prior right to the house, etc. is taken is the whole intestate estate after payment of debts and expenses. The definition is not subject to the limitation in s.1(2) which applies only to Pt I of the Act. Accordingly, when it applies, the prior right of a surviving spouse under s.8 is the first item to come out of a deceased person's estate. All other rights to share in a deceased's estate are postponed.

The prior rights under ss.8 and 9 apply only on the total or partial intestacy of the deceased. Unlike legal rights they do not prevail against a contrary will by the deceased. If the intestacy is only partial, prior rights apply only in so far as the property affected is included in the portion of the estate which has not been disposed of by will.

The effect is that the surviving spouse is entitled to receive, subject to any burdens affecting it, the ownership or tenancy of any one house owned, or tenanted otherwise than under the Rent Acts, by the deceased spouse, plus its furniture and plenishings. The surviving spouse, but not necessarily the deceased spouse, must have been ordinarily resident in the house in question at the date of death of the intestate (s.8(4)). To meet cases where the surviving spouse was ordinarily resident in more than one house, separate provisions are made in s.8(1) and (3) permitting the survivor to choose the house which will be taken under s.8(1) and the house from which the furniture and plenishings will be taken. The spouse may choose one of the houses and the furniture of the other.

There are maximum values for the benefit conferred on the surviving spouse. These are currently £130,000 in respect of the house itself and £22,000 in respect of the furniture and plenishings. If the deceased's interest in the house is worth £130,000 or less, the surviving spouse receives that interest (s.8(1)(a)(i)). If the value is over £130,000, the surviving spouse receives that sum in lieu of the house itself (s.8(1)(b)).

Similarly, the surviving spouse takes the whole of the furniture and plenishings if their value does not exceed £22,000, but may select furniture and plenishings to a value not exceeding £22,000 if the total value is over that sum (s.8(3)). There is provision in s.8(5) for arbitration in cases of dispute as to the value.

In the cases specified in s.8(2), even where the value of the deceased's interest in the house is £130,000 or less, the surviving spouse receives only the value of the deceased's interest and not that interest itself (s.8(1)(a)(ii)). The commonest case for this exception is that of the farmhouse under s.8(2)(b). The value of a farm, if the farmhouse were not available to a purchaser, would be likely to be reduced by an amount greater than the value of the farmhouse as such, and thus the "value of the estate as a whole would be likely to be substantially diminished" within the meaning of s.8(2)(b) if the farmhouse were transferred to the surviving spouse.

Prior right of surviving spouse to financial provision on intestacy

'9.—[2](1) Where a person dies intestate and is survived by a husband or wife, the surviving spouse shall be entitled to receive out of the intestate estate—

 (a) if the intestate is survived by issue, the sum of £35,000[3] or such larger amount as may from time to time be fixed by order of the Secretary of State, or

 (b) if the intestate is not survived by issue, the sum of £58,000[4] or such larger amount as may from time to time be fixed by order of the Secretary of State,

together with, in either case, interest at the rate of 7 per cent[5] per annum or at such rate as may from time to time be fixed by order of the Secretary of State on such sum from the date of the intestate's death until payment:

Provided that where the surviving spouse is entitled to receive a legacy out of the estate of the intestate (other than a legacy of any dwelling house to which the last foregoing section applies or of any furniture and plenishings of any such dwelling house), he or she shall, unless he or she renounces the legacy, be entitled under this subsection to receive only such sum, if any, as remains after deducting from the sum fixed by virtue of paragraph (*a*) of this subsection or the sum fixed by virtue of paragraph (*b*) of this subsection, as the case may be, the amount or value of the legacy.

(2) Where the intestate estate is less than the amount which the surviving spouse is entitled to receive by virtue of subsection (1) of this section the right conferred by the said subsection on the surviving spouse shall be satisfied by the transfer to him or her of the whole of the intestate estate.

(3) The amount which the surviving spouse is entitled to receive by virtue of subsection (1) of this section shall be borne by, and paid out of, the parts of the intestate estate consisting of heritable and moveable property respectively in proportion to the respective amounts of those parts.

(4) Where by virtue of subsection (2) of this section a surviving spouse has right to the whole of the intestate estate, he or she shall have the right to be appointed executor.

(5) The rights conferred by the Intestate Husband's Estate (Scotland) Acts 1911 to 1959 on a surviving spouse in his or her deceased spouse's estate shall not be exigible out of the estate of any person dying after the commencement of this Act.

(6) For the purposes of this section—

(a) the expression "intestate estate" means so much of the net intestate estate as remains after the satisfaction of any claims under the last foregoing section; and

(b) the expression "legacy" includes any payment or benefit to which a surviving spouse becomes entitled by virtue of any testamentary disposition; and the amount or value of any legacy shall be ascertained as at the date of the intestate's death.

NOTES

[1] Saved by the Prescription and Limitation (Scotland) Act 1973, s.6(2), Sched.1, para. 2(f).

[2] As amended by the Law Reform (Miscellaneous Provisions) (Scotland) Act 1968 (c.70), Sched.1 (estate of any person dying on or after November 25, 1968); the Succession (Scotland) Act 1973 (c.25), s.1(1)(b), the Law Reform (Miscellaneous Provisions) (Scotland) Act 1980 (c.55), s.4, the Law Reform (Parent and Child) (Scotland) Act 1986 (c.9), Sched.2 and S.I. 1993 No. 2690 (persons dying on or after November 26, 1993).

[3] As amended by S.I. 1999 No. 445. Earlier values: September 10, 1964 to May 22, 1973—£2,500; May 23, 1973 to December 30, 1977—£4,000; December 31, 1977 to July 31, 1981—£8,000 (S.I. 1977 No. 2110); August 1, 1981 to April 30, 1988—£15,000 (S.I. 1981 No. 806); May 1, 1988 to November 25, 1993—£21,000; November 26, 1993 to April 1, 1999—£30,000.

[4] As amended by S.I. 1999 No. 445. Earlier values: September 10, 1964 to May 22, 1973—£5,000; May 23, 1973 to December 30, 1977—£8,000; December 31, 1977 to July 31, 1981—£16,000 (S.I. 1977 No. 2110); August 1, 1981 to April 30, 1988—£25,000 (S.I. 1981 No. 806); May 1, 1988 to November 25, 1993—£35,000; November 26, 1993 to April 1, 1999—£50,000.

[5] As from August 1, 1981 the rate of interest is fixed at 7 per cent.: see S.I. 1981 No. 805. (Earlier rate (1964–81) 4 per cent.).

DEFINITIONS

"intestate": s.36(1).
"intestate estate": ss.9(6)(a) and 36(1) and (2). See also s.37(1)(a) and (b).
"issue": s.36(1).
"legacy": s.9(6)(b).

GENERAL NOTE

The prior right to a financial provision under s.9 applies only to the intestate estate of the deceased spouse. It is postponed to the s.8 housing right by virtue of the definition in subs.(6)(a) and is taken from any intestate estate which may be left after the housing right has been satisfied. The surviving spouse is entitled to £35,000 if there is issue of the deceased or to £58,000 if no issue of the deceased survived. In both cases the right will be satisfied by such lesser sum as may be left in the estate. Interest is due at 7 per cent from the date of death until payment. The capital sums involved may be increased and the rate of interest may be varied in either direction by order of the Secretary of State. The increases in the house values from £15,000 in 1964 have not kept pace with the changes in values since then.

Until further reform does finally abolish the distinction between heritage and moveables in succession, it remains necessary to establish the value of any moveable estate still remaining after a spouse's rights under ss.8 and 9 have been satisfied. Thus subs.(3) requires the amount payable to a surviving spouse under this section to be borne rateably by the heritage and moveables remaining after the s.8 rights have been satisfied.

If there is only a partial intestacy, legacies (other than of the dwelling-house in which the surviving spouse was ordinarily resident) must be deducted from the monetary prior right (subs.(1), proviso).

Provisions supplementary to sections 8 and 9

¹**9A.** Any order of the Secretary of State, under section 8 or 9 of this Act, fixing an amount or rate—

(a) shall be made by statutory instrument which shall be subject to annulment in pursuance of a resolution of either House of Parliament; and

(b) shall have effect in relation to the estate of any person dying after the coming into force of the order.

NOTE
¹Added by the Law Reform (Miscellaneous Provisions) (Scotland) Act 1980 (c.55), s.4.

Abolition of terce and courtesy, and calculation of legal rights

10.—(1) The right of courtesy of a surviving husband in his deceased wife's estate and the right of terce of a surviving wife in her deceased husband's estate shall not be exigible out of the estate of a person dying after the commencement of this Act.

(2) The amount of any claim to *jus relicti, jus relictae* or legitim out of an estate shall be calculated by reference to so much of the net moveable estate as remains after the satisfaction of any claims thereon under the two last foregoing sections.

10A. [*Added by the Law Reform (Miscellaneous Provisions) (Scotland) Act 1968 (c.70), s.2, in respect of estates of persons dying on or after 25th November 1968, and repealed by the Law Reform (Parent and Child) (Scotland) Act 1986 (c.9), Sched.2.*]

DEFINITION
"estate": ss.36(2) and 10(2).

GENERAL NOTE
The former legal rights of courtesy and terce were to income from the other spouse's heritable estate. These rights were abolished for deaths on or after September 10, 1964, but as there was no change to the legal rights of *jus relictae, jus relicti* and legitim, they remain exigible from moveables only. See s.33 for the construction of deeds referring to legal rights.

If the prior rights under ss.8 and 9 exhaust the estate, there will be no estate from which to pay legal rights(subs.(2)).

Representation in, and division of, legitim

¹**11.**—(1) Subject to the next following subsection, where a person (hereinafter in this section referred to as "the deceased") dies predeceased by a child who has left issue who survive the deceased, and the child would, if he had survived the deceased, have been entitled to legitim out of the deceased's estate, such issue shall have the like right to legitim as the child would have had if he had survived the deceased.

(2) If, by virtue of the foregoing subsection or otherwise, there are two or more persons having right among them to legitim, then the legitim shall—

(a) if all of those persons are in the same degree of relationship to the deceased, be divided among them equally, and

(b) in any other case, be divided equally into a number of parts equal to the aggregate of—

    (i) those of the said persons who are nearest in degree of relationship to the deceased (in this paragraph referred to as "the nearest surviving relatives") and

    (ii) any other persons who were related to the deceased in that degree and who (if they had survived him) would have been entitled to legitim out of his estate, but who have predeceased him leaving issue who survive him and are entitled to legitim out of his estate; and, of those parts, one shall be taken by each of the nearest surviving relatives, and one shall be taken *per stirpes* by the issue of each of the said predeceased persons, being issue who are entitled as aforesaid.

(3) Nothing in the last foregoing subsection shall be construed as altering any rule of law as to collation of advances; and where any person is entitled to claim legitim out of the estate of a deceased person by virtue of subsection (1) of this section he shall be under the like duty to collate any advances made by the deceased to him, and the proportion appropriate to him of any advances so made to any person through whom he derives such entitlement, as if he had been entitled to claim such legitim otherwise than by virtue of the said subsection (1).

(4) For the avoidance of doubt it is hereby declared that where any person is entitled by virtue of subsection (1) of this section to legitim out of the estate of the deceased, and the deceased is not survived by any child, the proportion of the estate due to any surviving spouse in respect of *jus relicti* or *jus relictae* shall be ascertained as if the deceased had been survived by a child.

NOTE

[1]As amended by the Law Reform (Miscellaneous Provisions) (Scotland) Act 1968 (c.70), Sched.1, in respect of estate of any person dying on or after November 25, 1968, and by the Law Reform (Parent and Child) (Scotland) Act 1986 (c.9), Sched.2.

GENERAL NOTE

Until the 1964 Act came into force, there was no representation in claims for legitim. Only the surviving immediate children of the deceased qualified, with the result that a single surviving child was entitled to the whole of the legitim fund to the exclusion of the issue of predeceasing children, but also shared with them in the distribution of the dead's part. The introduction of infinite representation now means that issue of predeceasing members of the class entitled to legitim will take their parent's share. The rule of division in subs.(2) is the same as that in s.6 and suffers from the same defects, which become particularly obvious when one attempts to calculate "the proportion appropriate to him" of advances to a representative's parent for the purpose of collation (subs.3). See Meston, *The Succession (Scotland) Act 1964* (5th ed.), Chapter 5.

Jus relictae or *relicti* is reduced to one-third of the available moveables if issue are entitled to legitim by virtue of representation (subs.(4)). There is no provision for representation in either of the legal rights of spouses.

Legitim not to be discharged by ante-nuptial marriage contract

12. Nothing in any ante-nuptial contract of marriage executed after the commencement of this Act shall operate so as to exclude, on the occurrence of the death of either party to the marriage, the right of any child of the marriage (or of any issue of his coming in his place by virtue of the last foregoing section) to legitim out of the estate of that party unless such child or issue shall elect to accept in lieu of legitim the provision made in his favour under the contract.

This section abolished the previous anomaly that the right of a child to legitim might be discharged prospectively by the ante-nuptial marriage contract of its parents. See *Galloway's Trs v. Galloway,* 1943 S.C. 339 and *Callander v. Callander's Exr,* 1972 S.L.T. 209 for examples of how it was possible to evade the protective function of legitim.

The date of execution of such a contract is its actual date of execution (s.36(3)).

Equitable compensation

¹**13.** Every testamentary disposition executed after the commencement of this Act by which provision is made in favour of the spouse or of any issue of the testator and which does not contain a declaration that the provision so made is in full and final satisfaction of the right to any share in the testator's estate to which the spouse or the issue, as the case may be, is entitled by virtue of *jus relicti, jus relictae* or legitim, shall (unless the disposition contains an express provision to the contrary) have effect as if it contained such a declaration.

NOTE
¹As amended by the Law Reform (Miscellaneous Provisions) (Scotland) Act 1968 (c.70), Sched.1, in respect of estate of any person dying on or after November 25, 1968, and by the Law Reform (Parent and Child) (Scotland) Act 1986 (c.9), Sched.2.

GENERAL NOTE
In the case of wills actually executed (s.36(3)) after the commencement of the Succession (Scotland) Act 1964, this section removes most of the practical effect of the abstruse doctrine of equitable compensation.

In a typical case before the Succession (Scotland) Act 1964 where a testamentary liferent was rejected in favour of a claim for a capital sum as the legal right, and vesting of the fee was not thereby accelerated, the income would accumulate. Over a substantial period the accumulated income might amount to enough to restore to the estate what was lost by paying out the capital sum. In that case, the liferent again became available to the beneficiary unless there was a clause in the will declaring that its provisions were in full satisfaction of legal rights. Section 13 now implies such a clause in every will, unless there is an express declaration to the contrary. The result is that in the vast majority of cases, equitable compensation cannot be claimed, but there may still be equitable compensation for other beneficiaries adversely affected by a claim for legal rights. (*Munro's Trs, Petrs,* 1971 S.L.T. 313).

PART III

ADMINISTRATION AND WINDING UP OF ESTATES

Assimilation for purposes of administration, etc., of heritage to moveables

14.— (1) Subject to subsection (3) of this section the enactments and rules of law in force immediately before the commencement of this Act with respect to the administration and winding up of the estate of a deceased person so far as consisting of moveable property shall have effect (as modified by the provisions of this Act) in relation to the whole of the estate without distinction between moveable property and heritable property; and accordingly on the death of any person (whether testate or intestate) every part of his estate (whether consisting of moveable property or heritable property) falling to be administered under the law of Scotland shall, by virtue of confirmation thereto, vest for the purposes of administration in the executor thereby confirmed and shall be administered and disposed of according to law by such executor.

¹(2) Provision shall be made by the Court of Session by act of sederunt made under the enactments mentioned in section 22 of this Act (as extended by that section) for the inclusion in the confirmation of an executor, by reference

to an appended inventory or otherwise, of a description, in such form as may be so provided, of any heritable property forming part of the estate.

(3) Nothing in this section shall be taken to alter any rule of law whereby any particular debt of a deceased person falls to be paid out of any particular part of his estate.

NOTE
¹The Administration of Estates Act 1971, s.6, provides:

"6.—(1) It shall be competent to include in the inventory of the estate of any person who dies domiciled in Scotland any real estate of the deceased situated in England and Wales or Northern Ireland, and accordingly in section 9 of the Confirmation of Executors (Scotland) Act 1858 the word 'personal' wherever it occurs is hereby repealed.

(2) Section 14(2) of the Succession (Scotland) Act 1964 (act of sederunt to provide for description of heritable property) shall apply in relation to such real estate as aforesaid as it applies in relation to heritable property in Scotland".

GENERAL NOTE
This section made the important change, now regarded as if it had always existed, that heritage as well as moveable property vests in the executor as such by virtue of confirmation to the deceased's estate.

Provisions as to transfer of heritage

15.—(1) Section 5(2) of the Conveyancing (Scotland) Act 1924 (which provides that a confirmation which includes a heritable security shall be a valid title to the debt thereby secured) shall have effect as if any reference therein to a heritable security, or to a debt secured by a heritable security, included a reference to any interest in heritable property which has vested in an executor in pursuance of the last foregoing section by virtue of a confirmation:
¹Provided that a confirmation (other than an implied confirmation within the meaning of the said section 5(2)) shall not be deemed for the purposes of the said section 5(2) to include any such interest unless a description of the property, in accordance with any act of sederunt such as is mentioned in subsection (2) of the last foregoing section, is included or referred to in the confirmation.

(2) Where in pursuance of the last foregoing section any heritable property has vested in an executor by virtue of a confirmation, and it is necessary for him in distributing the estate to transfer that property—

(a) to any person in satisfaction of a claim to legal rights or the prior rights of a surviving spouse out of the estate, or

(b) to any person entitled to share in the estate by virtue of this Act, or

(c) to any person entitled to take the said property under any testamentary disposition of the deceased,

the executor may effect such transfer by endorsing on the confirmation (or where a certificate of confirmation relating to the property has been issued in pursuance of any act of sederunt, on the certificate) a docket in favour of that person in the form set out in Schedule 1 to this Act, or in a form as nearly as may be to the like effect, and any such docket may be specified as a midcouple or link in title in any deduction of title; but this section shall not be construed as prejudicing the competence of any other mode of transfer.

NOTE
¹As amended by the Law Reform (Miscellaneous Provisions) (Scotland) Act 1968, s.19.

GENERAL NOTE
Confirmation creates a valid title in the executor to heritage included in the confirmation. This is achieved by providing that references to heritable securities in s.5(2) of the 1924 Act are to be construed as including any interest in heritage which has vested in an executor by virtue of s.14 of

the Succession (Scotland) Act. Problems over what was required as a description of the property were resolved by s.19 of the Law Reform (Miscellaneous Provisions) (Scotland) Act 1968.

Subsection (2) introduced a new procedure, which has proved very popular and effective, permitting an executor to transfer heritage to a beneficiary merely by endorsing a docket on the confirmation—or more usually on a certificate of confirmation relating only to the property in question. Such a docket is a valid link in title, although it cannot be recorded directly.

Provisions relating to leases

'**16.**—(1) This section applies to any interest, being the interest of a tenant under a lease, which is comprised in the estate of a deceased person and has accordingly vested in the deceased's executor by virtue of section 14 of this Act; and in the following provisions of this section "interest" means an interest to which this section applies.

(2) Where an interest—

(a) is not the subject of a valid bequest by the deceased, or

(b) is the subject of such a bequest, but the bequest is not accepted by the legatee, or

²(c) being an interest under an agricultural lease, is the subject of such a bequest, but the bequest is declared null and void in pursuance of section 16 of the Act of 1886 or section 11 of the 1991 Act, or becomes null and void under section 10 of the Act of 1955,

and there is among the conditions of the lease (whether expressly or by implication) a condition prohibiting assignation of the interest, the executor shall be entitled, notwithstanding that condition, to transfer the interest to any one of the persons entitled to succeed to the deceased's intestate estate, or to claim legal rights or the prior rights of a surviving spouse out of the estate, in or towards satisfaction of that person's entitlement or claim; but shall not be entitled to transfer the interest to any other person without the consent—

(i) in the case of an interest under an agricultural lease, being a lease of a croft within the meaning of section 3(1) of the Act of 1955, of the Crofters Commission;

(ii) in any other case, of the landlord.

(3) If in the case of any interest—

(a) at any time the executor is satisfied that the interest cannot be disposed of according to law and so informs the landlord, or

(b) the interest is not so disposed of within a period of one year or such longer period as may be fixed by agreement between the landlord and the executor or, failing agreement, by the sheriff on summary application by the executor—

²(i) in the case of an interest under an agricultural lease which is the subject of a petition to the Land Court under section 16 of the Act of 1886 or an application to that court under section 11 of the 1991 Act, from the date of the determination or withdrawal of the petition or, as the case may be, the application.

(ia) in the case of an interest under an agricultural lease which is the subject of an application by the legatee to the Crofters Commission under section 10(1) of the Act of 1955, from the date of any refusal by the Commission to determine that the bequest shall not be null and void,

(ib) in the case of an interest under an agricultural lease which is the subject of an intimation of objection by the landlord to the legatee and the Crofters Commission under section 10(3) of the Act of 1955, from the date of any decision of the Commission upholding the objection.

(ii) in any other case, from the date of death of the deceased, either the landlord or the executor may, on giving notice in accordance with the next following subsection to the other, terminate the lease (in so far as it relates to the interest) notwithstanding any provision therein, or any enactment or rule of law, to the contrary effect.

(4) The period of notice given under the last foregoing subsection shall be—

(a) in the case of an agricultural lease, such period as may be agreed, or, failing agreement, a period of not less than one year and not more than two years ending with such term of Whitsunday or Martinmas as may be specified in the notice; and

(b) in the case of any other lease, a period of six months:

Provided that paragraph (b) of this subsection shall be without prejudice to any enactment prescribing a shorter period of notice in relation to the lease in question.

(5) Subsection (3) of this section shall not prejudice any claim by any party to the lease for compensation or damages in respect of the termination of the lease (or any rights under it) in pursuance of that subsection; but any award of compensation or damages in respect of such termination at the instance of the executor shall be enforceable only against the estate of the deceased and not against the executor personally.

(6) Where an interest is an interest under an agricultural lease, and—

(a) an application is made under section 3 of the Act of 1931 or section 13 of the Act of 1955 to the Land Court for an order for removal, or

²(b) a reference is made under section 23(2) and (3) of the 1991 Act to an arbiter to determine any question which has arisen under section 22(2)(e) of that Act in connection with a notice to quit,

the Land Court shall not make the order, or, as the case may be, the arbiter shall not make an award in favour of the landlord, unless the court or the arbiter is satisfied that it is reasonable having regard to the fact that the interest is vested in the executor in his capacity as executor, that it should be made.

(7) Where an interest is not an interest under an agricultural lease, and the landlord brings an action of removing against the executor in respect of a breach of a condition of the lease, the court shall not grant decree in the action unless it is satisfied that the condition alleged to have been breached is one which it is reasonable to expect the executor to have observed, having regard to the fact that the interest is vested in him in his capacity as an executor.

²(8) Where an interest is an interest under an agricultural lease and is the subject of a valid bequest by the deceased, the fact that the interest is vested in the executor under the said section 14 shall not prevent the operation, in relation to the legatee, of paragraphs (a) to (h) of section 16 of the Act of 1886, or, as the case may be, section 11(2) to (8) of the 1991 Act, or, as the case may be, subsections (2) to (7) of section 10 of the Act of 1955.

²(9) In this section—

"agricultural lease" means a lease of a holding within the meaning of the Small Landholders (Scotland) Acts 1886 to 1931 or of the 1991 Act or a lease of a croft within the meaning of section 3(1) of the Act of 1955;

"the Act of 1886" means the Crofters Holdings (Scotland) Act 1886;

"the Act of 1931" means the Small Landholders and Agricultural Holdings (Scotland) Act 1931;

"the 1991 Act" means the Agricultural Holdings (Scotland) Act 1991;

"the Act of 1955" means the Crofters (Scotland) Act 1955;

"lease" includes tenancy.

NOTES

¹As amended by the Law Reform (Miscellaneous Provisions) (Scotland) Act 1968 (c.70), Sched.2 (estates of any person dying on or after 25th November 1968). See the Agriculture Act

1986 (c.49), Sched.2, para. 3. As regards notices to quit, see the Agricultural Holdings (Scotland) Act 1991 (c.55), s.25.

²As amended by the Agricultural Holdings (Scotland) Act 1991 (c.55), Sched.11, para. 24.

DEFINITION
  "estate": s.36(2).

GENERAL NOTE
  The right of a tenant under a lease is a heritable asset, and must be confirmed to by the executor—unless it is a "liferent lease" expiring on the tenant's death (s.36(2)) and *Rotherwick's Trs v. Hope & Ors,* 1975 S.L.T. 187).

  Subsection (2) gives the executor power in the specified circumstances to assign the lease to any one of the persons entitled to succeed on intestacy. There is no longer a single heir-at-law to succeed and a landlord could not reasonably be expected to accept a multiplicity of tenants. The selection by the executor may assist in finding someone genuinely interested in continuing the tenancy. There are provisions in subss (6) and (7) to take account of the fact that the lease is vested in the executor only in the capacity of executor.

  Executors and beneficiaries should take particular note of the time-limits specified in subs.(3). Irrespective of any provisions in the lease, if the executor has not disposed of the interest in the lease within one year from one of the dates specified, the lease may be terminated either by the executor or, more significantly, by the landlord by giving the appropriate notice. If an executor simply delays too long, the lease is liable to be lost to the beneficiaries. See *Rotherwick's Trs,* above and *Gifford v. Buchanan,* 1983 S.L.T. 613.

Protection of persons acquiring title

  ¹**17.** Where any person has in good faith and for value acquired title to any interest in or security over heritable property which has vested in an executor as aforesaid directly or indirectly from—
   (a) the executor, or
   (b) a person deriving title directly from the executor,
  the title so acquired shall not be challengeable on the ground that the confirmation was reducible or has in fact been reduced, or, in a case falling under paragraph (*b*) above, that the title should not have been transferred to the person mentioned in that paragraph.

NOTE
  ¹Saved by the Law Reform (Miscellaneous Provisions) (Scotland) Act 1968 (c.70), s.7.

GENERAL NOTE
  This is an important protection for purchasers of heritage, and it is now common practice to arrange conveyances in such a way as to ensure that this protection is available. It will normally mean that there is no need for third parties to investigate the validity of a confirmation. Even if the confirmation was reducible, or has actually been reduced, the title obtained from the executor by a purchaser in good faith and for value is not challengeable on that ground.

Provisions as to entails and special destinations

  18.—¹(1) On the death of the heir of entail in possession of any property subject to an entail, the entailed property shall, if the executor of the deceased is confirmed thereto, vest in the executor for the purpose of enabling it to be conveyed to the heir of entail next entitled thereto under the entail (if such conveyance is necessary) and for that purpose only.

  ¹(2) On the death of a person entitled to any heritable property subject to a special destination in favour of some other person, being a destination which the deceased could not competently have, or in fact has not, evacuated by testamentary disposition or otherwise, the property shall, if the executor of the deceased is confirmed thereto, vest in the executor for the purpose of enabling

it to be conveyed to the person next entitled thereto under the destination (if such conveyance is necessary) and for that purpose only.

(3) Section 14(2) of this Act shall apply in relation to property to which this section refers as it applies to property to which the said section 14(2) refers.

(4) Sections 15 and 17 of this Act shall apply to property which has vested in an executor by virtue of this section as they apply to property which has vested in an executor by virtue of section 14 of this Act, as if the person next entitled to the first mentioned property were a person entitled to share in the estate of the deceased.

NOTE
[1]See the Inheritance Tax Act 1984 (c.51), s.209(1). Repealed in part by the Abolition of Feudal Tenure (Scotland) Act 2000 (asp 5), s.76.

19. [*Repealed by the Finance Act 1975 (c.7), Sched.13.*]

Executor dative to have powers of a trustee

20. An executor dative appointed to administer the estate of a deceased person shall have in his administration of such estate the whole powers, privileges and immunities, and be subject to the same obligations, limitations and restrictions, which gratuitous trustees have, or are subject to, under anyenactment or under common law, and the Trusts (Scotland) Acts 1921 and 1961 shall have effect as if any reference therein to a trustee included a reference to such an executor dative:

Provided that nothing in this section shall exempt an executor dative from finding caution for his intromissions or confer upon him any power to resign or to assume new trustees.

GENERAL NOTE
An executor dative clearly now qualifies as a trustee for the purposes of the Trusts (Scotland) Acts.

Evidence as to holograph wills in commissary proceedings

[1]**21.**—(1) Notwithstanding any rule of law or practice to the contrary, confirmation of an executor to property disposed of in a holograph testamentary disposition shall not be granted unless the court is satisfied by evidence consisting at least of an affidavit by each of two persons that the writing and signature of the disposition are in the handwriting of the testator.

(2) This section shall not apply to a testamentary document executed after the commencement of the Requirements of Writing (Scotland) Act 1995.

NOTE
[1]As amended by the Requirements of Writing (Scotland) Act 1995 (c.7), Sched.4, para. 38 (effective August 1, 1995: s.15(2)).

Evidence as to testamentary documents in commissary proceedings

[1]**21A.** Confirmation of an executor to property disposed of in a testamentary document executed after the commencement of the Requirements of Writing (Scotland) Act 1995 shall not be granted unless the formal validity of the document is governed—

(a) by Scots law and the document is presumed under section 3 or 4 of that Act to have been subscribed by the granter so disposing of that property; or

(b) by a law other than Scots law and the court is satisfied that the document is formally valid according to the law governing such validity.

NOTE

¹Inserted by the Requirements of Writing (Scotland) Act 1995 (c.7), Sched.4, para. 39 (effective August 1, 1995: s.15(2)).

Court of Session may regulate procedure in commissary proceedings

¹**22.**—(1) The powers exercisable by the Court of Session by act of sederunt under section 18 of the Confirmation of Executors (Scotland) Act 1858, section 16 of the Sheriff Courts and Legal Officers (Scotland) Act 1927 and section 34 of the Administration of Justice (Scotland) Act 1933 (which empower the court to regulate *inter alia* procedure in proceedings in the sheriff court and in proceedings for the confirmation of executors) shall include power to regulate the procedure to be followed, and to prescribe the form and content of any petition, writ or other document to be used, in connection with the confirmation of executors in cases where, by virtue of this Act, heritable property devolves upon the executor.

(2) Without prejudice to the generality of the powers conferred on the court by the said sections and by this section, the power conferred by the said section 34 to modify, amend or repeal by act of sederunt enactments relating to certain matters shall include power so to modify, amend or repeal any enactment relating to the procedure to be followed in proceedings for the confirmation of executors in such cases as aforesaid.

(3) [*Repealed by the Law Reform (Miscellaneous Provisions) (Scotland) Act 1966 (c.19), Sched.,Part I.*]

(4) [*Repealed by the Finance Act 1975 (c.7), Sched.13.*]

NOTE

¹See S.I. 1964 No. 1143 and S.I. 1971 No. 1165.

PART IV

ADOPTED PERSONS

Adopted person to be treated for purposes of succession, etc., as child of adopter

¹**23.**—(1) For all purposes relating to—

(a) the succession to a deceased person (whether testate or intestate), and

(b) the disposal of property by virtue of any *inter vivos* deed,

an adopted person shall be treated as the child of the adopter and not as the child of any other person.

In this subsection and in the following provisions of this Part of this Act any reference to succession to a deceased person shall be construed as including a reference to the distribution of any property in consequence of the death of the deceased person and any claim to legal rights or the prior rights of a surviving spouse out of his estate.

(2) In any deed whereby property is conveyed or under which a succession arises, being a deed executed after the making of an adoption order, unless the contrary intention appears, any reference (whether express or implied)—

  (a) to the child or children of the adopter shall be construed as, or as including, a reference to the adopted person;

  (b) to the child or children of the adopted person's natural parents or either of them shall be construed as not being, or as not including, a reference to the adopted person; and

  (c) to a person related to the adopted person in any particular degree shall be construed as a reference to the person who would be related to him in that degree if he were the child of the adopter and were not the child of any other person:

Provided that for the purposes of this subsection a deed containing a provision taking effect on the death of any person shall be deemed to have been executed on the date of death of that person.

(3) Where the terms of any deed provide that any property or interest in property shall devolve along with a title, honour or dignity, nothing in this section or in the Children Act 1975 or in the Adoption (Scotland) Act 1978 shall prevent that property or interest from so devolving.

(4) Nothing in this section shall affect any deed executed, or the devolution of any property on, or in consequence of, the death of a person who dies, before the commencement of this Act.

(5) In this Part of this Act the expression "adoption order" has the same meaning as in section 38 of the Adoption (Scotland) Act 1978 (whether the order took effect before or after the commencement of this Act); and "adopted" means adopted in pursuance of an adoption order.

NOTE
[1]As amended by the Adoption (Scotland) Act 1978 (c.28), Sched.3, para. 4. See also the Legitimation (Scotland) Act 1968 (c.22), ss.2(6), 6(2). Excluded by the Law Reform (Miscellaneous Provisions) (Scotland) Act 1966 (c.19), s.5.

GENERAL NOTE
  The anomalously unfair lack of provision for adopted children prior to the Succession (Scotland) Act was one of the prime reasons for the appointment of the Mackintosh Committee on the Law of Succession (cmd.8144). Adopted children had no rights in the succession to their adopting parents and retained any rights which they had in the estates of their biological parents.

  Adopted children now are treated as children of the adopter or adopters and not as children of any other person. They have full rights of succession, including legal rights, to the adopting parents and lose all rights in the estates of the natural parents. Children adopted by overseas adoptions are included (*Salvesen's Trs, Petrs*, 1993 S.L.T. 1327).

  The one major exception is succession to titles, honours and dignities. These are not affected by the Act (s.37(1)(a)) and therefore no right of succession to titles, etc. was conferred on adopted children by the Act. If a deed prescribes that property is to devolve along with a title, nothing in the adoption legislation prevents that (subs.(3)).

Provisions supplementary to section 23

[1]**24.**—(1) For the purposes of the law regulating the succession to any property and for the purposes of the construction of any such deed as is mentioned in the last foregoing section, an adopted person shall be deemed to be related to any other person, being the child or the adopted child of the adopter or (in the case of a joint adoption) of either of the adopters,

  (a) where he or she was adopted by two spouses jointly and that other person is the child or adopted child of both of them, as a brother or sister of the whole blood;

  (b) in any other case, as a brother or sister of the half blood.

²(1A) Where, in relation to any purpose specified in section 23(1) of this Act, any right is conferred or any obligation is imposed, whether by operation of law or under any deed coming into operation after the commencement of the Children Act 1975, by reference to the relative seniority of the members of a class of persons, then, without prejudice to any entitlement under Part I of the Law Reform (Miscellaneous Provisions) (Scotland) Act 1968 of an illegitimate child who is adopted by one of his parents,

(a) any member of that class who is an adopted person shall rank as if he had been born on the date of his adoption, and

(b) if two or more members of the class are adopted persons whose dates of adoption are the same, they shall rank as between themselves in accordance with their respective times of birth.

³(2) Notwithstanding anything in the last foregoing section, a trustee or an executor may distribute any property for the distribution of which he is responsible without having ascertained that no adoption order has been made by virtue of which any person is or may be entitled to any interest therein, and shall not be liable to any such person of whose claim he has not had notice at the time of the distribution; but (without prejudice to section 17 of this Act) nothing in this subsection shall affect any right of any such person to recover the property, or any property representing it, from any person who may have received it.

(3) Where an adoption order is made in respect of a person who has been previously adopted, the previous adoption shall be disregarded for the purposes of the last foregoing section in relation to the devolution of any property on the death of any person dying after the date of the subsequent adoption order, and in relation to any deed executed after that date whereby property is conveyed or under which a succession arises.

(4) *[Repealed by the Adoption (Scotland) Act 1978 (c.28), Sched.4.]*

NOTES
¹Saved by the Legitimation (Scotland) Act 1968 (c.22), ss.2(6), 6(2).
²Added by the Children Act 1975 (c.72), Sched.2, para. 5.
³As amended by the Adoption Act 1964 (c.57), s.1(1).

PART V

FINANCIAL PROVISIONS ON DIVORCE

25–27. *[Repealed by the Divorce (Scotland) Act 1976 (c.39), Sched.2.]*

PART VI

MISCELLANEOUS AND SUPPLEMENTARY

28. *[Repealed by the Age of Legal Capacity (Scotland) Act 1991 (c.50), Sched.2.]*

Right of tenant to bequeath interest under lease

29.—(1) A bequest by a tenant of his interest under a tenancy or lease to any one of the persons who, if the tenant had died intestate, would be, or would in any circumstances have been, entitled to succeed to his intestate estate by virtue of this Act shall not be treated as invalid by reason only that there is among the conditions of the tenancy or lease an implied condition prohibiting assignation.

¹(2) This section shall not prejudice the operation of section 16 of the Crofters Holdings (Scotland) Act 1886, or section 11 of the Agricultural Holdings (Scotland) Act 1991 (which relate to bequests in the case of agricultural leases), or of section 10 of the Crofters (Scotland) Act 1955 (which makes similar provision in relation to crofts).

NOTE
¹As amended by the Law Reform (Miscellaneous Provisions) (Scotland) Act 1968 (c.70), Sched.2 (estate of persons dying after the commencement of that Act), and the Agricultural Holdings (Scotland) Act 1991 (c.55), Sched.11, para. 25.

Effect of testamentary dispositions on special destinations

30. A testamentary disposition executed after the commencement of this Act shall not have effect so as to evacuate a special destination (being a destination which could competently be evacuated by the testamentary disposition) unless it contains a specific reference to the destination and a declared intention on the part of the testator to evacuate it.

GENERAL NOTE
This brief section is particularly important. Despite its importance, however, it is frequently ignored. Special destinations are an abomination and ought to be abolished, but while they exist their functions and effects cannot be ignored. If their nature is understood, they can be used sensibly but far too many cases have arisen in which it would appear that they have been either not understood or merely ignored (see *Weir v. J.M. Hodge & Son*, 1990 S.L.T. 266).

Many special destinations in the titles to land will be contractual, for example a survivorship destination when both spouses contribute to the purchase of a house. If so, there is no power to revoke the destination, and no reference in a will, however formal, can evacuate it.

If power to revoke does exist, this section makes it clear that it cannot be revoked by implication. There must be a specific reference in the will to the destination and a declared intention on the part of the testator to revoke it (see *Stirling's Trs & Ors*, 1977 S.L.T. 229).

Presumption of survivorship in respect of claims to property

31.—(1) Where two persons have died in circumstances indicating that they died simultaneously or rendering it uncertain which, if either, of them survived the other, then, for all purposes affecting title or succession to property or claims to legal rights or the prior rights of a surviving spouse,

(a) where the persons were husband and wife, it shall be presumed that neither survived the other; and

(b) in any other case, it shall be presumed that the younger person survived the elder unless the next following subsection applies.

(2) If, in a case to which paragraph (*b*) of the foregoing subsection would (apart from this subsection) apply, the elder person has left a testamentary disposition containing a provision, however expressed, in favour of the younger if he survives the elder and, failing the younger, in favour of a third person, and the younger person has died intestate, then it shall be presumed for the purposes of that provision that the elder person survived the younger.

GENERAL NOTE
This was the first provision in Scots law for determining the order of death in the case of common calamities. The form of the provision is to create "presumptions", but they are in fact rules of law which cannot be rebutted. This is because they arise only where there is no actual

proof of survivorship, so that by definition there cannot be evidence to rebut the presumptions see *Lamb v. Lord Advocate*, 1976 S.L.T. 151).

The general rule in subs.(1)(b) is that where two persons die in circumstances indicating that they died exactly simultaneously (which will be almost impossible to establish) or rendering it uncertain which survived the other, the younger is treated as having survived the elder.

There is different provision for husbands and wives (s.31(1)(a)). In this situation there is a positive presumption that neither survived the other. This has the effect that in a common calamity with no proof of survivorship, the estate of each spouse will be wound up on the basis that the other did not survive and is therefore not a beneficiary. However if their wills make provision for the situation of the other "predeceasing", these cannot receive effect as failure to survive does not prove predecease.

Subsection (2) creates another, and somewhat complex, exception for the situation mentioned there. Whether this provision is worth having is of some doubt.

Certain testamentary dispositions to be formally valid

¹**32.**—(1) For the purpose of any question arising as to entitlement, by virtue of a testamentary disposition, to any relevant property or to any interest therein, the disposition shall be treated as valid in respect of the formalities of execution.

(2) Subsection (1) above is without prejudice to any right to challenge the validity of the testamentary disposition on the ground of forgery or on any other ground of essential invalidity.

(3) In this section "relevant property" means property disposed of in the testamentary disposition in respect of which—

(a) confirmation has been granted; or

(b) probate, letters of administration or other grant of representation—

　(i) has been issued, and has noted the domicile of the deceased to be, in England and Wales or in Northern Ireland; or

　(ii) has been issued outwith the United Kingdom and had been sealed in Scotland under section 2 of the Colonial Probates Act 1892.

NOTE
¹Substituted by the Requirements of Writing (Scotland) Act 1995 (c.7), Sched.4, para. 40.

Construction of existing deeds

¹**33.**—²(1) Subject to subsection (2) of this section, any reference in any deed taking effect after the commencement of this Act to *jus relicti, jus relictae* or legitim shall be construed as a reference to the right to *jus relicti, jus relictae* or legitim, as the case may be, as modified by Part II of this Act; and any reference in any such deed to courtesy or terce shall be of no effect.

³(2) Any reference to legal rights in a marriage contract made before the commencement of this Act and taking effect in consequence of a decree of divorce granted in an action commenced after the commencement of this Act shall be construed as a reference to any right which the husband or the wife, as the case may be, might obtain by virtue of the provisions of section 26 of this Act or section 5 of the Divorce (Scotland) Act 1976 or section 29 of the Matrimonial and Family Proceedings Act 1984 or section 8 of the Family Law (Scotland) Act 1985.

NOTES
¹As amended by the Law Reform (Miscellaneous Provisions) (Scotland) Act 1968 (c.70), Sched.1, in respect of estate of any person dying on or after 25th November 1968.
²As amended by the Law Reform (Parent and Child) (Scotland) Act 1986 (c.9), Sched.1, para. 7(1) and Sched.2, with effect from 8th December 1986.

'As amended by the Divorce (Scotland) Act 1976 (c.39), Sched.1, para. 2, the Matrimonial and Family Proceedings Act 1984 (c.42), Sched.1, para. 6, and the Family Law (Scotland) Act 1985 (c.37), Sched.1, para. 4.

Modification of enactments and repeals

34.—(1) Subject to the provisions of section 37 of this Act, the enactment mentioned in Schedule 2 to this Act shall have effect subject to the modifications specified in that Schedule, being modifications consequential on the provisions of this Act.

(2) [*Repealed by the Statute Law (Repeals) Act 1974 (c.22).*]

Transfer of certain jurisdiction to Sheriff of Chancery

35.—(1) If at any time it appears to the Secretary of State expedient to do so he may by order transfer to the Sheriff of Chancery the jurisdiction of any other sheriff in relation to the service of heirs.

(2) An order made under this section may contain such consequential provisions as appears to the Secretary of State to be necessary, including provisions for the consequential repeal or consequential modification of any enactment relating to the matters dealt with in the order.

(3) Any order made under this section shall be made by statutory instrument.

Interpretation

36.—(1) In this Act the following expressions shall, unless the context otherwise requires, have the meanings hereby respectively assigned to them, that is to say—

"deed" includes any disposition, contract, instrument or writing, whether *inter vivos* or *mortis causa*;

"an intestate" means a person who has died leaving undisposed of by testamentary disposition the whole or any part of his estate, and "intestate" shall be construed accordingly;

"intestate estate", in relation to an intestate, means (subject to sections 1(2) and 9(6)(a) of this Act) so much of his estate as is undisposed of by testamentary disposition;

"issue" means issue however remote;

"Land Court" means the Scottish Land Court;

"lease" and "tenancy" include sub-lease and sub-tenancy, and tenant shall be construed accordingly;

"legal rights" means *jus relicti, jus relictae,* and legitim;

"net estate" and "net intestate estate" means respectively so much of an estate or an intestate estate as remains after provision for the satisfaction of estate duty and other liabilities of the estate having priority over legal rights, the prior rights of a surviving spouse and rights of succession, or, as the case may be, the proportion thereof properly attributable to the intestate estate;

"owner" in relation to any heritable property means the person entitled to receive the rents thereof (other than rents under a sub-lease or sub-tenancy);

"prior rights", in relation to a surviving spouse, means the rights conferred by sections 8 and 9 of this Act;

"testamentary disposition" in relation to a deceased, includes any deed taking effect on his death whereby any part of his estate is disposed of or under which a succession thereto arises.

(2) Any reference in this Act to the estate of a deceased person shall, unless the context otherwise requires, be construed as a reference to the whole estate, whether heritable or moveable, or partly heritable and partly moveable, belonging to the deceased at the time of his death or over which the deceased had a power of appointment and, where the deceased immediately before his death held the interest of a tenant under a tenancy or lease which was not expressed to expire on his death, includes that interest:

Provided that—

(a) where any heritable property belonging to a deceased person at the date of his death is subject to a special destination in favour of any person, the property shall not be treated for the purposes of this Act as part of the estate of the deceased unless the destination is one which could competently be, and has in fact been, evacuated by the deceased by testamentary disposition or otherwise; and in that case the property shall be treated for the purposes of this Act as if it were part of the deceased's estate on which he has tested; and

(b) where any heritable property over which a deceased person had a power of appointment has not been disposed of in exercise of that power and is in those circumstances subject to a power of appointment by some other person, that property shall not be treated for the purposes of this Act as part of the estate of the deceased.

(3) Without prejudice to the proviso to section 23(2) of this Act, references in this Act to the date of execution of a testamentary disposition shall be construed as references to the date on which the disposition was actually executed and not to the date of death of the testator.

(4) References in this Act to any enactment shall, except where the context otherwise requires, be construed as references to that enactment as amended by or under any other enactment, including this Act.

²(5) Section 1(1) (legal equality of children) of the Law Reform (Parent and Child) (Scotland) Act 1986 shall apply to this Act; and any reference (however expressed) in this Act to a relative shall be construed accordingly.

NOTES

¹As amended by the Law Reform (Parent and Child) (Scotland) Act 1986 (c.9), Sched. 2.

²Includes inheritance tax: see the Inheritance Tax Act 1984 (c.51), Sched.6, para. 1.

³Added by the Law Reform (Parent and Child) (Scotland) Act 1986 (c.9), Sched.1, para. 7(2), with effect from 8th December 1986.

Exclusion of certain matters from operation of Act

37.—¹(1) Save as otherwise expressly provided, nothing in this Act or (as respects paragraph (*a*) of this subsection) in the Children Act 1975 or the Adoption (Scotland) Act 1978 shall—

(a) apply to any title, coat of arms, honour or dignity transmissible on the death of the holder thereof or affect the succession thereto or the devolution thereof;

(b) [*Repealed by the Law Reform (Miscellaneous Provisions) (Scotland) Act 1968, Sched.3 (estate of any person dying after the commencement of that Act)*];

(c) affect any right on the part of a surviving spouse to claim from the representatives of his or her deceased spouse payment of aliment out of the estate of that spouse;

²(d) affect the administration, winding up or distribution of or the making up of title to any part of the estate of any person who died before the commencement of this Act or the rights of succession to such an estate

or any claim for legal rights or terce or courtesy or any rights arising under the Intestate Husband's Estate (Scotland) Acts 1911 to 1959, out of such an estate or the right to take any legal proceedings with respect to any such matters;

(e) affect any claim for legal rights arising out of an action of divorce commenced before the commencement of this Act;

and in relation to the matters aforesaid the law in force immediately before the commencement of this Act shall continue to have effect as if this Act had not passed.

(2) Nothing in this Act shall be construed as affecting the operation of any rule of law applicable immediately before the commencement of this Act to the choice of the system of law governing the administration, winding up or distribution of the estate, or any part of the estate, of any deceased person.

NOTES

[1] As amended by the Children Act 1975 (c.72), Sched.2, para. 5, and the Adoption (Scotland) Act 1978 (c.28), Sched.3, para. 5.

[2] Saved by the Law Reform (Miscellaneous Provisions) (Scotland) Act 1980 (c.55), s.6.

Citation, extent and commencement

38.—(1) This Act may be cited as the Succession (Scotland) Act 1964.

(2) This Act shall extend to Scotland only.

(3) This Act shall come into operation on the expiration of the period of three months beginning with the date on which it is passed.

SCHEDULES

SCHEDULE 1

Section 15

FORM OF DOCKET

NOTE

[1] As amended by the Requirements of Writing (Scotland) Act 1995 (c.7), Sched.4, para. 41 (effective August 1, 1995: s.15(2)).

I AB, being by virtue of the within confirmation [*or certificate of confirmation*] the executor on the estate of the deceased CD so far as specified in the confirmation [*or certificate or inventory attached hereto*] hereby nominate EF [*designed*] as the person entitled—

(a) in [part] satisfaction of his claim to prior rights, as a surviving spouse, on the death of the deceased,

(b) in [part] satisfaction of his claim to legal rights on the death of the deceased,

(c) in [part] satisfaction of his share in the said estate,

(d) in [part] implement of a trust disposition and settlement, [*or will, or as the case may be*] of the deceased dated and registered in the Books of Council and Session

to the following item of estate, that it to say, [*short description*] being number of the items of the estate specified in the said confirmation [*or certificate or inventory*].

Testing clause*

*Note—Subscription of the document by the granter of it will be sufficient for the document to be formally valid, but witnessing of it may be necessary or desirable for other purposes (see the Requirements of Writing (Scotland) Act 1995).

SCHEDULE 2

Section 34

MODIFICATION OF ENACTMENTS

GENERAL MODIFICATIONS

¹1.Subject to the specific modifications made by the following provisions of this Schedule, references in any enactment to the heir-at-law of a deceased person in relation to any heritable property shall be construed as references to the persons who by virtue of this Act are entitled to succeed to such property on intestacy.

NOTE

¹As amended by the Law Reform (Miscellaneous Provisions) (Scotland) Act 1968 (c.70), Sched.3 (estate of any person dying after the commencement of that Act).

2. Subject as aforesaid references in general terms in any enactment to the heirs of a deceased person shall include—
   (a) the persons entitled by virtue of this Act to succeed on intestacy to any part of the estate of the deceased; and
   (b) so far as is necessary for the purposes of Part III of this Act, the executor of the deceased.

3. References in any enactment relating to the confirmation of executors or the administration of the moveable estates of deceased persons to the moveable or personal property or estate of a deceased person shall, except where the context otherwise requires, be construed as references to the whole estate of the deceased person.

4. References in any enactment (other than in this Act) to courtesy or terce shall be of no effect.

NOTE

See the Registration of Leases (Scotland) Act 1857, ss.8, 9 and Scheds. C, F. Titles to Land Consolidation (Scotland) Act 1868, s.20. Conveyancing (Scotland) Act 1924, ss.32, 33.

APPENDIX 1

RULES OF DIVISION, ACCORDING TO THE LAW OF SCOTLAND, OF THE ESTATE OF A PERSON WHO HAD DIED INTESTATE ON OR AFTER SEPTEMBER 10, 1964

NOTE
Figures applicable to person dying on or after April 1, 1999. For earlier figures see notes to ss. 8 and 9 of the 1964 Act.

References to a section are to that section of the Succession (Scotland) Act 1964. There being three different sets of rules, any or all of which may be called into play in a given succession, those applied are indicated against each entry by the following abbreviations:

PR—Prior rights to a house, furniture and a monetary provision under sections 8 and 9.

LR—Legal rights of *jus relicti, jus relictae* and legitim under common law as amended by the 1964 Act and other statutes.

FE—Succession to the free estate, heritable and moveable, under Part I of the 1964 Act.

I. SUCCESSION BY A SURVIVING SPOUSE

If the person dies, leaving	Rules Applicable	The estate is divided thus
1. Spouse only.	PR LR FE	Whole to spouse. Comprising (1) prior right under section 8 to deceased's interest in the house in which surviving spouse was ordinarily resident (maximum £130,000), and to the deceased's interest in the furniture and plenishings of that house (maximum £22,000); (2) prior right under section 9 to £58,000; (3) *jus relicti* or *jus relictae* (1/2) from balance of moveables, and (4) whole free estate under section 2(1)(e). (See note 8.)
2. Spouse and the deceased's child whether by marriage to the surviving spouse or not, and whether legitimate or not.	PR LR FE	Spouse has (1) prior right under section 8 to deceased's interest in the house in which the surviving spouse was ordinarily resident (maximum £130,000) and to the deceased's interest in the furniture and plenishings of that house (maximum £22,000); (2) if net balance of the estate is less than £35,000, prior right under section 9 to whole balance; if balance is over £35,000, prior right to £35,000 therefrom, taken rateably from heritage and moveables; and (3) legal right of *jus relicti* or *jus relictae* to one-third of the moveable estate remaining after the prior rights under sections 8 and 9 have been met. Child (or children equally among them)

175

If the person dies, leaving	*Rules Applicable*	*The estate is divided thus*
		receive the whole remainder of the estate, comprising (a) legitim—a further one-third of the moveable estate remaining after the spouse's prior rights under sections 8 and 9, and (b) free estate—the remaining one-third of the moveables plus the heritage not required for prior rights. (See note 5 and note 8.)
3. Spouse and that spouse's children by marriage to deceased and prior marriages.	PR LR FE	Spouse entitled to rights as in No. 2 Remainder (legitim and free estate as above) to deceased's children equally.
4. Spouse and children and issue of predeceasing children.	PR LR FE	Spouse entitled to rights as in No. 2. Remainder (legitim and free estate) to surviving children *per capita* and issue of predeceasing children *per stirpes*. (See note 5 for issue of predeceasing illegitimate children.)
5. Spouse and grandchild or grandchildren.	PR LR FE	Spouse entitled to rights as in No. 2. Remainder (legitim and free estate) to grandchild or among grandchildren equally. (See note 5.)
6. Spouse and remoter issue.	PR LR FE	Spouse entitled to rights as in No. 2. Remainder (legitim and free estate) to members of the nearest class of issue of which there are survivors, *per capita*, and to issue of predeceasing members of that class, *per stirpes*. (See note 5.)
7. Spouse and brothers and sisters. (See note 3 at end).	PR LR FE	Spouse has (1) prior right under section 8 to deceased's interest in the house in which the surviving spouse was ordinarily resident (maximum £130,000) and to the deceased's interest in the furniture and plenishing of that house (maximum £22,000); (2) If the net balance of the estate is less than £58,000, prior right under section 9 to the whole balance: if the balance is over £58,000, prior right to £58,000 therefrom, rateably from heritage and moveables, and (3) legal right of *jus relicti* or *jus relictae* to one-half of the moveable estate remaining after the prior rights under sections 8 and 9 have been met. Brothers and sisters share the whole remainder of the estate equally between them as free estate. (See note 8.)
8. Spouse and brothers and sisters and/or issue of predeceasing brothers and sisters.	PR LR FE	Spouse entitled to rights as in No. 7. Remainder to surviving brothers and sisters *per capita* and issue of predeceasing brothers and sisters *per stirpes*. If all brothers and sisters have predeceased, and there is issue of some or all of them, the remainder to members of the nearest class of issue of which there are survivors, *per capita*, and to issue of predeceasing members of that class, *per stirpes*.
9. Spouse and parent or parents, and brothers and sisters and/or issue of predeceasing brothers and	PR LR FE	Spouse entitled to rights as in No. 7. Remainder, one-half to surviving parent or to both parents equally between them, and one-half to brothers and sisters equally (or to their issue on

If the person dies, leaving	*Rules Applicable*	*The estate is divided thus*
sisters.		principles noted in No. 8).
10. Spouse and parent or parents.	PR LR FE	Spouse entitled to rights as in No. 7. Remainder to surviving parent or to both parents equally between them.
11. Spouse and uncles and aunts (or issue thereof) and/or grandparents or remoter ancestors.	PR LR FE	Whole to spouse (as in No. 1).

II. SUCCESSION BY DESCENDANTS

(Illegitimate Person—see Note 5).

If the person dies, leaving	*Rules Applicable*	*The estate is divided thus*
12. Children only.	LR FE	Whole estate to children equally. (One-half of moveable estate as legitim, noting that the division of legitim may be unequal if advances have been made. Whole balance of estate as free estate.)
13. Children and issue of predeceasing children.	LR FE	Whole estate to surviving children *per capita* and issue of predeceasing children *per stirpes*. (Legitim and free estate as in No. 12.)
14. Grandchildren.	LR FE	Whole estate (being legitim and free estate as in No. 12) to grandchildren equally.
15. Remoter issue.	LR FE	Whole estate (being legitim and free estate as in No. 12) to members of the nearest class of issue of which there are survivors, *per capita*, and to issue of predeceasing members of that class, *per stirpes*.
16. Issue and spouse	PR LR FE	See Nos. 2 to 6.
17. Issue and collaterals.	LR FE	Whole to issue as in Nos. 12 to 15.
18. Issue and ascendants.	LR FE	Whole to issue as in Nos. 12 to 15.

III. SUCCESSION BY COLLATERALS

If the person dies, leaving	*Rules Applicable*	*The estate is divided thus*
19. Brothers and sisters.	FE	Whole estate equally among them.
20. Brothers and sisters and nephews and nieces, being issue of predeceasing brothers and sisters.	FE	Whole estate to brothers and sisters *per capita* and nephews and nieces *per stirpes*.

If the person dies, leaving	*Rules Applicable*	*The estate is divided thus*
21. Nephews and nieces.	FE	Whole estate equally among them.
22. Remoter issue of brothers and sisters.	FE	Whole estate to members of the nearest class of issue of which there are survivors, *per capita*, and to issue of predeceasing members of that class, *per stirpes*.
23. Brothers and sisters (or their issue) and issue of the intestate.	LR FE	Brothers and sisters (or their issue) are excluded: whole to issue. (See No. 17 and Nos. 12–15.)
24. Brothers and sisters (or their issue) and spouse.	PR LR FE	See Nos. 7 and 8.
25. Brothers and sisters (or their issue), spouse and parent or parents.	PR LR FE	See No. 9.
26. Brothers and sisters and parent or parents.	FE	One-half of the estate to brothers and sisters equally; one-half to surviving parent or to both parents equally.
27. Brothers and sisters, nephews and nieces, and parent or parents.	FE	One-half of the estate to brothers and sisters *per capita* and nephews and nieces *per stirpes*; one-half to surviving parent or to both parents equally.
28. Remoter issue of brothers and sisters, and parent or parents.	FE	One-half of the estate to members of the nearest class of issue of brothers and sisters of which there are survivors, *per capita*, and to issue of predeceasing members of that class, *per stirpes*; one-half to surviving parent or to both parents equally.
29. Brothers and sisters (or their issue), and uncles and aunts or remoter ascendants.	FE	Whole estate to brothers and sisters or their issue, the division being to members of the class nearest to the intestate of which there are survivors, *per capita*, and to issue of predeceasing members of that class, *per stirpes*.
30. Brothers and sisters, full blood, and brothers and sisters of half blood (consanguinean and uterine).	FE	Whole estate to brothers and sisters of full blood equally among them.
31. Brothers and sisters of half blood (consanguinean and uterine).	FE	Whole estate equally among them, with no distinction between consanguinean and uterine.
32. Brothers and sisters of half blood (consanguinean and uterine), and/or issue of same.	FE	As for full blood. See Nos. 19 to 22.
33. Brothers and sisters of half blood (consanguinean and uterine), spouse and other relations of intestate.	PR LR FE	As for full blood. See Nos. 23 to 29.

IV. SUCCESSION BY ASCENDANTS

If the person dies, leaving	*Rules Applicable*	*The estate is divided thus*
34. Father only.	FE	Whole estate to father.
35. Mother only.	FE	Whole estate to mother.
36. Father and mother.	FE	Whole estate equally between father and mother.
37. Parent or parents, uncles and aunts (paternal and maternal) and their descendants.	FE	Whole estate to the surviving parent or to both parents equally as in Nos. 34 to 36.
38. Parent or parents and grandparents (paternal and maternal) or remoter ancestors.	FE	Whole estate to the surviving parent or to both parents equally as in Nos. 34 to 36.
39. Paternal and maternal uncles and aunts, and issue of predeceasing uncles and aunts.	FE	Whole estate to uncles and aunts (paternal and maternal) *per capita* and to cousins *per stirpes*.
40. Cousins only (on paternal or maternal sides), or their issue.	FE	Whole estate to cousins (paternal or maternal) or their issue, the division being to members of the class nearest to the intestate of which there are survivors, *per capita*, and to issue of predeceasing members of that class, *per stirpes*.
41. Paternal and maternal uncles and aunts, or their issue and paternal and maternal grandparents or remoter ancestors.	FE	Whole estate to uncles and aunts (paternal and maternal) *per capita* and to cousins *per stirpes*.
42. Paternal and maternal grandparents, great uncles and great aunts.	FE	Whole estate to grandparents (paternal and maternal) equally among them.
43. Paternal and maternal great uncles and great aunts (or issue of such) and great grandparents or remoter ancestors (or issue of collaterals of such).	FE	Whole estate to great uncles and great aunts (paternal and maternal) or their issue, the division being to members of the class nearest to the intestate of which there are survivors, *per capita*, and to issue of predeceasing members of that class, *per stirpes*.
44. Great grandparents or remoter ancestors and issue of collaterals of such.	FE	Infinite search, with division on the principles illustrated in Nos. 34 to 43; lineal ancestors on paternal or maternal sides succeeding before their collaterals and division among such collaterals and their issue being to members of the class nearest to the intestate of which there are survivors, *per capita*, and to issue of predeceasing members of that class, *per stirpes*.
45. Parent or parents and spouse.	PR LR FE	See No. 10.

If the person dies, leaving	*Rules Applicable*	*The estate is divided thus*
46. Remoter ascendants and spouse.	PR LR FE	See No. 11.
47. Ascendants and issue of intestate.	LR FE	See No. 18 and Nos. 12 to 15.
48. Parent or parents and collaterals.	FE	See Nos. 26 to 28.
49. Remoter ascendants and collaterals.	FE	See No. 29.

V. CROWN

If the person dies, leaving	*Rules Applicable*	*The estate is divided thus*
50. No other successor.	FE	Whole to Crown as *ultimus haeres*.

NOTES

1. *Estate affected*

This table applies to the whole of the intestate estate, both heritable and moveable, of a deceased person so far as it is estate the succession to which falls to be regulated by the law of Scotland. There are, however, certain specialties.

(a) *Tenancies of crofts.* Crofting tenancies were originally excluded from the operation of the Succession Act, but in respect of the estates of persons dying on or after November 25, 1968, they now fall to be dealt with under the Act (Law Reform (Miscellaneous Provisions) (Scotland) Act 1968, s.22(3)).

(b) *Titles, coats of arms, etc.* The 1964 Act does not apply to the succession to any title, coat of arms, honour or dignity transmissible on the death of the holder thereof. Accordingly these items fall to be regulated by the pre-existing law (section 37(1)(a)).

2. *Private international law*

Briefly, this table applies to the devolution of the moveable estate of persons who die domiciled in Scotland and to the devolution of all immoveable property in Scotland, whatever the domicile of the deceased. The pre-existing rules for choice of law are preserved by section 37(2).

3. *Collaterals of the half blood*

The previous differentiation between collaterals of the half blood consanguinean and those of the half blood uterine has been removed by the 1964 Act. Accordingly, where brothers and sisters of an intestate, or of a parent or other ancestor of an intestate, have right to the whole, or one-half as the case may be, of the free intestate estate, collaterals of the whole blood are entitled to succeed thereto in preference to collaterals of the half blood, but where collaterals of the half blood are entitled to succeed they rank without distinction as between the half blood consanguinean and the half blood uterine (section 3).

4. *Representation*

Prior to the 1964 Act, representation was unlimited in intestate heritable succession but was severely limited in moveable succession. The effect of the Act is to apply a modified version of the previous rules of intestate moveable succession to the total free estate, heritable and moveable, of an intestate. One of the modifications is the removal of the anomalies in representation. Accordingly, infinite representation has been introduced in legitim (section 11) and also in the distribution of the free estate (sections 5 and 6). There is no representation in a surviving spouse's prior rights, nor in *jus relicti* and *jus relictae*. A class (*e.g.* children) through which representation would otherwise apply is ignored if all members have predeceased (sections 6 and 11).

5. *Illegitimate children*

Substantial changes in the succession rights of illegitimate children were effected by the Law Reform (Miscellaneous Provisions) (Scotland) Act 1968 in respect of the estates of persons dying on or after November 25, 1968 and the Law Reform (Parent and Child) (Scotland) Act 1986 in respect of persons dying on or after December 8, 1986. Briefly, from 1968 to 1986 illegitimate children were on a basis of formal equality with legitimate children in the succession to both parents, but could not represent a predeceasing parent and had no collaterals. From December 8, 1986 the status of illegitimacy is abolished in succession and all rights of succession are determined by biological blood relationship rather than by marriage of the parents. The child formerly classed as illegitimate now has complete rights of succession, including representation, and has collaterals like any other child.

6. *Adopted children*

While the previous position was that an adopted child had no rights on the intestacy of the adopting parents and retained any rights which it had in the estates of its natural parents, the 1964 Act sets out to ensure that for the purposes of succession, or of the disposal of property by deed *inter vivos*, any adopted person is to be treated as the lawful child of the adopter and that rights in the estates of its natural parents are cut off. The detailed provisions for achieving this appear in Part IV of the Act.

7. *Interest*

Interest is payable on the ascertained amounts of the legal rights of *jus relicti, jus relictae* and legitim from the date of death until paid, usually at the rate earned by the estate. No interest is payable on the value of a surviving spouse's prior right to the deceased's dwelling-house and its furniture and plenishings under section 8 of the 1964 Act. Interest is, however, payable on the £35,000 or £58,000 available to a surviving spouse as a prior right under section 9 at a rate which was fixed at 4 per cent for deaths before August 1, 1981, but is now variable and is 7 per cent (SI 1981/805). This interest runs for the period from the date of death until payment. There is, of course, no interest on the value of the rights of succession to the free estate.

8. *Prior rights to a house and its furniture and plenishings*

A house to which section 8 applies is any one dwelling-house in which the surviving spouse of the intestate was ordinarily resident at the date of death of the intestate (section 8(4)). The deceased's "relevant interest" therein which may pass to the surviving spouse is the interest of an owner or of a tenant, other than one whose tenancy is subject to the Rent Acts, and is subject to any heritable debt secured over the interest. The right is applicable to only one house even if the survivor was ordinarily resident in more than one, and the maximum benefit which the surviving spouse may receive under this head is £130,000. If the value of the deceased's interest in the house is greater, the survivor receives that sum and not the house itself (section 8(1)(b)). Even if the value does not exceed the limit, in the cases specified in section 8(2) the survivor receives not the house itself, but the substituted value thereof. The survivor is also entitled to the deceased's interest in the furniture and plenishings (excluding heirlooms—section 8(6)(b) and (c)) of any one house in which the survivor was ordinarily resident. A maximum limit of £22,000 is placed on the value of the furniture and plenishings to be transferred under this head. Should the value be greater, the surviving spouse may choose items to a value not exceeding that sum.

EXAMPLES OF THE DIVISION OF INTESTATE ESTATES

Some simplified examples are given of the division of typical estates to illustrate points which arise in practice. Unless otherwise stated, the values shown are the net values of the estate after taxation, payment of debts and expenses of administration. In addition the examples are worked out as if the distribution of the estate occurred on the day of death, so that no account is taken of the interest payable on prior and legal rights from the date of death until payment, nor of any income arising after the date of death. The distinction between heritage and moveables is preserved where it is still relevant, *i.e.* in prior and legal rights.

X is the intestate. Square brackets indicate that the person concerned predeceased the intestate. The deceased was domiciled in Scotland and all the assets are situated in Scotland.

Example 1. Surviving spouse's prior rights exhaust the estate.

Family [X] = W
        ┌──────┴──────┐
        S   D

Estate (Net values after debts, etc.)

	Heritage £	*Moveables* £
Deceased's house(widow ordinarily resident therein)	120,000	
Furniture and plenishings thereof . .		20,000
Other moveable estate.		30,000
	120,000	50,000

(1) Prior rights (section 8)

	Heritage	*Moveables*
Widow — house (she being ordinarily resident and value being under £130,000)	120,000	
Widow — its furniture and plenishings (subject to £22,000 limit on value)		20,000
Balance	—	30,000

	Heritage £	Moveables £
(2) Prior rights (section 9)		
Widow — preferential right to £35,000 (there being issue of the deceased), if so much is available		30,000
Balance	—	—

The estate is not large enough for there to be a surplus after the spouse's prior rights and thus the widow takes the whole estate and the children receive nothing. Their rights are postponed to those of the deceased's spouse (s.9(2)). If there had been a will in favour of the widow, there would have been no prior rights and the children would have been entitled to legitim of one-third of the total moveable estate, but if there was no destination-over of the gift to the wife, she might have been able to create an intestacy by renouncing her benefit under the will (*Kerr, Petr*, 1968 S.L.T. (Sh.Ct.) 61).

Example 2 All rules of intestate succession operate.

Family   [X] = W
           |
    ┌──────┴──────┐
    S   D

Estate

	Heritage £	Moveables £
Deceased's house (widow ordinarily resident)	150,000	
Furniture and plenishings thereof .		15,000
Holiday house	25,000	
Other estate (bank a/cs; shares, etc.)		110,000
Gross estate	175,000	125,000
Less Debts		
Loan secured over matrimonial home	20,000	
Suppliers' accounts		10,000
Net estate	155,000	115,000
(1) Prior rights s.8		
Widow — deceased's interest in house (value £130,000 after heritable debt: s.(8)(6)(d))	130,000	
Widow — furniture and plenishings .		15,000
Net after s. 8	25,000	100,000

	Heritage £	Moveables £
(2) Prior rights s.9		
Widow — right to £35,000, rateably from heritage and moveables.		
Total estate available 125,000.		
Of which heritage is 1/5 and bears 1/5	7,000	
Of which moveables are 4/5 and bear 4/5		28,000
Net after prior rights	18,000	72,000
(3) Legal rights		
Widow — *jus relictae* (1/3rd of moveables)	24,000	
Children — legitim 1/3 moveables	24,000	
		48,000
Net after legal rights	18,000	24,000
(4) Free estate		
Heritage and moveables assimilated		42,000
S receives 1/2 (s.2)	21,000	
D receives 1/2 (s.2)	21,000	42,000
		£ —

Scheme of Division

Widow

Prior rights	£	
section 8(1)	130,000	
section 8	15,000	
section 9	35,000	
	180,000	
jus relictae	24,000	204,000

Son

Legitim	12,000	
Free estate (s.2)	21,000	33,000

Daughter

Legitim	12,000	
Free estate	21,000	33,000
		270,000

Example 3. Same family as in example 2 but with foreign assets.

Family [X] = W

S   D

The deceased was domiciled in Scotland. The matrimonial home, the furniture and plenishings and the holiday cottage in Scotland are the same as in example 2. There is a villa in Spain owned by the deceased and the moveable estate of £110,000 includes a yacht moored in Spanish waters near the villa. Hence the estate is as follows:

Deceased's house (widow ordinarily resident)	150,000
Furniture and plenishings thereof	15,000
Holiday house in Scotland.	25,000
Spanish Villa	30,000
Yacht in Spain	10,000
Other estate (bank A/cs; shares, etc.) . . .	100,000
Gross estate	330,000

Less Debts		
Loan secured over matrimonial home	20,000	
Suppliers' accounts	10,000	30,000
Net estate		300,000

It is assumed that the villa in Spain is classified as immoveable by Spanish law (the *lex situs*). Hence the rights of inheritance to it are governed by Spanish law, not Scots law. Section 37(2) of the Act expressly preserves the previous rules about choice of law. Thus the Spanish villa is not taken into account for the purposes of the Succession (Scotland) Act. Evidence of the devolution of the villa under Spanish law is required and any equivalent of legal rights in the villa are those pointed out by Spanish law — as also are the procedural requirements for completion of title. The ordinary form of Scottish will is probably not sufficient to transfer title.

It is also assumed that Spanish law would classify the yacht which is physically in Spanish waters as moveable in the international sense. Thus the yacht forms part of the deceased's moveable estate governed by Scots law as the *lex domicilii*.

The result is that the estate distributed according to Scots law is exactly the same as in Example 2 with the same result. The net heritable estate is still £155,000 and the net moveable estate is still £115,000. The villa devolves according to Spanish law and even if this should result in the whole or any part of the villa being transferred to the widow, that fact has no effect upon the amount or value of the prior and legal rights under Scots law. She would be entitled to both.

Example 4. Advances and collation *inter liberos* when there is representation in legitim (see also Chap. 5).

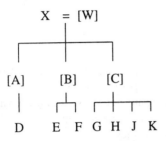

The intestate has died, predeceased by his spouse and all three of his children, but is survived by seven grandchildren, in families of one, two and four respectively. All seven have chosen legitim. During his lifetime, X had made an advance of £3,000 to A. The legitim fund derived from the estate owned by X at the date of his death amounts to £18,000. Although only £18,000 is available for distribution as legitim at the date of death, the total after collation *inter liberos* is £21,000.

The existence of collation demonstrates that the right to legitim is not necessarily co-extensive with the right to share in the free estate and that it is not appropriate to lump together the legitim fund and the free estate and then to divide the total.

If A had survived his father, he would have been entitled to 1/3 of £21,000 = £7,000 less the £3,000 advance, *i.e.* £4,000 and this might have passed down to his only child D.

As A has predeceased his father, along with all the other children of X, the effect of section 11(2) is that there is not true representation by division into thirds, one part going to each of the families of A, B and C. Instead there is equal division into 1/7 shares among the seven grandchildren, although D would have been entitled to 1/3 of the fund if any of A, B or C had survived their father X.

In these circumstances, D is entitled to only 1/7 of the combined fund of legitim plus advance (£21,000), *i.e.* £3,000. However, as a condition of that entitlement, section 11(3) requires him to collate "the proportion appropriate to him" of any advances to his ancestor A. The advance to A was of exactly the amount to which D would be entitled from the combined fund. If the "appropriate" proportion which D must collate is the whole of the advance (as seems likely despite the unfairness) then D receives nothing, although he would have received £4,000 if his father had not been inconsiderate enough to die before the grandfather.

Example 5. Heritable securities in the calculation of legal rights.

H = [X]

S   D

X dies intestate leaving a net estate consisting of a debt of £35,000 due to her, secured by a standard security and also moveable assets worth £35,000, making a total of £70,000. There being no house or furniture owned by the intestate, her husband is entitled to a section 9 prior right of £35,000 plus *jus relicti* of one-third of the remaining moveables.

The heritable security is heritable for the purposes of *jus relicti* and legitim, but is moveable for all other purposes of succession. This leaves the executor with an insoluble problem when allocating funds to meet the husband's prior right, as his possible courses of action lead to different total shares for the husband. The problem is that the heritable security is moveable for the purposes of prior rights. Three possible courses of action may be envisaged.

I. *The heritable security is allocated to the prior right*

Prior right s.9 (the security is allocated to this right, and there remains £35,000 of moveables)	£35,000
Jus relicti (1/3 of remainder)	£11,666
Total for husband	£46,666

II. *Moveables other than the security allocated to the prior right*

Prior right s.9 (the moveables other than the security are allocated to this right, and there remains the heritable security of £35,000)	£35,000
Jus relicti (security not subject to legal rights)	—
Total for husband	£35,000

III. *Security treated as if it were heritable at all stages*

	Heritage £	Moveables £	Husband
	35,000	35,000	
Prior right s. 9 apportioned	17,500	17,500	35,000
	17,500	17,500	
Jus relicti		5,833	5,833
	Total for husband		£40,833

Situation I gives the husband £46,666, Situation II gives him only £35,000 and Situation III gives him £40,833. Although there is nothing to require an executor to make one choice rather than another, the only rational answer seems to be the third course, treating the heritable security as a heritable asset at all stages.

Example 6. Partial intestacy.

[F] = M

X = W

[S]

X has died, survived by his wife and his mother, but predeceased by his only child and by his father. His estate (net of debts) consisted of the matrimonial home in which W is ordinarily resident, valued at £150,000; the furniture and plenishings of that house, valued at £30,000 and other moveable estate of £200,000.

X's will leaves the house, furniture and plenishings and a legacy of £50,000 to his wife, and the residue to his son, with no alternative provision. The result is a partial intestacy of the residue amounting to:

		150,000

Prior Rights

s.8 No house or furniture etc included in intestate estate.		—
s.9 Widow entitled to	58,000	
less legacy (s.9(1) proviso))	50,000	8,000

		142,000

Note: The fact that the values of the testamentary gifts of the house, furniture and plenishings are greater than the *maxima* which would have applied if they had been part of the intestate estate is of no consequence. The proviso to section 9(1) states that no deduction is made from the widow's right under section 9 in respect of a legacy of "any" house to which section 8 applies or of "any" furniture, etc of such a house. It is not limited to the maximum values specified in section 8.

Legal Rights

Widow's *jus relictae* — One half	71,000
	71,000

Free Estate

Whole to deceased's mother (s.2(1)(d))	71,000
	—

INDEX

References are to page number